The Philosophy of Motion

Foundations of the Philosophy of the Arts
Series Editor: Philip Alperson, Temple University

The Foundations of the Philosophy of the Arts series is designed to provide a comprehensive but flexible series of concise texts addressing both fundamental general questions about art as well as questions about the several arts (literature, film, music, painting, etc.) and the various kinds and dimensions of artistic practice.

A consistent approach across the series provides a crisp, contemporary introduction to the main topics in each area of the arts, written in a clear and accessible style that provides a responsible, comprehensive, and informative account of the relevant issues, reflecting classic and recent work in the field. Books in the series are written by a truly distinguished roster of philosophers with international renown.

1. The Philosophy of Art, *Stephen Davies*
2. The Philosophy of Motion Pictures, *Noël Carroll*

Forthcoming:
The Philosophy of Literature, *Peter Lamarque*
The Philosophy of Music, *Philip Alperson*
Black is Beautiful: A Philosophy of Black Aesthetics, *Paul Taylor*

The Philosophy of Motion Pictures

Noël Carroll

Blackwell
Publishing

© 2008 by Noël Carroll

BLACKWELL PUBLISHING
350 Main Street, Malden, MA 02148-5020, USA
9600 Garsington Road, Oxford OX4 2DQ, UK
550 Swanston Street, Carlton, Victoria 3053, Australia

The right of Noël Carroll to be identified as the author of this work has been asserted in accordance with the UK Copyright, Designs, and Patents Act 1988.

First published 2008 by Blackwell Publishing Ltd

1   2008

Library of Congress Cataloging-in-Publication Data

Carroll, Noël, 1947–
    The philosophy of motion pictures / Noël Carroll.
        p. cm. — (Foundations of the philosophy of the arts)
    Includes bibliographical references and index.
    ISBN 978-1-4051-2024-1 (hardcover : alk. paper) — ISBN 978-1-4051-2025-8 (pbk. : alk. paper)
1. Motion pictures—Philosophy. I. Title.
    PN1995.C3574 2008
    791.4301—dc22

                                                2007019837

A catalogue record for this title is available from the British Library.

Set in 11.5/13pt Perpetua
by SPi Publisher Services, Pondicherry, India
Printed and bound in Singapore
by C.O.S. Printers Pte Ltd

The publisher's policy is to use permanent paper from mills that operate a sustainable forestry policy, and which has been manufactured from pulp processed using acid-free and elementary chlorine-free practices. Furthermore, the publisher ensures that the text paper and cover board used have met acceptable environmental accreditation standards.

For further information on
Blackwell Publishing, visit our website at
www.blackwellpublishing.com

To Loretta and Maureen
for taking care of my brothers

Contents

Acknowledgments

The author would like to acknowledge the helpful comments, criticisms, and suggestions offered in the preparation of parts of this book by Philip Alperson, Susan Feagin, Margaret Moore, Jonathan Frome, Vitor Moura, Jinhee Choi, Murray Smith, Gregory Currie, Aaron Smuts, Tom Wartenberg, Cynthia Freeland, Annette Michelson, Jeff Dean, George Wilson, Elisa Galgut, Ward Jones, Amy Coplan, Patrick Keating, and Deborah Knight. They helped make this a better book. I'm the one who made it worse.

Introduction

From Film Theory to the Philosophy of the Moving Image

Though the philosophy of the motion picture – or, as I prefer to say, the moving image – began early in the twentieth century, perhaps arguably with the publication in 1916 of *The Photoplay: A Psychological Study* by Hugo Munsterberg (a Harvard professor of philosophy and psychology in the department of William James), the philosophy of motion pictures did not become a thriving sub-field of philosophy until quite recently. Although Ludwig Wittgenstein enjoyed movies and attended them often – he especially liked westerns – he did not philosophize about them. But as of late, the discussion of movies by philosophers has become quite literally voluminous.[*]

Why?

At least two factors may account for this, one demographic and the other intellectual.

The demographic consideration is this: for the philosophy of motion pictures to take root in any serious way, a substantial cadre of philosophers steeped in motion pictures was necessary in order for a deep and informed philosophical conversation to be sustained. Historically speaking, that condition did not begin to be satisfied sufficiently until the late 1960s and 1970s. By then there was at least one generation of philosophers who had grown up going to the movies in their neighborhood playhouses, and also a second generation who had access, through television, to a wide selection of the history of their own national and/or regional cinema

---

[*] See for example the bibliography assembled by Jinhee Choi in *Philosophy of Film and Motion Pictures*, edited by Noël Carroll and Jinhee Choi (Oxford: Blackwell Publishing, 2006).

traditions. Thus, toward the end of the twentieth century there were – suddenly – enough philosophers with enough knowledge about motion pictures for rich and wide-ranging philosophical debates to begin and for positions to be refined dialectically.

The demographic situation that I've just described, of course, not only explains the emergence of the field of the philosophy of motion pictures. It also accounts for the evolution of cinema studies (or moving image studies, or just media studies) as a rapidly expanding academic enterprise. However, though cinema scholars initially followed in the footsteps of the major film theorists (such as Rudolf Arnheim, Sergei Eisenstein, V. I. Pudovin, André Bazin, and Siegfried Kracauer, among others), by the 1980s cinema studies, like other branches of the humanities, took what has come to be called "the cultural or social turn." That is, academics in cinema studies decided to reorient their field in the direction of what came to be known as "cultural studies." And in doing so, they left in mid-air many of the discussions of a lot of the issues that had perplexed earlier film theorists.

Intellectually, a vacuum appeared. And as Richard Allen, a former chairperson of the New York University Department of Cinema Studies, has pointed out, philosophers stepped into that gap. In effect, the professors of cinema studies have ceded what was once a central part of their field to philosophers of the moving image.

Perhaps needless to say, the philosophical appropriation of many of the topics of the earlier film theorists is by no means a matter of an alien colonization. For traditional film theory was always mixed through and through with philosophy. For example, to take a position on whether film is or is not art presupposes a philosophy of art. Film theorists also helped themselves to theses from many other branches of philosophy as well. Philosophy was never far from the thinking of classical film theorists. So, in this respect, the philosophy of the moving image is a legitimate heir to film theory, and not a usurper.

Many of the topics in this book – especially in terms of the questions asked – reflect the legacy of traditional film theory for the contemporary philosophy of the moving image. The first chapter addresses the question of whether or not film can be art. This is undoubtedly the question that got film theory and the philosophy of the motion pictures rolling in the early decades of the twentieth century. As we shall see, the issue has been revived of late due to some recent, highly sophisticated theories about the nature of photography. As in the past, showing that film can be an art forces us to look at and think closely about the nature of our object of study. In this way, meeting the charge that film is somehow precluded from the order of art in fact becomes an opportunity to deepen our understanding of the moving image.

The second chapter concerns what can be called the "medium specificity thesis." This is the view that the artistic exploration of cinematic possibilities must follow the implicit directives of the medium in which those possibilities are realized. The precise medium that figures in debates like this is typically film – that is, photographically or celluloid based motion pictures. The claim is that the nature of this medium has normative consequences with regard to that which moviemakers should pursue and avoid in their artistic endeavors. Quite simply, it is argued, they should strive to be cinematic and shun being un-cinematic (a condition that is often also equated with being theatrical). Because this was an article of faith for so long in the history of film and because the position appeals so seductively to common sense, it is worth a chapter to scrutinize the medium specificity hypothesis in depth.

Chapter 3 focuses on the question, "What is cinema?" The title, of course, comes from the legendary collection of essays by André Bazin, one of the most renowned theorists in the history of the moving image. It probably goes without saying that nearly every major film theorist has organized his or her thinking about cinema around this question.

In this chapter, I defend the notion that cinema is best understood in terms of the category of the moving image. "The moving image?" you might ask: "In contrast to what?" The short answer is: in contrast to *film* – that is, to be more explicit, in contrast to celluloid-mounted, photographically based film. I will argue that our object of study here is more fruitfully conceptualized under the broader category of the *moving image* than it is under the rubric of *film*, narrowly construed.

Film, properly so called, was undoubtedly the most important early implementation of the moving image (a.k.a. *movies*), but the impression of movement – including moving pictures and moving stories – can be realized in many other media including kinetoscopes, video, broadcast TV, CGI, and technologies not yet even imagined. Of course, ordinary folks don't haggle over whether a videocassette is a movie or not. And neither, I will argue, should philosophers.

This, of course, is a conceptual point. It is not my intention to initiate a crusade for linguistic reform. That would be quixotic. In everyday speech, many use the label *film* to designate things that are really the product of other media. For example, they may refer to a high-definition video as a film.

This is rather like the use of the name "Coke" for any cola, or "Xerox" for any copying machine, or "Levi" for all jeans, or "zipper" for every slide fastener. In these cases, the names of the earliest, most popular entrants to a field get used – in an inaccurate way, strictly speaking – to refer to their successors and even their competitors. Because of this tendency, we understand why sometimes digital cinematography will get called film, though it does not involve the use of film (i.e., the use of a filmstrip). There is little damage here in the daily course of events. Nevertheless, as we shall see, it can and does cause philosophical mischief.

Chapter 4 follows the discussion of the nature of cinema with an analysis of the nature of the cinematic image, construed as a single shot. Obviously, these two topics are related, if only because throughout the history of motion pictures, the temptation has endured to treat movies as if they were equivalent to photographs, where photographs, in turn, are conceived of as modeling single shots.* That is, many have attempted to extrapolate the nature of cinema *tout court* from the nature of the photographic shot. Thus, it is imperative for the philosopher of the moving image to get straight about the nature of the shot.

Of course, typical motion pictures, excluding experiments like Andy Warhol's *Empire*, are usually more than one shot in length. Shots are characteristically strung together in cinematic sequences, usually by means of editing. Chapter 5 examines prevailing structures of cinematic sequencing from a functional point of view. In this regard, one might see the analysis here as returning to an exploration of the terrain that was of the greatest interest to the montage theorists of the Soviet period.

Moreover, in composing the image series in a motion picture, one not only standardly combines shots to construct sequences but then also joins sequences to build whole movies. Consequently, in the second part of chapter 5 we turn to the most common way of connecting sequences to make popular, mass-market movies – a process that we call erotetic narration, that is, a method of generating stories by means of questions the narrator implicitly promises to answer.

Just as chapter 5 revisits, with a difference, the concerns of the montagists, so chapter 6 also tackles a subject near and dear to the heart of Sergei Eisenstein – the way in which cinema addresses feeling. Unlike Eisenstein, however, in this chapter I will take advantage of recent refinements in the philosophy of mind and cognitive science in order to appreciate the wide gamut of ways in which movies can engage our affective reactions. I will try

---

* For example, we call an afternoon photographing fashion models "a shoot" and a successful photo a "nice shot."

to be precise where Eisenstein was often impressionistic. Nevertheless, at the end of the chapter, I will attempt to argue that at least one of Eisenstein's insights into the mechanics of influencing audience affect was spot-on. These audience responses are what we can call mirror reflexes; and Eisenstein was dead right about their significance.

The last chapter in the book focuses on the evaluation of motion pictures. Though many might be tempted to maintain that they are wholly a subjective affair, I will try to demonstrate that quite often movie evaluations can be shown to be rational and objective. Often, this relies upon determining the category in which the movie under discussion is to be correctly classified. Since more than one category comes into play when evaluating the range of available motion pictures, the position defended in our last chapter is called the *pluralistic-category approach*.

The pluralistic-category approach contrasts sharply with traditional approaches which attempt to identify a single category – often called *the cinematic* – into which all movies allegedly fall and in accordance with which all motion pictures can be evaluated. The pluralistic-category approach, instead, accepts that there are many categories of motion pictures – from comedies and splatter films to travelogues and onto instructional videos about install- ing software or wearing condoms – and that, inasmuch as specimens of these different categories are designed to fulfill different functions, they call forth different criteria of evaluation.

In the past, the theory (or philosophy) of cinema was often pursued in a very top-down manner. One identified the essence of cinema – usually understood in terms of photographic film – and then attempted to deduce accounts of every other feature of film on the basis of that essence.

The conception of the moving image championed in this book is much looser. Although I attempt to define the moving image, I do so in a way that remains wide open not only to the media in which moving images may be realized, but also in terms of the purposes moving images may legitimately serve. Our characterizations of the elements of the moving image – the shot, the sequence, the erotetic narrative, and its modes of affective address – are not deduced from first principles. Rather, we proceed from topic to topic in a piecemeal fashion.

Thus, the end product is in nowise as unified as the philosophies of our very distinguished predecessors in film theory. Instead, our results are pluralistic. Nevertheless, that appears to be where the argument leads us.

Of course, whether or not that is really so is for you to decide.

Therefore, read on.

Suggested Reading

There are several anthologies that may be useful for readers interested in exploring the field of the philosophy of the motion pictures. A very serviceable introductory text is *The Philosophy of Film: Introductory Text and Readings*, edited by Thomas E. Wartenberg and Angela Curran (Oxford: Blackwell Publishing, 2005). A slightly more advanced textbook is *The Philosophy of Film and Motion Pictures*, edited by Noël Carroll and Jinhee Choi (Oxford: Blackwell Publishing, 2006). Also valuable are any of the many editions of Oxford University Press's *Film Theory and Criticism*, edited by Marshall Cohen, Gerald Mast, and later Leo Braudy. For philosophical purposes, the earlier editions are to be preferred to the later ones.

Two anthologies that present a wide selection of topics in the discipline of the philosophy of motion pictures are *Philosophy and Film*, edited by Cynthia Freeland and Thomas E. Wartenberg (New York: Routledge, 1995), and *Film Theory and Philosophy*, edited by Richard Allen and Murray Smith (Oxford: Oxford University Press, 1997). The journal *Film and Philosophy*, edited by Daniel Shaw, also publishes essays in this area of inquiry on a regular basis.

Although the present volume is concerned with the philosophy *of* motion pictures, many philosophers are also interested in the prospect of philosophy *in* motion pictures. This involves the interpretation of specific motion pictures as illustrations of – and sometimes even as original proposals of – philosophical themes. An example of this approach might be a reading of *Groundhog Day* as a version of Nietzsche's myth of the eternal return. Many of the articles in the journal *Film and Philosophy* are in this genre. An important recent collection devoted to the topic of philosophy in film is *Thinking Through Cinema: Film as Philosophy*, edited by Murray Smith and Thomas E. Wartenberg (Oxford: Blackwell Publishing, 2006). This book derives from the special issue of the *Journal of Aesthetics and Art Criticism* 64:1 (Winter 2006).

Chapter One

Film as Art

The philosophy of the motion picture was born over the issue of whether or not film can be art. The question here, of course, was not whether all films are art – surely raw surveillance footage is not. Rather the question was whether *some* films could be art. At the beginning of the twentieth century, the lurking suspicion in many quarters was that, since films are photographic, they are somehow precluded from the order of art. That is, photography as a medium – and film as an extension of photography – lacked the capacity to create art, properly so called. Thus, no films could possibly be artworks, since photographic media, whether still or moving, by their very nature, are incapable of producing art. This debate, moreover, was (and remains) a philosophical one, because it presupposes views about what is required of an object, if it is to be legitimately classified or categorized as an instance of the concept of art.

To contemporary ears, the contention that no films can be art undoubtedly sounds bizarre insofar as some films – such as *Citizen Kane* – number among our paradigms of twentieth-century art. We are sure that some films are art because we think we've seen a number of straightforward cases; in fact, we believe we've seen quite a few. We even call some films – such as Robert Bresson's *Mouchet*, Federico Fellini's *8½*, and Hou Hsiao Hsien's *Millennium Mambo* – art films. But things were far less obvious when film first arrived on the cultural scene. For in the first decade of the twentieth century there were not that many, if any, agreed-upon masterpieces of cinema for the friend of cinema to cite.

However, the problem went deeper than merely the lack of available evidence. Skeptics concerning the possibility of film art thought that they had prior reasons that conclusively established that no film could be an artwork. Those reasons had to do with the supposition that film was essentially photographic in nature. Moreover, cinematography, on their view, was merely photography that moved. So, since these skeptics were convinced that photographs, given their essential nature, could not be art, they therefore surmised that moving photographs couldn't be either.

That is, the argument that films could not be art rested upon antecedent arguments – arguments that had been voiced throughout the nineteenth century – which maintained that photography could not be art. That the first moving pictures were *films* – the very name of which betrays their photographic (celluloid) basis – encouraged skeptics who contemplated the prospects for film art to extrapolate their reservations about the possibility of photographic art to the products of the new technological medium of motion pictures. The skeptics did so just because they believed that motion pictures were nothing more than moving photographs. Thus, in this chapter, in order to discuss the possibility of film art, we will have to spend a very great deal of time talking about photography.

Against Photography

So why, from the outset, did skeptics challenge the artistic credentials of photographs? Even in the nineteenth century were there not already photographs – by people like Julia Cameron Mitchell, for example – which were undeniably artworks? However, for often subtle reasons, many skeptics were not prepared to grant this.

Skeptics about the potential for an art of photography begin by taking note of the fact that photographs are mechanical productions. Photographs are the causal consequences of a series of physio-chemical processes – the exposure of silver haloids to light. A photograph was the sheer physical output of the operation of brute laws of nature. Thus, the skeptics concluded that photography precluded the creative, imaginative, subjective, expressive contribution of the photographer. Photographic images, according to the skeptic, were the automatic product of a machine, not of a mind. Press a button and you get a picture. But art is not made thusly. Art requires an artist who expresses herself through her work and who imposes form or style upon her materials. Yet that cannot be achieved by a machine slavishly grinding its way through a sequence of physical states.

According to the philosopher, Benedetto Croce, "if photography be not quite art, that is precisely because the element of nature in it remains more or less unconquered and ineradicable" in a way that blocks the transmission of artistic intuitions and points of view. The visual artist gives form to his subject, grouping its elements in a way predicated upon securing a specific effect. But the photograph allegedly does nothing more than mechanically reproduce the formless flow of reality as it passes before the lens of the camera.

This view of photography, moreover, was confirmed for many by the earliest film screenings, such as the newsreels of the Lumière Brothers in France. Called *actualités*, these one-minute shorts captured street scenes from home and abroad, travelogue footage, domestic affairs, folkways, historic events, everyday details, and the like. These films appeared to be little more than documentary records of whatever flitted before the cameras of the itinerant Lumière photographers. People wandered in and out of the frame. Audience fascination was with the reproduction of reality in all its shapeless bustle. Putatively, it was not as though some comment or feeling on the part of the photographers regarding their subjects emerged from the screen. What there was to see and wonder at was arguably nothing more than the simulacra of reality mechanically reproduced with neither the intervention of a subjective artistic interpretation nor formal invention.

On the one hand, the skeptic argued that inasmuch as photography was mechanical, it foreclosed the opportunity for creativity – both expressive and formal – on the part of the artist. An objective physical process, it left no space for the subjective influence of the artist. Photography was simply a mechanism. Moreover, the skeptic also drew attention to the kind of mechanism it is. It is a machine for automatically reproducing whatever finds its way in front of the camera lens. In this regard it is nothing but a recording device. When the camera is pointed at a street scene, it mechanically records reality. And, the skeptic maintains, just as reality comes without expressivity or form, so does a mere mechanical recording of it.

But what of the case where what the motion picture camera is trained upon is not an everyday street scene, but a dramatic enactment of a fiction? Might not that be an artwork? After all, aren't the actors expressing their thoughts and feelings about the characters they are playing? However, the skeptic rejects this possibility, again by stressing that photography, moving or otherwise, is essentially a process of exact recording and, therefore, incapable of being art in its own right.

Consider the case of the museum-shop postcard of Munch's painting *The Scream*. It is not an artwork in its own right, though *The Scream* is. The postcard is at best the photographic reproduction of an artwork. It is not an artwork itself. Likewise, a CD of Bizet's *Carmen* is not an artwork itself; it is the recording of one. The postcard and the CD give us access to already pre-existing artworks, but they are not artworks themselves. They are recording media, not artistic media.

The photograph of *The Scream* does not make art; it only preserves art. Photographs and, by extension, films are recordings; they are rather like time capsules – temporal containers – that convey artistic achievements that are far away in space and/or time from us. But just as the jar in which the caviar is sold is not the delicacy itself, neither is the photographic recording of the artwork – whether of a painting or a dramatic fiction – the work of art. No one would mistake the photographic plates in an art history book for the works of art they showcase. Furthermore, this argument can be applied to dramatic films. If a filmed drama is thought to be an artwork, then it is not the film that is the pertinent artwork. Rather it is the drama – enacted before the camera and preserved on film – that is the artwork proper. Fiction films are not artworks under their own steam; they are at best slavish, mechanical recordings of theatrical or dramatic artworks – that is, recordings of artworks staged in front of the camera.

For decades, many contended that the German expressionist film *The Cabinet of Dr. Caligari* was not really an example of cinematic art, but only the mechanical recording of a stage play. Yes, the sets are expressive – expressive of a kind of existential claustrophobia. But this, it was said, is the product of the work of the set designers; the filmmaker simply photographed the antecedently expressive sets that stood before the camera. Similarly, the acting is expressive. But that is the contribution of the performers. The filmmakers merely mechanically recorded that which the actors creatively invented.

Whatever artistry is attributable to *Caligari*, the skeptic protests, belongs to the enactment of the narrative and the design of the stage sets which were automatically imprinted on the film stock as the camera routinely cranked on. Surely, the skeptic charges, exposing film is not the work of an artist. If there is art in *Caligari*, then it is due to the work of the writers, the actors, and the set designers and not to the people running the cameras. If the director, Robert Wiene, added art to the proceedings, it is as a theatrical director of actors and not as a cinematic director of cameras that he makes his mark. The film as such simply preserves an already existing dramatic accomplishment for posterity. It does not make art itself; at best it makes available art from elsewhere in space and/or time. *The Cabinet of Dr. Caligari* is just like the postcard of Munch's *Scream*, except that it moves.

Because photography, still or moving, was regarded as the mere mechanical recording or copying of reality, its potential for creating art was denied. For it seems reasonable to presuppose that art requires the addition of artistic expression and/or formal articulation to its subject matter. And a mere copy adds nothing. Unlike a painting of a street scene, the Lumière *actualité* reproduces mechanically the look of said reality sans artistic invention. On the other hand, where the subject of a film is a fiction, such as *The Cabinet of Dr. Caligari*, then, allegedly, the art is in the dramatic enactment of the story as it played in front of the camera. The art is not in the camerawork – not in the film as film. In contrast to theater, which creates artistic fictions, film at best records their performance.

To summarize: if a film is a nonfiction – say, a Lumière newsreel – it cannot be art, since art, properly so called, affords the scope for artistic expression and/or formal invention. Machine reproductions do not afford the scope for artistic expression and/or formal invention, since they are, by definition, automatic mechanical transcriptions of how things look. So insofar as non-fiction films are machine reproductions, they cannot be artworks.

Nor, on the other hand, argues the skeptic, are fiction films art. Again, the problem is that film is essentially a recording medium. Where a fiction film is said to be art, the skeptic maintains that this confuses the recording of something artistic – namely, the performance of a drama – with an artwork in its own right. If Charlie Chaplin created art when in *The Gold Rush* he made us see his boot as a turkey dinner, it was his pantomime before the camera and not the filming of it that belonged to the Muses. But in that case, there is no art of the film as such; there is only theater art – in Chaplin's case mime – captured on film.

Of course, many remained unconvinced by these skeptical arguments against photography and then film. And in the process of resisting the skeptic's case, the philosophy of film took flight. For in addressing the skeptic's allegations that films could not be art on a priori grounds, the friends of film began to clarify the ways in which films could qualify as authentic candidates for the status of artworks.

Some theorists, like Rudolf Arnheim, pointed out that in spite of their mechanical dimensions, both photography and film were not perfect replicas of that which they represented and that, in virtue of the ways in which they diverged from being perfect mechanical recordings, photographs and films could be expressive. A low-angle shot, for example, can portray a typewriter as massive, thereby commenting upon it. In his *The General Line*, Sergei Eisenstein uses shots like this to underscore the *oppressiveness* of the bureaucracy that employs such typewriters. Similarly, a filmmaker can use a distorting lens to make a point; laughing faces can be made to appear hideous by means of a wide-angle lens, thereby unmasking the cruelty that can lurk underneath a smile.

Moreover, as silent film theorists frequently emphasized, film is not reducible to moving photography. Editing is at least as important to film as we know it. But since film editing can rearrange the spatio-temporal continuum, including the sequence of events in a play, a film need not be a mere slavish recording of anything – of either an actual everyday event or the theatrical performance of a fictional one. Editing gives the film-maker the capacity to rearrange reality creatively as well as to body forth imaginatively alternative fictional worlds – worlds of works of art.

Considerations like these have by now won the day – hardly anyone presently questions whether or not the motion picture is an artform. Indeed, some maintain that it was *the* artform of the twentieth century. Nevertheless, the arguments of the skeptics should not be dismissed as nothing but cranky conservatism. The skeptics recognized certain profound features of film whose possible implications enthusiasts sometimes failed to appreciate. Thus, one can learn about film from the skeptics, even in the process of trying to refute them. So, for the rest of this chapter, I will be taking a long look at the skeptic's case against the possibility of film art both in order to see how it goes wrong and what it gets right.

The Skeptical Argument

The skeptic's leading argument against the possibility of film art has three major movements. It goes like this:

1 Photography is not art.
2 A film is at best a photographic recording of a work of dramatic art.
3 Therefore, film itself is not art.

This skeptical argument, in turn, is supported by three further arguments, each of which is intended to bolster the first premise of the leading argument. For convenience sake, let us call these three supporting arguments respectively: (1) the causation argument; (2) the control argument; and (3) the aesthetic interest argument. Typically the skeptic does not appear to have additional arguments to reinforce the second premise of the lead argument. This premise is sometimes treated as if it were absolutely unobjectionable. This, however, is not so, and we will return to this lacuna after reviewing the three arguments in behalf of the first premise of the skeptic's master argument.

The Sheer Physical Causation Argument

Crucial for the skeptic's case against film is the premise that photography is not an art. One way in which the skeptic supports this is by means of *the sheer physical causation argument* (henceforth, usually just called "the causation argument"). The skeptic presupposes that anything worthy of being classified as art is necessarily an expression of thought – the expression of an idea, a feeling, an attitude, a point of view, or the articulation of a formal conception. If the snowflakes falling in my driveway assemble themselves in such a way that the results look exactly like one of Rodin's statues of Balzac, the skeptic would argue (and I think that most of us would agree) that that thing in my driveway is not a work of art. Unlike Rodin's statue of Balzac, there is no thinking, expression, or formal invention behind our putative snow "sculpture." Indeed, does it even make sense to call it a *sculpture*, since, given the case as we've described it, there was no sculpting involved. And, in any event, it is not the product of a sentient human agency. It is a natural event, the result of a mindless sequence of causes and effects, the outcome, albeit freakish, of the sheer operation of physical laws. That it resembles Rodin's Balzac, or, for that matter, Balzac, is an accident.

True, things that look like my snowdrift are usually the product of a mind – but not always. There are shadows cast by the mountains of the moon that from a certain angle are said to resemble a face. But such anomalies are not even representations, let alone artworks, the skeptics argue, since they are not the products of mental acts. They are not the result of human intentions, but of the sheer movement of matter. They do not express thought, since they do not express anything. If expression involves bringing something that is inside, such as a thought, outside, these stochastic flukes have nothing inside to manifest outside. They are completely the product of the random operation of physics, not psychology. They involve no thinker; they express no thinking; they are neither portraits nor artworks properly so called.

But what does this have to do with photography, including moving photography? A photograph can occur sans human agency. Imagine a camera falling off the back of a truck in such a way that it starts to click off perfectly focused snapshots. These images would not meet the skeptic's criterion for art status, since they express no thoughts. How could they? No one is taking the picture.

Likewise airport surveillance cameras do not require operators; they may be fully automated. That is why, in the normal course of things, we do not count that footage as art. For, once again, it is not plausible to suppose that any thought is expressed by an automated surveillance camera. Perhaps an artist can take such footage and re-edit it in such a way that it counts as art. But that is another story. Raw surveillance footage is not art, if only because it is mindless. So again: that a photographic image of *x*, moving or otherwise, enables us to recognize *x* in it does not entail that the image of *x* is an intentional product. Thus, we might also call this argument the *absence of intentionality argument*.

A photograph need not be the product of an intentional agent; it may be the consequence of a concatenation of sheer physical events. For example, we might imagine certain improbable but nevertheless logically possible instances of photographs that express no thoughts. Think of a cavern in the recesses of which there is a puddle of photographic salts; overhead there is a tiny crack in the ceiling of the cave that admits a ray of light. This light, in turn, functions like a pin-hole camera and fixes the outline of a neighboring volcano on the floor of the cave. A randomly occurring, "natural" photograph like this would not require a human photographer nor a human intention. And for that reason, we would not count an image such as this as an artistic representation of a volcano, no matter how nicely it appeared to resemble one. For, since it lacks a photographer, it expresses no thought about the volcano.

What these examples are intended to show is that photography does not necessarily require a camera operator. There could be cases of things that we would be perfectly willing to call photographs – i.e., genuine products of the process of photography – that are the outcome of a sequence of physical causes without any human intervention. Stripped down to its essence then, a photograph does not require human input, and, consequently, need not involve the expression of human thought or the implementation of human intentions. The expression of thought, in other words, is not an essential feature of photography. Therefore, with respect to its essential nature, photography is not art.

In this regard, what might be called the essential photograph differs profoundly from the essential painting, which, for the purposes of argument, we may take to be paradigmatic of art status. All paintings putatively have the property of *intentionality* which means, according to the skeptic, that paintings are (1) about something because (2) the painter intends this. A painting is intentional both in the sense that it is directed at something and in the sense that it is a vehicle for the thought of its maker (such as a comment on or interpretation of whatever the painting is about). But essential photographs are not intentional in either of these senses. They can be the result of completely causal processes lacking any intentional/ mental mediation. Nor is the appearance of the volcano in our fanciful example of the aforesaid "natural" photograph *about* anything; it is just a happenstance collision of events with no more content than a lightning bolt. Such an essential photograph could not express the thought that the volcano is awesome, as a painting of a volcano might, since an essential photograph of the sort imagined lacks an author to bear the thought, whereas a genuine painting, according to the skeptic, requires a sentient artificer by definition.

So the sheer physical causation argument ultimately boils down to this:

1   If something is art, then it must involve the expression of thought.
2   If something involves the expression of thought, it requires a mental dimension, also known as intentionality.
3   Intentionality is not an essential feature of photography.
4   Therefore, photography (including moving photography) is not essentially or necessarily art.

But if photography is not essentially art, then photography – whether still or moving – is not art qua photography, i.e., not in virtue of being photography.

Furthermore, whereas a painting can depict imaginary things, a photograph allegedly always delivers up the appearance of something that quite literally stood before the camera. Photographs present the spectator with what philosophers call referentially transparent contexts – in other words, in the typical case, the photograph P is the effect of cause C (a volcano, for instance) in such a way that the existence of P allows us to infer the existence of C (a volcano or, at least, something that looks like a volcano).

Paintings, in contrast, are referentially opaque. From the painting of a satyr, you are not advised to infer the existence of a satyr. Paintings can be about whatever painters imagine; their subjects do not necessarily exist. This too is a feature of intentionality, sometimes called intentional inexistence. On the other hand, that which gives rise to a photographic image must have existed and the photograph gives one inferential grounds to affirm it. Thus, this is another way in which the photograph lacks intentionality.

But painting is a representational artform in large measure because it involves intentionality – which feature of painting is intimately related to its capacity authorially to express thoughts concerning its subjects. Instead, photography, seen in terms of its minimal or essential nature, produces its images by means of mechanical causation rather than by means of intentionality. Consequently, photography as such – photography qua photography – is not a representational artform and neither is film, since film is basically to be understood as merely moving photography.

The Control Argument

In addition to the causation argument, the skeptic may also bring forward *the control argument* to elaborate the case against photographic art. According to the skeptic, an artist working in a medium requires control over the medium. Why? If art is the expression of thought, then in order to express one's thought clearly, you need to have control over every detail of the medium. If one lacks control, wayward effects may intrude into the results, undermining the thought or the feeling one intends to express. To articulate clearly one's thoughts, one must have a handle on the elements that go into presenting such thoughts. Ideally, it is said, every element in a genuine artwork either serves or should be capable of serving the expression of the artist's thoughts. To express a thought or a feeling is to clarify it; to clarify a thought or a feeling requires the capacity to hone every element that makes the thought or feeling more definite, and the capacity to expel or modify any element that might render it ambiguous. That is, art as the expression or articulation of thought or feeling requires consummate control over the relevant medium.

Painting evinces the requisite degree of control, since everything in a painting is ostensibly there because the painter *intentionally* put it there. Also, as we have seen, the painter – again in virtue of intentionality – can clarify her ideas or emotions by imagining whatever she needs to sharpen her thoughts, not restrained by what is. However, the photographer, including the cinematographer, supposedly has nothing approaching these resources. The photographer/cinematographer is at the mercy of what is in a way that it seems a painter never is.

The camera is akin to a mirror; the lens captures whatever looms before it, whether or not the camera operator is aware of the details she records and/or whether she intends to photograph them. For this reason, many historical spectacles are marred by the intrusion of unwanted anachronisms. A telephone pole, for example, may appear in the background of a medieval romance to the embarrassment of the camera crew just because it was a detail of the actual *mise en scène*,* albeit not one the cinematographer noticed or desired to record. However, since photography is a causal process, if something stands before the camera, the physical procedure guarantees, all things being equal, that it will appear in the image, no matter what the cinematographer intended.

---

* The scenographic layout – what is next to what and in front of what else, etc.

Were a telephone pole to appear in the background of a painting of what otherwise looked to be a medieval scene, we would suppose the painter intentionally drew it there and then go on to interpret what the painter meant by doing so. But when comparable anachronisms erupt in historical films, as they do with unnerving frequency, we infer that they arrived there because things got out of control. Since we know that the photographic process is automatic, abiding blindly by the laws of chemistry and optics, we understand that things appear, to the chagrin of filmmakers, in motion picture images that were never meant to be there.

There are so many things in front of the motion picture camera that may make an inadvertent debut in the final print of a film. Indeed, there are typically far too many details – large and small – for the cinematographer to keep track of. Many surprises appear uninvited in the finished film and the filmmaker just has to learn to live with them. On the other hand, everything in a painting is putatively there because that is what the painter intended. The painter is not surprised by what she finds in her painting, because she put it there. What would we make of a painter who, looking at her medieval scene, asked: "How did that telephone pole get there?" The painter has ultimate control over what inhabits her canvas.

Not so the photographer/cinematographer. Details appear in the photographic image, whether still or moving, just because they were in the camera's visual field even if no one on the film crew took heed of their presence. Furthermore, there are always an indefinitely large number of potential gaffs lying in wait for the unwary cinematographer. In this regard, the painter must be said to exert far more control than either the still or moving picture photographer.

Since paintings are intentionally produced, painters enjoy a degree of control such that there is nothing whose appearance in her pictures takes her aback. But photographers are often startled by what they *find* in their photos, because the causal process they initiate evolves in utter obliviousness of whatever the photographer believes, desires, or intends.

The photographer not only falls far short of the level of control the painter imposes over what can show up in her image; the photographer also lacks the painter's imaginative freedom to picture whatever she will – absolutely unrestrained by what is – inasmuch as the photographer can only present what can be placed before a camera. The painter can picture a werewolf for us; the filmmaker can only give us a photographic picture of a man got up in a werewolf outfit. The painter, in this regard, has greater freedom than the photographer, which, in turn, entails greater control over shaping her subject matter and the expression of her thinking about it.

Because art involves the expression of thought, only media that afford a high level of control are suitable for the purposes of artmaking. The clarification of thought requires a degree of plasticity. To get across an idea or a feeling clearly you may have to depart from the way the world is – either by adding to it or by subtracting from it. Photographic media, however, are inhospitable in this regard. They are tied to what is and they incorporate details, like inadvertent telephone poles, that are beyond the photographer's ken. Unlike painting, photography is not an artform; it lacks the degree of control evinced by an unquestionable artform like painting. And for the same reasons, moving photography suffers the same liabilities as does still photography. So, once again, we must conclude that film is not an art.

The Aesthetic Interest Argument

A third skeptical argument to the conclusion that photography/cinematography is not art can be labeled the *aesthetic interest argument*. An aesthetic interest is an interest that we take in something *for its own sake*, that is, because of the kind of thing it is. We take an aesthetic interest in the novel *Remembrance of Things Past* when we are preoccupied by the kind of thing it essentially is – an expression of thought – rather than as a set of books the color of the covers of which contrasts appealingly with the drapes in our living room.

According to the skeptic, photography cannot command aesthetic interest because a photograph is strictly analogous to a mirror. When we are interested in a mirror the object of our interest is whatever is reflected there and not the mirror itself. When one brushes off one's jacket in front of the looking glass, one is concerned with whether there is any telltale lint anywhere. We look into the glass in order to learn something about our jacket; our interest is in our jacket, not in the mirror reflection for its own sake. We are only interested in the mirror reflection because of what it tells us about something else, namely our jacket. Thus, the interest one typically has in a mirror is not an aesthetic interest.

Moreover, the skeptic argues that what is true of mirrors is also true of photographs. We are interested in them for what they show – historical events, atrocities, family weddings, dead relatives, and so on – and not for their own sake. It is the object in the photograph and not the photograph as an object that engages our attention.

With respect to the art of painting, it is the painting as object (indeed, as art object) that commands our attention and it does so because it is an expression of thought. Mirrors are not expressions of thought; they are optical appliances whose images are produced naturally, not intentionally. They relay appearances to us mechanically. There is no point in taking an interest in them in the way that we care about paintings. In fact, the only way to take an interest in the images in mirrors, if our interest is not scientific, is to be occupied by what they show us – like the police cruiser with the flashing blue light in our rear-view mirror.

Likewise, the skeptic argues that photos record appearances; they do not convey thoughts. We are interested in a photograph of x – say of Osama Bin Laden – because we are interested in seeing the way he looks. We are not interested in the photograph for itself, but only as a mechanism that transmits appearances. The interest is not aesthetic, since it is not an interest in the kind of thing the photograph is, but rather an interest in the person whose appearance it delivers.

Another way to make the skeptic's point here is to say that the skeptic is claiming that photographs, properly so called, are *transparent*. We have already seen that photographs are referentially transparent in contrast to the referential opacity characteristic of the productions of intentionality. That is, there is a causal connection between the photo and the object that gives rise to it such that the photo supplies grounds for inferring the existence of the object in the photo. My appearance in the surveillance footage supplies evidence that I was in the bank on the night of the robbery. All things being equal, the jury will legitimately infer it was so. But in addition to providing this inferential warrant, skeptics are also maintaining that photography as it is usually employed – what has been called "straight photography" – is also transparent in the sense that it provides us with indirect perceptual access to the object it represents. Just as seeing an object *through* a rear-view mirror is a special, indirect way of seeing the police cruiser behind me, so a photograph is a special way of seeing an object.

That is, we see objects *through* photographs just as I see objects through mirrors. In this way, photographs, like mirrors, are perceptually transparent. But, the skeptic adds, if photographs are perceptually transparent, then it is not the photograph in its own right that preoccupies us. It is the object to which the photograph gives us perceptual access that interests us, either for its own sake, or otherwise. In either case, our interest is not an aesthetic interest. We are not interested in the photograph as an object; we are not interested in the photograph as an artwork; we are interested in it because of what it shows and not how it shows it. Moreover, if a photograph cannot support aesthetic interest, then why suppose it is an artwork? For, the skeptic presumes, an artwork is just the kind of thing that enjoins aesthetic interest — that is, an artwork is the kind of thing in which we are interested because of the kind of thing (the kind of object) it is (rather than because of the kind of object to which it affords us perceptual access).

Suppose that the object of a photograph is something very beautiful — like a flowering rose — of the sort whose appearance we are typically said to value for its own sake. The skeptic maintains that the putative aesthetic interest here is the beautiful rose. Our attention is not drawn to the photograph itself — as it would be were it a genuine artistic object — but to the appearance of the flower which the photograph serves up transparently and mechanically. It is not, so to speak, a beautiful photograph but a photograph of a beautiful thing. And it is the beautiful thing in the photograph that is the object of our aesthetic interest, properly speaking. Likewise, when the movie presents us with a beautiful vista, it is the vista that is the object of our aesthetic interest, not the movie that allegedly merely records it.

The Soviet filmmaker Dziga Vertov called film the "microscope and telescope of time." Just as perceptual apparatuses like microscopes and telescopes enable us to penetrate very small and very large spaces, photographic processes enable us to "see into" the past, to "bridge" temporal distances at a glance. But, equally, just as in the normal course of affairs neither the microscope nor the telescope is the object of our interest, unless we are optical technicians or repairmen, neither, the skeptic maintains, is the photographic or cinematographic image. With respect to these things, we are meant to see "through" them; they are transparent.

To sum up: we are not interested in the photograph — as we are interested in genuine art objects — for the sake of the object it is. The photograph does not sustain aesthetic interest on its own. It is not an instance of genuine representational art. Consequently, if film, as its name indicates, is basically, essentially photographic in nature, then it is not a representational artform in its own right either. If a given film appears to elicit aesthetic interest — as *The Cabinet of Dr. Caligari* does — that is because it is a transparent photographic record of a dramatic (theatrical) representation. It is the dramatic representation itself — as it was staged and enacted in front of the motion picture camera — that grips our interest, just as it is Groucho Marx's monologues and not the moving picture recording of them of them that is the locus of our aesthetic interest in *Animal Crackers*. To suspect otherwise is to confuse the box that contains the cookies for the cookies themselves.

Responding to the Skeptics

These three arguments – the causation argument, the control argument, and the aesthetic interest argument – are the basis for the skeptic's brief against the possibility that some films are artworks. These arguments, however benighted they may appear, call our attention to intriguing features of film, even if the skeptic does not always draw the right conclusions from his observations. The arguments often sound convincing, but are they decisive? Let us review them critically in order to locate their potential shortcomings.

Round Two: The Causation Argument

First, let us reconsider the causation argument. The skeptic correctly points out that the production of a photograph, properly so called, does not necessarily require the intentional contribution of an agent. A photograph, still or moving, could result from a series of physical events with no intentional input. A malfunctioning camera might switch on when dropped, or, more fantastically, photographs might appear in nature as the result of a sequence of statistically improbable but logical possible events as discussed earlier in the case of our natural "cave" photo of the volcano. These cases suggest that intentionality is not an essential feature of photos. That is, there can be photos stripped of intentionality altogether which are nevertheless still appropriately classified as photos. But if there is no intentionality involved, they cannot be expressions of thought, for they are bereft of thought content (something they are about). Thus, what might be called essential or minimal photographs are not necessarily artworks, where to be an artwork requires, *ex hypothesi*, being an expression of thought.

So there are *conceivable* photographs that are not artworks. But, granting that there *may* be such a case, what about actual photographs rather than merely conceivable ones? When we admire the photos of Edward Steichen as works of art, we are talking about actually existing photographs and not just conceivable ones. Moreover, in the cases of the actually existing photographs that we classify as artworks, do we not believe, with good cause, that the intentions of the relevant photographer are expressed in his images? Steichen's photos convey thoughts and feelings about the content toward which they draw our attention and we believe they are undoubtedly intended to do precisely that by their maker.

As Walter Benjamin noted, Atget's photographs, for example, express thoughts about Parisian cityscapes. The pertinent photographs, in other words, possess intentionality in the ways the skeptic mandates, and said photographs should, consequently, count as works of art in accordance with the terms the skeptic's argument dictates. What difference does it make to the artistic status of actually existing photographs that express thought, as Atget's do, that there are some other conceivable photographs that do not?

That some photographs express thoughts is enough to establish that some photographs are art. The fact that there may be conceivable photographs, like those we have explored, that do not express thought at best shows that not all photographs must necessarily be art. But, on the one hand, no one wants to prove that; even the greatest fan of photography will concede that not every photograph is or must be art. Who thinks the photos on standard automobile licenses are art?

On the other hand, the skeptic has to prove more than just the proposition that some photos are not or may not be art. The skeptic is committed to proving that necessarily no photograph is art nor can it be. But how will the skeptic show that? What the skeptic, invoking the notion of an essential or minimal photograph, has demonstrated is that intentionality is not necessarily involved in producing something that we would be willing to categorize as a photograph. But it does not follow logically from the proposition that intentionality is not necessarily involved in producing some photographs that necessarily intentionality is not involved in the production of any photographs. The fact that a surveillance camera at a traffic light records a scofflaw automatically – without the intervention of any intention – does not entail that intentionality and intentions do not come into play productively when I select the subject of my snapshot, choose the lens, film stock and aperture setting that I desire, and adjust the lighting for my purposes at the same time as I prepare to execute my photograph. To imagine that the lack of intentionality in the case of the surveillance camera must imply a lack of intentionality in the shoot I've just described is a logical error (called a *modal fallacy* because it is an error in alethic modal logic, i.e., the logic of necessity and possibility).

From the fact that mere photographic status does not necessarily require intentionality, it does not follow that anything legitimately classified as photography must necessarily lack intentionality. Though the skeptic appears to presume this inference, it is a non sequitur. Technically, it is a fallacy of alethic modal logic to attempt to move from (1) photography is not *necessarily* an intentional product to (2) *necessarily* photography is not an intentional product. But the skeptic seems to attempt, erroneously, to make precisely this inferential leap.

Against the skeptic, we can argue that even if certain conceivable photos lack intentionality and are not artworks for that very reason, this does not even remotely suggest that all actual photos are equally compromised. For as we have just seen, if we did not know already, some actual photos can and do have intentional content and can be and have been intentionally produced, thereby satisfying even the skeptic's criteria for art status. And if still photographs can be representational artworks on these grounds, so can films, even films considered as merely essentially moving photographs.

Perhaps the skeptic will argue that anything short of what we've called an essential or minimal film should not count as an authentic specimen of the medium. But when adjudicating the question of whether some photos are artworks, why would we grant greater weight to how they might have been made as opposed to how they were actually made?

Moreover, the skeptic cannot plausibly argue that if causation is implicated in the production of a work, then that precludes the kind of intentionality requisite for art status. For were that so, virtually no medium could be said to be capable of producing art, since almost all of them possess an ineliminable causal dimension. Consider: even a paintbrush is a tool; once an artist touches his brush to the canvas, a causal process is set in motion; the paint flows at a rate determined by chemical law. The sculptor is beholden to physics. The organ, of course, is a machine. But in none of these cases do the facts that there are causal processes involved preclude the expression of thought. So, if in countless cases of already acknowledged artistic media their causal or mechanical aspects do not foreclose the possibility of expressing thought, then why does the skeptic suppose matters to stand differently with photography and film?

The Control Argument Revisited

The skeptic emphasizes that the expression of thought – for him, the *sine qua non* of art status – requires control. If there is no control over the medium in question, the skeptic contends, then one is simply not expressing one's own thought. This seems fairly persuasive. For if there is no control whatsoever, then it is doubtful that any thought is being expressed at all. Furthermore, if you believe that there is an essential connection between the expression of thought and the possession of style, then if one lacks control over one's medium, what one produces lacks style, with the upshot: no control, no style, no art. Such is the control argument.

An initial response to the control argument must be that it is utopian. If what is required for art status is *total* control of a medium, then we will be compelled to discount as artforms most of the practices that we esteem as such. Most artists have to negotiate compromises with their medium – to adjust to the material at hand. A theater director will have to cast her drama with the available actors; these may not be and often are not exactly how she imagined the characters upon her first reading of the script. But she will make do. A director does not have total control; she has to work within parameters set by others and by circumstances.

Likewise a choreographer has just these dancers and just these spaces. Whatever dreams she had for her dance must be brought down to earth, so to say. Virtually every particular artistic element comes with limitations. Even the writer has to work within the confines of a specific language. The composer has to work with the array of existing instruments and the musician has to work with the peculiarities of his tool. Architects and sculptors are evidently very constrained physically in terms of the amount of leeway they have for exerting their will on their materials, while even the painter will have to live with the resources to which she has access – such as the available varieties of paint – and their attendant properties. Though critics may speak of this or that artist as controlling every aspect of her creation, this is, in the main, journalistic hyperbole – a feel-good fantasy for the Sunday arts and leisure section.

Few artforms, if any, realize the fantasy of total control. Are we to say, then, that no medium is capable of producing art? Surely a more reasonable tack is to lower our sights – to require only that a medium permit its practitioners sufficient control, rather than total control. But this adjustment then reframes the terms of the debate – to wit: does the film medium allow enough control for the filmmaker to project intentional content – i.e., to express thoughts and feelings and/or to structure formally his subject matter?

We can start to formulate a positive response to this by reminding ourselves of some of the points that we made in the process of refuting the causation argument. We noted that the photographer has a number of variables at her disposal that enable her to articulate and, thereby, express her thoughts. She can select her subject matter, for instance. Certainly it is not random statistical coincidence that explains the undeniable consistency in the work of a Diane Arbus. Also, the photographer may choose the type of camera, lens, film stock, aperture setting, and lighting effects that she determines to be suitable for whatever thoughts and/or feelings she means to express. And, in addition, the photographer may set up the shot – staging it, establishing the right subject-to-camera distance, electing the props, costumes, and make-up, and, indeed, often the very models who then strike the pose in this regalia.

Frequently, the photographer makes a series of photos of a given subject, settling ultimately on the one from an array of alternatives that most realizes her conception. And once she shoots the film, she can then go on to clarify more specifically her expression by deploying a gamut of laboratory processes, including printing on various papers, cropping, air-brushing, and so forth.

At each step in the creation of a photograph, there are choices that can be made, each of which will inflect the expression of thought and/or feeling embodied in the picture. Opting for one of these alternatives rather than another – a wide-angle lens rather than a long lens – may make a difference that expresses with greater precision the content and/or qualities of the thoughts and/or feelings that the photographer endeavors to convey. Should not all this count as enough control of the medium to warrant regarding photography as a representational artform?

One reason to think so is that there is a striking inventory of correlations between many of the acknowledged variables for modifying paintings expressively and those that obtain with respect to photography, including choice of subject, lighting, scale, framing, and so on. Moreover, we already know that variations along these expressive dimensions have proven rich enough to differentiate the thoughts and feelings that an August Sandler intends to express from those of a Robert Mapplethorpe.

Whether a medium grants sufficient control to be categorized as a representational art can be put to the test by gauging if there exist enough alternative variables of articulation for us to identify distinctive stylistic or expressive profiles. That we can isolate stylistic and expressive contrasts between photos by Cindy Sherman and Walker Evans and then go on to associate these with the expression of different thoughts strongly supports the conjecture that photography possesses the degree of control sufficient to qualify as a medium capable of artmaking.

The style or form of a work of art is the ensemble of choices that function to realize its point or purpose – for example, the expression of thought and/or affect. Control is required in order to possess a style and to express thoughts. The level of control is a function of having at one's disposal a range of articulatory options such that the choice of one of these strategies with respect to the pertinent variable rather than another makes for stylistic and/or expressive differences; for it is choice from a field of alternative elements with contrasting qualities and associations that clarifies thought and particularizes style.

Photography possesses multiple expressive channels, replete with alternative, contrasting strategies of construction at each level of articulation. This wealth of options affords the creative wherewithal for the photographer to implement her intentions by strategic decisions. Furthermore, such has proven to be more than enough control for artistic purposes, since it has enabled us to locate the divergent "authorial intentionalities" of a Man Ray, a Nan Goldin, a Weegie, and a Moholy-Nagy.

The cinematographic image, moreover, offers even more levers of stylistic control and choice than does the still photographic image. For example, camera movement allows the cameraman the opportunity to explore the array, bracketing this or that detail for special attention. Of course, neither medium grants absolute control. But, as indicated, the real argument is over the issue of whether the relevant medium permits sufficient control. And for the reasons just rehearsed, we can insist against the skeptic that photography and film appear to satisfy the requisite level of control justifiably expected of an artform, representational or otherwise.

Back to the Aesthetic-Interest Argument

Plato demeaned the seriousness of mimetic painting and poetry by analogizing them to mirrors. Similarly, the skeptic disparages the pretensions of photography, still and moving, to the status of art by alleging that cameras are little more than mirrors artlessly reflecting whatever wanders into their purview. For if photos and films are like mirrors, then they no more express thoughts than does the glass on the front of your bathroom medicine cabinet. A mirror trades in mere appearances rather than intentionality. Thus, if photography and film are strictly analogous to mirrors, then we do not care about them for their own sake; we do not take an aesthetic interest in them. Rather, we care about them or take an interest in them for the sake of the objects they show us. I do not care about the curling, sepia snapshot of my beloved grandmother as a photograph but as a reminder of Nanny.

The capacity of film and photography to afford a window into the past has been called "photographic transparency." The notion of photographic transparency provides the basis for the skeptic's assertion that photography and film are not artforms, representational or otherwise, because they are not capable of commanding our attention to the kind of objects they are in their own right. Consequently, neither photography nor film can sustain aesthetic interest. For if they are transparent, then we see through them and our interest lands on the appearance of whatever they are images of.

If the photograph is of President Bush's inauguration, then my interest lies in his inauguration. It supposedly makes no sense for me to be interested in the photograph as such, since it is transparent – i.e., we see through it.

But there seems to be a dubious presupposition underlying the skeptic's polemic, namely, that if a photograph, still or moving, is transparent, then it is invisible. Here "invisible" means something like seeing an object through a photograph is *just like* seeing the object in question face to face. That is, the mediating agency of the photograph goes undetected by the human eye, and, since we allegedly don't see it, we don't take an interest in it, where *it* is the photograph as such – the photograph as an object of attention in its own right and not merely the image of some other object.

Yet even if we grant that photographs are transparent, it would not follow that they are invisible. In fact, not even all mirrors are invisible in the way the skeptic suggests. When I look into one of those convex mirrors that enables one to see around corners in parking lots, I may see through it to the car that is racing toward me; however, I also see the distortion in the mirror. Such a mirror is hardly invisible even if it is transparent; transparency does not entail invisibility. But the skeptic's aesthetic interest argument against photography only gains traction if photos are invisible; alleging they are simply transparent is not enough. Moreover, the case for the invisibility of photographic mediation is even more unlikely than the case for the invisibility of mirror mediation.

Throughout most of the history of photography, both still and moving, most photographs were black and white. This feature of photos was scarcely invisible. Looking at a photograph of the blood-spattered body of the Archduke Ferdinand was not *just like* seeing a dead body staring you in the face. It was obvious to everyone that the absence of color was a feature of the photographic mediating process.

Needless to say, one could take an interest in this aspect of a certain photograph – noticing whether the blacks and whites contrasted starkly and brutally, or whether they were subtly mapped along the grey scale. Moreover, a photographer could intentionally design a photograph in such a way as to reward attention to photographic features like this. That is, photographers could make photos that could support taking an aesthetic interest in such objects in their own right. In short, there is no reason to suspect that the photographer cannot meet the skeptic's challenge on the skeptic's own terms.

Photography may be transparent, but even if it is, it may still be interesting because of the ways in which the medium displays views of objects that depart, in various respects, from the ways in which those objects would appear to "photographically unassisted" or "normal" vision. The photograph, even on the transparency thesis, need not be thought to disappear; the image need not collapse into the object of which it is an image. Thus, it is possible to take an interest in a photographic object for its own sake – an aesthetic interest, that is, in a photographic art object. Taking an aesthetic interest in a photograph as an object in its own right, moreover, will be especially apposite where the photograph has been designed to encourage such an interest.

If we are willing to say that we see objects through photographs, then that kind of seeing, like seeing through a mirror, is indirect, rather than direct. Furthermore, indirect "photographic seeing" is different in kind from direct seeing – seeing that involves a close encounter of the third kind, a face-to-face brush with the object of attention. Photographs, for example, lift the object out of its natural context and reframe or bracket it, often enabling us to see the object afresh in ways denied to us in routine face-to-face encounters with it. Photographs freeze the object in a moment, potentially disclosing aspects of it that might be otherwise typically occluded in everyday life. And the object pictured in a photograph is absent from the viewer, inviting an opportunity for scrutiny that in "real life," where the object is present to the viewer, might be dangerous, callous, insensitive, impolite, or confusing. Moreover, it is this feature of absence that can make nostalgia an appropriate emotional response to the someone or something depicted in the photograph, whereas nostalgia would be an absurd reaction were they "in our face."

In virtue of the differences between photographic seeing and face-to-face seeing, features of the photographic medium can defamiliarize the objects whose appearances they convey. Defamiliarization, in turn, may serve as an artistic strategy for expressing thoughts about the relevant objects, persons, events, actions, and places captured on film. Even if photographs are said to be transparent, their departure from face-to-face or direct seeing leaves open the possibility of artistic defamiliarization and, thence, the expression of thought and feeling. Furthermore, if a photograph by means of features of the photographic medium expresses a thought and/or emotion about its objects, then we may take an interest in the photograph qua photograph – that is, we may take an aesthetic interest in the way in which the photograph at hand mobilizes characteristic features of its medium to express thought.

Our concern, in other words, need not be presumed to be absorbed solely in the appearance of the object as it has been relayed to us by the photograph. The defamiliarizing resources of the photographic medium can be harnessed to express thoughts about the objects portrayed and this process, in consequence, can give rise to ruminating aesthetically about the way in which the kind of object a photograph is has given birth to a thought. That photographs may defamiliarize opens the possibility for them to express thoughts about the object they depict, contrary to what the skeptic assumes about the alleged transparency of photography. Moreover, the process of expressing thoughts not only gives us a renewed interest in the object upon which the photograph comments, but an interest in the photograph itself as viewers ask themselves how the use of various features of the medium has managed to engender thought.

Like the still photograph, the motion picture shot has an estimable repertoire of devices that diverge from the direct face-to-face perception of objects. These include the close-up, high- and low-angle shots, lenses of various types, filters, traveling shots, alternating camera distances, and so forth. Each of these devices makes possible the expression of thought and/or feeling about the objects presented in the shots. If such shots are transparent, they can nevertheless be expressive, since there is no coherent view of transparency that implies that the photographic image, still or moving, is plausibly indiscernible from that of which it is an image. But that is what the aesthetic interest argument that the skeptic advances would appear to require. And that is just unconvincing.

The skeptic argues that an aesthetic interest is an interest that we take in an object because of the kind of thing it is. Photographs do not afford aesthetic interest because whatever interest we have in photographs, still or moving, collapses into the interest we have in the objects of which they are photographs. Two things need to be said about this.

First, as has already been emphasized, we may take an interest in the photograph qua photograph in virtue of the ways in which it has exploited the photographic (or cinematographic) medium to express a thought or feeling.

However, we may also wish to challenge the skeptic's conception of an aesthetic interest. For the skeptic, it seems that an aesthetic interest in an object must be about the kind of object it is; so it must be an interest in the modes and materials that comprise the object. An aesthetic interest in an oil painting must be one that takes notice of how oil paint has been used to achieve a certain effect. This seems to imply that an aesthetic interest in an artwork requires insider knowledge about properties of the modes and materials of the artform in which the object is created.

But this seems to be an overly stipulative conception of what counts as an aesthetic interest. Surely, I have an aesthetic interest in a film if I am absorbed by its expressive properties. For example, I think many viewers had legitimate aesthetic interests in the "hot chocolate" number in *Polar Express*, taken as they were with its infectious exuberance and good spirits. And yet I suspect that few viewers, including myself, have much of an understanding of how it was made. However, even though we might not be able to be interested in the object in terms of the immensely technical achievement it is, our interests were still aesthetic in the usual sense of that term.

Moreover, the relevance of this for the prospects of taking an aesthetic interest in photography should be clear-cut. Photography, still and moving, can manifest expressive properties of objects that might otherwise go unremarked, especially in direct, face-to-face encounters with said objects in quotidian experience. People are very often absorbed in these qualities as revealed by a master photographer or cinematographer, like Gregg Toland. Thus, it is false to suggest, that photographs, whether still or moving, cannot reward aesthetic attention and sustain aesthetic interest.

What about the Skeptic's Second Premise?

Thus far we have been bickering with the first premise of the skeptic's master argument. This has been a fairly intricate exercise because the skeptic supports this opening move with an elaborate set of considerations. But the skeptic's case also depends upon the truth of the second premise in the argument – namely, that film is at best a photograph (a moving photograph) of a dramatic representation. Without this premise, the skeptic cannot extrapolate what he alleges to be the limitations of photography to the case of film. That is, without this second premise the argument that film cannot be art falters.

Luckily sketching our reservations about the second premise in the skeptic's argument need not be as complex as unhorsing his defense of the first premise, since the skeptic presents little by way of motivating the claim that films are nothing more than moving photographs of dramatic representations. The skeptic appears to regard this as self-evident, which it truly extraordinary, since it seems so palpably mistaken.

Films are not mere *photographs* of dramatic representations for the painfully obvious reason that films are not merely photographs. Photography, that is, is not the only constituent element that comprises film. In addition, there is, among other things, most notably, also editing. So even if all the arguments against photography had won the day, those objections could not be transferred to the case against film, since the edited dimension of cinema can express thoughts and feelings, is not transparent, can facilitate a more than sufficient level of artistic control, and can abet a locus of aesthetic interest, both in the skeptic's narrow sense and in the broader, more ordinary sense. The Odessa Steps sequence of Eisenstein's film *Potemkin* expresses a viewpoint about the event that it is implausible to suppose any stationary-camera position on the actual event in 1905 could have delivered. Perhaps skeptics will carp that editing is not really film art, but something else. However, to deny that editing is a characteristic element of the motion picture begs the question. But it also invites the question: if not film, what else?

Nor can the rich repertoire of techniques available to the contemporary filmmaker for coordinating the audio with the visual components of film be reduced to the photographic aspect of the medium. When the horror-suspense filmmaker of *The Descent* introduces frightening, off-screen sounds, how is the emotional anxiety she is provoking simply attributable to photography. The *frisson* would not occur without the sound. And the sound design of a movie is patently not part of its photographic dimension.

Film, in sum, has many more dimensions than the photographic one. So even if photography/cinematography was as sullied artistically as the skeptic insinuates, it would still not follow that cinema is comparably incapacitated as a player in the art game.

But another problem with the skeptic's second premise is that it presupposes that the image track of film is exclusively photographic. Undoubtedly, in the main, for most of film history, this has been true of most movies. But it is not *necessarily* true of motion picture images, as one realizes when one contemplates the development of new moving picture technologies, such as computer-generated mattes. As seen in *Sky Captain and the World of Tomorrow*, not to mention recent installments of *Star Wars* and *Lord of the Rings*, whole cities, armies, and air fleets can be created without primary recourse to the mediation of traditional photography/cinematography. These things can be concocted out of thin air, digitally fabricated, if you will. Indeed, in the future, entire feature-length motion pictures are likely to be constructed in the computer. I say that this is likely if only because it is so economically attractive. Producers will not have to drag casts and crews to expensive locations, and trouble-some, highly paid actors can be retired in favor of digitally synthesized ones. I can see the producers smiling already.

Again, the skeptic may say that these are not really films, since they are not celluloid-based. But I doubt that most people will hesitate to call moving picture narratives that look like the movies of yesteryear film. They will continue to call them *film* for the same reason they continue to call blue jeans "Levis," copiers "Xeroxes," and cola "Coke." *Film* was one of the first names we had for this sort of thing and it will stick, just as we continue to call those things "zippers" after their inventor.[*]

Of course, although it might be more accurate to call the optical creations made possible by computer technology and whatever new inventions come down the pike in the future "moving images," most people, I predict, will continue indiscriminately to call motion picture narratives, however they are produced, *films* in honor of the first medium that made these moving spectacles popular.

But it is important to remember that photographic film is not the only delivery system for what we call film (a.k.a. motion pictures) in the broader sense. And since some of these delivery systems need not employ photographic film in any way, it is false to allege that a dramatic film is a photograph of a dramatic representation. It could be a computer-generated representation in its own right. Moreover, this has always been a logical possibility for the film medium, even if the mass production of such work awaits the future.

Furthermore, it should be evident that computer-generated imagery faces none of the challenges that the skeptic levels at straight photography. Such imagery may mirror nothing, nor can it always be said to be transparent because sometimes it creates its own objects. What appears on screen is as much under the control of the CGI specialist as what appears on the canvas is under the control of the painter. Nor can there be any question of whether computer-generated imagery can express thoughts. It can do so in the same ways that a painting does.

At this point, the skeptic may reject these claims on the grounds that computer-generated imagery and anything else like it that is invented in the future is not really film, but, perhaps, animation or even painting. But at that point, the skeptic is in danger of exiting a genuine philosophical debate about the evolving practice of motion picture making and indulging in, at best, an antiquarian and primarily verbal debate about some of its earliest stages.

---

[*] For example, I doubt anyone, including both ordinary and informed viewers, will hesitate to call the last section of Kiarostami's 1997 *Taste of Cherry* "film" just because it was shot on video. "Film" has just become another way of saying "moving image," irrespective of the provenance of its material process of production, Or so I conjecture.

In short, the second premise of the skeptic's master argument is as troubled as the first one. Consequently, at this point in the dialectic, it seems fair to say that the skeptics have failed to carry their point. Thus, we may continue to share the common-sense conviction that (some) films (some motion pictures or moving images) are art. The burden of proving otherwise belongs to the skeptic.

In sum, throughout this chapter we have been engaged in addressing the arguments of skeptics who contend that art cannot be made by means of film. Though this debate, from the outset, may not have seemed particularly alive to many readers, it is to be hoped that in considering the skeptic's brief a number of interesting and heuristically valuable claims about photography and photographically based cinematography have been brought to light – such as their alleged transparency. As we will see in ensuing chapters, these claims will continue to figure in other debates concerning the moving image.

However, until further notice, the debate about whether film, or, more precisely, the moving image, is art is closed. Motion pictures can be art. It is important to establish this unequivocally from the outset, since I doubt that we would have any interest at all in developing a philosophy of motion pictures were it not the case that this particular technology (or set of technologies) had evolved into a genuine artistic practice.

Suggested Reading

If some of the topics in this chapter have intrigued you and stimulated your interest in pursuing them in greater depth, let us offer some further readings for your consideration. If the skeptical position about the possibility of an art of film appears worth a second look, by far the most sophisticated version of it can be found in "Photography and Representation," by Roger Scruton in his book *The Aesthetic Understanding* (South Bend, IN: St. Augustine Press, 1998), 119–48. A discussion of the historical background of the prejudice against photography and then cinematography as art can be found in the first chapter of *Philosophical Problems of Classical Film Theory* by Noël Carroll (Princeton, NJ: Princeton University Press, 1988). A particularly effective and extremely historically influential answer to the traditional charges that neither photography nor film is art is *Film as Art* by the indomitable Rudolf Arnheim (Berkeley, CA: University of California Press, 1956).

Powerful responses to Roger Scruton's arguments include Berys Gaut, "Cinematic Art," *Journal of Aesthetics and Art Criticism* 60:4 (Fall 2002), 299–312, and Dominic McIver Lopes, "The Aesthetics of Photographic Transparency," *Mind* 112:447 (July 2003), 433–48.

The idea of photographic transparency is developed in Patrick Maynard, "Drawing and Shooting: Causality in Depiction," *Journal of Aesthetics and Art Criticism* 44:2 (Winter 1985/6), 115–29, and Kendall Walton, "Transparent Pictures: On the Nature of Photographic Realism," *Critical Inquiry* 11:2 (Dec. 1984), 246–77. Kendall Walton has defended criticisms of his view in the article, "On Pictures and Photographs: Objections Answered," in *Film Theory and Philosophy*, edited by Richard Allen and Murray Smith (Oxford: Oxford University Press, 1997).

Of classical film theorists, the author who comes closest to articulating the "transparency" view is Andé Bazin. See his "The Ontology of the Photographic Image," in *What Is Cinema?*, vol. 1, trans. Hugh Gray (Berkeley, CA: University of California Press, 1967). Consider also Stanley Cavell, *The World Viewed* (Cambridge, MA: Harvard University Press, 1971, 1974, 1979).

Chapter Two

Medium Specificity

The topic of this chapter is the doctrine of medium specificity or, as it is sometimes better known, the problem of the purity of the medium – the view that artists should be true to the medium in which they work, or, in other words, they should not pursue effects that belong to some other medium. Needless to say, the medium that concerns us is the one that is usually labeled alternatively film, cinema, or the movies. Traditionally, purists with regard to film are particularly anxious that filmmakers not dilute the cinematic medium with that of theater.

What is a Medium?

A medium is something that mediates. The word itself derives from the Latin word *medius*, which means "middle." The medium is a middleman, a go-between betwixt one thing and another. In the arts, it is that which brings the artist's conception to the audience, or, more exactly, it is generally what makes the artist's vision physically manifest for reception. With respect to the debates to be canvassed in this chapter, the notion of media is to be understood primarily in terms of *physical* media.

Media, on this construal, are (1) the materials (the stuff) out of which works are made and/or (2) the physical instruments employed to shape or to otherwise fashion those materials. The medium of painting, in the *material* sense, is paint, including watercolor, pastels, acrylic, gouache, tempera, oil, and so forth. The medium of painting in the *instrument* sense includes brushes, palette knives, air guns, fingers, etc. With respect to cinema, the celluloid-based, photographic filmstrip, coated with silver haloids, is – or at least was for many years – the most obvious material medium; the film camera is a physical instrumentality that gives shape to the emulsion on the filmstrip in a manner roughly analogous to the way in which the brush gives form – or informs – the oil paint on the canvas.

Editing, the literal piecing together of discrete shots, is also a physical means by which films are composed, much as collage is a physical technique in fine art.

(Here it is important to emphasize that, for the most part, given the nature of the debate regarding cinema as it has evolved, we shall be discussing the physical media from which artworks are constructed and not what might be call the *artistic* media – that is to say, the conventions, such as the reversal of fortune in tragedy, which are employed in the production of certain genres of artworks. The reason for this is simply that conventions cross media, materially or instrumentally construed.)

Medium Specificity

The idea of medium specificity is that each artform has its own specific medium – as painting has paint, and film has film. These media, to a great extent, individuate artforms. Furthermore, it is believed, the media of specific artforms possess a definite range of effects – things they can do especially well and other things that they cannot do, or, at least, that they cannot do as well as the media that correlate with some other artform or artforms. For example, it is frequently said that, in virtue of its medium (especially editing), film represents physical action – such as chases, races, and intergalactic dog-fights – exceedingly well, but intricate speeches less well, notably in contrast with theater.

According to the doctrine of medium specificity, each artform, given its physical medium – in either the material and/or instrumental sense – has a range of representational, expressive, and/or formal capacities. Some of these may overlap with the representational, expressive, and formal capabilities associated with the media of other artforms. However, some of these possibilities are said to be *distinctive* of the medium that serves to identify or to individuate the artform in question. By "distinctive" is meant that certain of the effects of the relevant medium are managed both (1) better than the other things it (the medium) does *and* (2) better than said effects are managed by the media possessed by any other artform. The medium-specificity thesis recommends that artists exploit the distinctive possibilities of the medium in which they ply their trade and that they abjure the effects that are discharged better or equally well by the media of other artforms.

Because the doctrine of medium specificity advises the artist to exploit all and only those effects that are distinctive, in the preceding sense, to her medium, the doctrine is a form of purism. It instructs artists to operate within the pristine boundaries of their chosen medium and warns them not to flirt with counterfeiting the characteristic effects of the media that belong to other artforms.

An artist must be true to her medium. For example, the sculptor should not attempt to imitate the effects of bronze in plastic. In German, this doctrine is sometimes referred to as *Materialgerechtigkeit*, which translates as "doing justice to the nature of the material." That is, the medium has a distinctive nature with specific capacities – ones that differentiate it from the media of other artforms – and it is precisely these possibilities that the artist ought to explore rather than the effects that are distinctive of the media that identify or individuate other artforms. For example, metal engravings should not attempt to fake the grainy look of woodwork.

Artforms are distinguished in terms of their physical media. Paint is different from film. Artforms should, normatively speaking, be true to the possibilities governed by the physical media that serve as the basis of what individuates them.

Why?

Considerations on Behalf of Medium Specificity

One suggestion on behalf of medium specificity is ostensibly prudential: namely that trafficking in the distinctive effects that belong to the medium of another artform is a prescription for failure. A blizzard, for example, is an apt subject for painting, but not for sculpture. Painting can capture the lightness of snow; stone cannot shed its own heaviness. A painting can portray individual snowflakes; a sculpture made of a white block of stone will look more like a giant, milky ice cube than it will look like a flurry of snowflakes. If a sculptor trespasses into the domain of painting, so the story goes, he courts disaster.

This way of thinking underwrites the traditional account of the failure of early talking pictures. The charge is that these movies were artistic catastrophes exactly because they were nothing more than canned theater – that is, theater in a film can. Actors awkwardly declaimed their lines, rigidly arrested in space so as not to wander out of range of the microphone; the camera was equally static, too large to move because it was housed in a heavy, trailer-like, soundproof structure.

Producers bought up theater properties – actors, writers, and scripts – in order to give the audience something to hear. But, the writing was crafted for the stage, and the actors, accustomed to reciting it there, were scarcely prone to movement. Nor did these films exploit the fluid possibilities of changing camera positions. The cinematic grace of the silent film, which emphasized the putatively unique art of motion pictures, was betrayed for a mess of words.

That a great many early talkies were artistically wooden and aesthetically stilted no one disputes. However, the proponent of medium specificity adds that they were failures precisely because they eschewed the "natural" inclinations of the cinema – which exploits movement in every dimension (hence, *moving* pictures) – while simultaneously and ill-advisedly these early talkies aspired to the condition of theater. As such, they fell stillborn from the projector and the putative reason for their failure is that they violated the dictates of medium specificity; they were impure to their medium. And the medium bit back.

The doctrine of medium specificity is a very bold idea. In its most radical version, it dares to predict which artistic endeavors will succeed and which will fail in a given artform. Only those strategies that exploit the distinctive possibilities of the pertinent medium have any prospect of success, while those which ignore or neglect the demands of their medium do so at their own peril – they will either fail, or, at least, will not go very well. In this regard, the doctrine, supposing it to be true, is extremely attractive, because it supplies the artist with general guidelines about what will fare nicely in her medium and what will supposedly go badly. The doctrine of medium specificity tells the artist what lines of exploration are promising and what directions should be shunned.

The doctrine is also seductive for critics-at-large and ordinary audience members, as we shall see in the last chapter of this book, because it gives them the means to account for why some films fly and others flop. Those that excel are *cinematic* – that is, they engage in and exploit the distinctive properties of the medium. Those that are insolvent can often be explained away on the grounds that they have failed to take advantage of the special resources and distinctive capabilities of film, often by stumbling into the realm of the medium of an adjacent artform (usually theater). Thus, someone might claim that the doctrine of medium specificity explains why Hitchcock's film *Psycho* is superior to his *The Paradine Case*. The latter, with all its palaver, crossed over into the domain of theater, whereas *Psycho* – remember the shower-sequence montage – is pure cinema (cutting, that is to say, editing, every inch of the way).

The doctrine of medium specificity also appears to have common sense on its side. It just seems intuitively right. Who would deny that an artist should be knowledgeable concerning her medium? If the filmmaker is shooting a scene in the dark, she should know the speed of her film stock, lest nothing show up on the screen. She should not attempt to make the medium do what it cannot do. It would be absurd to try to shoot at night with film stock that is too slow to do the job. Isn't that obvious?

Clearly, the artist must know her medium. She should be savvy enough to use the right tool for the right job. Using a piledriver to open a sardine can is likely to go awry. Similarly, it is argued that using cinema to render a story dominated by ornate and complicated language is a recipe for ennui; for, in order to enable the audience to follow such dialogue, the camera will have to hold on to it rather than taking the risk of distracting us away from it by shifting the camera's position in a gesture that could call attention to itself. But the result of this caution will be uncinematic; it will not do justice to the distinctive fluidity of cinema – its potential not only for character movement but for moving (shifting) camera set-ups as well. The film will feel stultifying; and the audience will squirm claustrophobically.

Moreover, the proponent of medium specificity adds, the reason for this is that our filmmaker is attempting to use the medium to do something for which the medium is not suited. She has opted for the wrong tool for the job. If this is the kind of script that interests her, then she should look toward Broadway, not Hollywood. It is just common sense that you should not try to make an instrument do what it cannot do. You don't use a machete to cut a diamond. Don't enlist film to do theater's work, nor vice versa.

The Legacy of Lessing

The idea of medium specificity was popularized in the eighteenth century, especially by Gotthold Ephraim Lessing in his 1776 treatise entitled *Laocoön*. In that book, Lessing compares, among other things, painting and poetry, and, he argues that, insofar as the basic elements of painting – daubs of paint – lie side by side, painting is *naturally* best suited to represent static states of affairs, like landscapes and frozen historical moments; whereas, since the basic building blocks in poetry – namely, words – follow each other sequentially in time, poetry, or literature in general, is the best means for representing events, i.e., things that unfold over time. In other words, the very structure of the medium putatively is such that in painting spatial arrangements are the ideal subject, while in poetry actions and events are.

Furthermore, artists invite trouble if they fail to respect the nature of their medium. Lessing worries that the statue after which his book is named may be flawed just because it attempts to depict an event that is too action-packed for sculpture – Laocoön and his sons struggling violently against the coiling serpent about to devour them. Such strenuous movement supposedly looks strange in stone; the subject is not right for the physical medium.

Early lovers of film were predictably drawn to the idea of medium specificity, because it gave them a framework in which to defend the possibility of film as art. It was simply a question of showing that there was some range of aesthetic results that film achieved best in virtue of its physical medium. Commentators often stressed editing as the essence of the film medium and pointed to all the kinds of things that film could represent with incomparable facility by means of editing that, in effect, were plausibly thought to be unequaled in neighboring artforms. Devices like crosscutting, for instance, permitted opportunities for the parallel development of simultaneous events virtually unrivaled by theater as conventionally staged.

But camera movement too can deliver distinctively cinematic effects. For instance, the follower of medium specificity might argue, at the end of *Sansho the Bailiff*, Mizoguchi's slowly rising camera, moving from the characters to the vista of the beach and sky overhead, secures its emotional punctuation in a way that is practically inconceivable by conventional theatrical means.

Lessing emphasized the suitability of a medium for representing certain kinds of things more perfectly than other media. For example, media whose basic elements follow each other in time supposedly represent temporal succession more perfectly than media whose basic elements are not related temporally. However, proponents of the art of cinema were – more often than not – concerned with the ways in which film departed from the perfect representation of its subject matter. This difference from Lessing, moreover, can be readily explained once we recall the arguments against the possibility of film art rehearsed in the previous chapter.

For, as we saw there, the worry was that if film were merely the perfect representation (recording) of whatever it represented, film could not be art at all, or, if it seemed to be, that was only because it was really a perfect representation/recording of some work of theater art. Thus, where Lessing was preoccupied with matching the properties of the medium with what it represents, the defender of film art purposefully zeroes in on the ways in which the inherent properties of the film medium result in deviations from the perfect replication of whatever it represents. The film lover argues in this way, as we have seen, in order to secure a space for artistic expression in the teeth of skeptical arguments about slavish, mechanical recording.

In the days of the silent film, the film theorist pointed out the way in which the film image of the talking woman departed from normal experience and then went on to suggest how this very silence might be used for expressive effect; for example, the actress would have to "speak" with her eyes. Likewise, the absence of sound effects impelled the filmmaker to find creative ways to communicate things such as the noise of a gunshot – for instance, by showing scores of frightened birds taking wing.

Because of the charge, discussed at length in the last chapter, that film was precluded from the ranks of the fine arts inasmuch as it was nothing but a recording machine, early defenders of film were at pains to exhibit and to delineate all the ways in which film *did not* record impeccably but also diverged from what it portrayed in ways that were potentially expressive and creative.

Were cinematic representation truly invisible, then there would putatively be no way for the filmmaker to express – that is, to make manifest or to mark – his thoughts and feelings regarding whatever it was he was representing. The object would look no different than it does in its everyday context where it dwells expressionlessly in reality. For expression to gain a foothold, there must be some difference between the object and its representation; the mediation cannot be invisible – leastwise, there is no way of signaling the addition of expression.

That is why twentieth-century expressionists have so often favored strategies of distortion. *Distortion* has the potential to make expression tangible. Similarly, the filmmaker uses the differences and divergences between the filmic mediation of what it represents and the normal perception thereof in order to render her expressive viewpoint upon the matter before her perceptible.

Film editing had special importance in this regard, since it clearly involves going way beyond mere recording; it is a means for creatively and assertively rearranging whatever events and objects the camera took in and, therefore, it affords wide latitude for artistic invention and creation. But cinematography itself already also has ample resources to enable the filmmaker to go beyond mere recording and to defamiliarize her subject matter. As we saw in the last chapter, the filmmaker may frame an object in a way that lifts it out of its ordinary context, enabling us to see it afresh – to apprehend certain of its properties that may have gone heretofore unnoticed in the normal course of perception. Likewise, freeze frames, slow and accelerated motion, high- and low-angle shots, as well as close shots and camera movement cannot be dismissed as nothing but the simulacra of an act of seeing with one's own eyes. They depart from reality noticeably and can, therefore, function as potential expressive devices.

The friends of film embraced the idea of medium specificity in the first instance because it supplied them with a clear-cut way in which to defend the artistic promise of the medium of cinema by demonstrating the kinds of artistic effects that its distinctive medium could deliver which, at the same time, did not have ready equivalents in the distinctive medium of other arts, as always, notably theater. Medium specificity – not to put too fine a point on the matter – was a conceptual framework made for enfranchising media artistically. But the proponents of film did not just dragoon medium specificity for the purpose of legitimatizing film art. They also bought into the further normative commitments of the medium-specificity program – the notion that being pure to the medium is the litmus test of success and failure as an artwork.

The Soviet montagists, enthusiasts of the belief that editing is the essence of cinema, hailed those films as cinematic successes that exploited cutting and castigated those that did not as retrograde. Films such as *Potemkin*, *Strike*, *By the Law*, *Fragment of Empire*, *Mother*, *The End of St. Petersburg*, *Earth*, and *Arsenal* were rated as masterpieces, whereas Russian films with long takes, for example *Father Sergius*, were dismissed as artistic fossils. Editing could not only reshape the spatio-temporal continuum; it could also be deployed to express attitudes – as Sergei Eisenstein does in his film *October* when he juxtaposes a shot of Kerensky against a statue of Napoleon.

In the late 1920s, a kind of international film style developed which reached a high point in works such as F. W. Murnau's *Sunrise*, Joe May's *Asphalt*, and Josef von Sternberg's *Last Command*, that combined stylish editing, sophisticated camera movement, special effects, assertive lighting and strikingly composed camera set-ups; these films celebrated emphatically the potential of the medium to depart from mere recording in order to defy the suspicions of the skeptic about the proposition that film could be art; and, in turn, cinematic extravaganzas of this sort were rewarded by medium-specificity advocates, like Rudolf Arnheim, with the highest aesthetic accolades.

Cinematic artifice was treated as the high road to art. The influence of the idea of medium specificity was so entrenched that one could still hear its undertones as late as the 1960s, when a film like Ingmar Bergman's *Winter Light* might be ranked artistically beneath Alfred Hitchcock's *To Catch a Thief* on the grounds that Hitchcock exploited the distinctive potential of cinema – Hitchcock's films were cinematic, whereas *Winter Light* was not. Moreover, it was often argued that Hitchcock was the greater artist, for this very reason. And to the extent that that conviction is still widespread among *cinéphiles*, the doctrine of medium specificity continues to have clout.

But what is the argument that gets us from a defense of the possibility of film art to the conclusion that motion pictures that exploit the distinctive capacities of the film medium (however those are to be specified) are better artworks than those that do not? This normative conclusion is quite spectacular when one comes to think about it. For it would seem to entail that a film like *Tarzan the Apeman* is a better work of art than Louis Malle's *My Dinner with André*, since the latter is arguably essentially a work of theater, an evening of talk, talk, talk only minimally relieved by the rhythm of the shot-counter-shot; whereas the jungle picture revels in the spatio-temporal liberty of the medium, representing Tarzan swinging across miles, vine by vine. And yet, many would feel uncomfortable with the judgment that the Tarzan film is a greater artistic achievement than Louis Malle's film. How can the medium-specificity advocate defend this conclusion?

The Medium-Specificity Argument

The argument begins by reminding us that film can be art precisely because, in both its cinematographic and its montage components, it can depart from the slavish, mechanical recording of that which stands before the camera and/or from what we would see if we encountered whatever stood before the camera face to face. Film is not bound to record – perfectly, automatically, and without deviation – anything, neither nature nor the products of other artforms. Film can express the thoughts and feelings of filmmakers because of certain distinctive features of the medium, ones that do not simply mirror whatever the camera is aimed at.

But if it is the exploitation of these features of the medium that makes the films in question art – specifically *film* art (as opposed to, say, theater art) – then certainly those films that possess the pertinent features (let us call them cinematic features) must be better *as* film (qua film) than films that lack those features.

Why so? With respect to the art of film, aren't films that are artworks better than films that are not art? That is, if a film qualifies as a work of film art, then, all things being equal, it would appear to stand to reason that it is better qua film art than a work that does not qualify as a work of film art. If Helen qualifies for the long-distance swimming team after a series of fair trials and Jane doesn't, then, all things being equal, Helen is a better long-distance swimmer than Jane. Similarly, a film that qualifies as a work of art is a better work of *film* art than a film that does not so qualify.

But recall: putatively films are works of *film* art only if they exploit those features of the medium that transcend mere recording. Those features are cinematic ones. So a cinematic film is better as a work of film art than an uncinematic film. Let us test this hypothesis by examining a pair of examples.

First, consider the Oceana Roll sequence in Charlie Chaplin's *The Gold Rush*. This is the scene in which the Tramp, in a dream, entertains Georgia and her friends on New Year's Eve by sticking two forks into two bread rolls in such a way that calls to mind feet, which "feet" the Tramp then sets to gigging through his graceful mime. The camera just stands by and takes in this glorious performance by Chaplin. Let us agree, for the sake of argument, that this is merely the recording of a stage pantomime. It is not particularly cinematic, since it does not transcend mere recording. On the other hand, the chase sequence of the Keystone Kops comedy *Lizzies of the Field* is unquestionably cinematic; at the very least, it is an exercise in editing. According to the medium-specificity theorist, the chase sequence of *Lizzies of the Field* is a better work of film art than the Oceana Roll routine from *The Gold Rush*.

Perhaps many can live with this conclusion. However, the strongest version of the medium-specificity thesis goes even farther. As art (not just film art, but art as such), the chase sequence is superior to the Oceana Roll sequence. That is, the thesis holds that, from

(a) If a film qualifies as a work of film art, then, all things being equal, it is better qua film art than a work that does not qualify as a work of film art

we are entitled to infer that

(b) If an artwork qualifies as an artwork in the medium in which it was created then, all things being equal, it is a better artwork qua art than an artwork that does not.

But what justifies the move from (a) to (b)?

The reasoning may go something like this: any artist aspires to expertise in a specific medium – a painter in paint, for example. What a painter knows about as an artist is how to express feelings and ideas, including ideas of form, by exploiting the distinctive advantages of the sensuous medium of paint. She might be another kind of artist in addition to being a painter. She might also be a drummer. But as a drummer, what she knows is how to express herself by means of drums. In short, an artist is always an artist in some medium.

An artist achieves excellence as the kind of artist she is by mastering the distinctive features of the medium that make hers the artform it is and not some other artform. Artistic accomplishment, in other words, is always relative to the medium in question. To be a great artist is to be someone accomplished in marshalling the distinctive capacities of one's medium to great effect. That is what artistic skill amounts to. A genuine artist, as such, is a mistress (or master) of her medium.

Furthermore, to say that one artwork qua artwork is better than another is to say that it is a greater artistic accomplishment – a greater accomplishment by an artist – than another. But this is to say that the artist being commended has done her – somewhat specialized – job better than someone else. Clearly an artist whose work qualifies as an artwork in the medium in which it has been created has done a better job in her medium than the artist whose work does not so qualify. But since artistry is always relative to a medium, then the artist who excels in her medium is better as an artist than one who does not. Her artistic accomplishment as such is greater. Therefore, her artwork is better.

With regard to film, then, a film that qualifies as a work of film art – which it does by the artist engaging the distinctive features of the film medium which transcend mere recording – achieves a greater level of artistic accomplishment than a film that does not, since artistry as such is always relative to mastery of a medium. Or, the chase sequence in *Lizzies of the Field* is a greater artistic accomplishment than the Oceana Roll sequence from *The Gold Rush*.

Resisting Medium Specificity

This is a conclusion that few will find palatable. Though the Keystone Kops chase is a perfectly respectable piece of film comedy, few would accord it anywhere near the admiration they believe the Chaplin turn deserves.

I wonder whether, if confronted with a Sophie's choice with regard to these two pieces of film, there are any film historians who would plump for the chase over the Oceana Roll geste? Chaplin's mime is more subtle, better observed, more imaginative, original, and more thematically dense than the simple, progressively deteriorating car chase that Mack Sennett's police force offers us. Though Sennett's gags are eminently serviceable ones, Chaplin's conception is possibly profound. An argument that concludes that *Lizzies of the Field*, or a part thereof, outranks even this moment of *The Gold Rush* is automatically suspect.

What appears to carry the medium-specificity advocate's argument over the finish line is the presupposition that "better as an artwork" means "a higher level of achievement by the artist in handling the medium in which the work is created than some other work in the medium." But what warrants this presupposition? It seems to be the idea that an artist as such just is someone who handles the distinctive medium of her artform. But an artist is not someone who just handles her medium; she does it to some effect. Surely her accomplishment as an artist is to be gauged by the quality of her effects. If Chaplin's effects are superior to Sennett's, what difference should it make that in some sense Sennett relied on distinctive features of the film medium that transcend recording and Chaplin did not?

The Oceana Roll sequence is excellent on film, even if it would also have been excellent on stage. The sequence is no less excellent for being on film. When we speak of artistic excellence as such, what warrants requiring that in addition to being fine the work must also be pure to its medium? Indeed, isn't defining "artistic excellence" or "better as an artwork" in the preceding manner merely begging the question in favor of the medium-specificity argument?

Nor is it compelling to say that an artist must always be the master of his medium. For surely there are artists whom we recognize to be better at manipulating their medium than some others, but who are nevertheless counted to be the lesser artists in our all-things-considered judgments. There were armies of hack Hollywood directors who handled the medium better than Marcel Pagnol but whose films were never the artistic equal of his *César*. Surely artistic excellence need not be tied to the medium. Even if a film that engages the medium more directly is better as film art, it is not evident that it follows that it is a better artwork qua art. For the quality of the artist as such and the artwork as such depends on the overall excellence of the output.

We know that there can be excellent artworks on film that medium-specificity advocates will maintain are not excellent works of *film* art.

If only for the purpose of the argument, let us grant them that, in a certain sense, this is true. Nevertheless, it does not follow from this concession that these are not excellent artworks, indeed, excellent artworks that may even be superior to works more beholden to the allegedly distinctive capacities of the medium. The medium-specificity advocate must tell us why considerations of the medium should be overriding in our all-things-considered judgments of said artworks as artworks. Why must considerations of the purity of the medium trump considerations of the excellence of the effect of the work, irrespective of the constraints of media?

The defender of medium specificity really has no convincing reason for valuing the purity of the medium over the excellence of the artistic effect. Both artists and artworks would appear to be validly assessed in terms of the excellence of the effects they achieve and not in terms of whether their means of securing of those effects are pure. The requirement of purity here seems to fetishize the medium.

This is an especially anomalous position for the defender of medium specificity to land in. It is as if she has forgotten what a medium is! For a medium is the kind of thing that is *instrumentally* valuable. If a medium is valuable, it is as the means to something else. Isn't this the very definition of a medium? The media that are associated with artforms are presumably valuable ultimately as means to artistic excellence. Thus, it would appear virtually self-contradictory for the medium-specificity theorist to maintain that respecting the medium is more important than the achievement of excellence. Doesn't that seem to reverse the means–ends relationship here? In demanding the purity of the medium, the medium-specificity proponent acts as though the medium were valuable for its own sake or intrinsically valuable, rather than being only instrumentally valuable. But that flies in the face of what it means to be a medium in the first place.

Earlier the integrity of the medium was defended by analogizing it to tools. But tools are instrumentally valuable, not valuable for their own sake. If you can achieve your end by using a hammer in a non-standard way – say, propping a door open with it – then its effectiveness is what warrants your use of it. If holding the door open is what you want, the observation that that is not what hammers are most suited for is beside the point. We do not respect tools for themselves, but for what they get done. Who values a screwdriver for its own sake? If the media associated with artforms are really analogous to tools, we should treat them likewise – that is to say, as only instrumentally valuable.

Undoubtedly, the friend of medium specificity will challenge the preceding observations. She may begin by claiming that our objections are based on imagining cases that will never occur, namely cases where there is authentic artistic excellence despite the artist's neglect of the distinctive capacities of the medium. But the defender of medium specificity is too confident here. There are such cases, as exemplified by the Oceana Roll sequence from Chaplin's *The Gold Rush*. Indeed, it might be argued that throughout his career, Chaplin was never a very cinematic director by the lights of medium-specificity theorists of a certain vintage, but nevertheless, on everyone else's hit list, he was one of the greatest artists ever to have worked in film.

At this point in the debate, the proponent of medium specificity is likely to say that Chaplin's work was never really all that good. But this will run afoul of received wisdom. Moreover, if the medium-specificity theorist says that Chaplin's work was not very good because Chaplin did not exploit the medium, then the theorist will again be accused of begging the question. The medium-specificity thesis often seems attractive because it looks like a powerful empirical theory that promises to predict what will work or not in cinema.* However, no one has ever succeeded fielding a medium-specificity hypothesis of any degree of detail that has not been immediately accosted by counterexamples.

Typically medium-specificity theorists attempt to fend off these counter-examples by denying that the masterpieces in question are genuinely estimable due to their compromised employment of the medium. But that merely assumes as a premise what should be the conclusion of the argument. It is an attempt to transform an empirical statement into a definition of what is good in cinema.

But how, the believer in medium specificity will demand, can it be that an artist who ignores what is distinctive about the medium can accomplish anything? Earlier it was emphasized that you cannot make a medium do that which it is beyond its realm of possibility. That is true, but only because it is a tautology – by definition, if something is impossible for *x*,

---

* Another way in which to see that being true to the medium – a.k.a. being cinematic – is not a guarantee of quality is to recall that most of the films and TV programs we see will pass the medium-specificity muster. But a great many of them are not very good at all; in fact many are bad. So being, as they say, cinematic, is not a reliable predictor of goodness. Moreover, interestingly enough, the reason they are bad often has to do with factors they share with other media – for example, they are badly plotted or acted, or poorly written. So, purity is not a key to artistic success, just as impurity is not a sure road to aesthetic perdition. Hence, we have yet another nail to hammer into the coffin of the medium-specificity thesis.

then x cannot do it. Yet it was not impossible for Chaplin to make the Oceana Roll sequence in the way he did. Had it been, he would not have been able to make it. The camera didn't explode when he mimed before it; the footage did not ignite when projected in theaters. In no logical or physical sense of *impossibility* was the Oceana Roll sequence impossible.

In fact, there would be no cause for the medium-specificity theorist to warn artists away from putatively impure uses of the medium, if said uses were truly impossible options. No artist can execute anything that is genuinely impossible. If the proponent of medium specificity is afraid of people doing the impossible, she should stop fretting and find some other crusade to rally.

Common sense is naturally attracted to the medium-specificity position because of the previously mentioned analogy between media and tools. Use hacksaws for cutting through steel; use jack-hammers for busting concrete. Similarly, use film for representing fast-moving action that occurs over large distances; use theater for presenting densely packed speeches with elaborate verbal textures.*

Behind the tool analogy, of course, there is some presiding notion of efficiency. Use the right tool for the right job.† But the media of the various

---

* By the way, it should be added that it is a mistake to think that elaborate verbal textures have no place in cinema. For, at the very least, the juxtaposition of complex verbiage with imagery can be immensely stimulating, as shown by, among other motion pictures, Yvonne Rainer's *Journeys to Berlin*, Peter Greenaway's *Prospero's Books*, Hans-Jürgen Syberberg's *Our Hitler*, and Jean-Luc Godard's *L'Histoire du cinéma*. Moreover, even medium purists will have to accept these examples, since audio-visual juxtaposition is an inherent possibility of the sound film (though, of course, not a possibility beyond the reach of theater).

† Another problem for the medium-specificity thesis may be that sometimes the apparently uncinematic choice may be the right artistic choice for a specific motion picture project. In *Dogville*, director Lars von Trier opts for highly theatrical sets, sets lacking walls, as one might find in a production of *Our Town*. That the movie is shot on a sound stage is pretty evident. And yet this highly theatrical style – indeed, this style that even alludes to theater – serves von Trier's artistic purposes perfectly. The absence of walls enables us to "see through" the town in both senses of the phrase; von Trier wants to get across the idea that we are seeing the town stripped of its façades, figuratively speaking, and the stagecraft literalizes this. Likewise, von Trier intends to present this specimen of Americana as a matter of roles, and the allusion to theater through the sets helps establish this conception. Were von Trier to forswear theatricality here in order to pay his dues to the cinematic, he would sacrifice the precise figuration that expresses

artforms are not tools with fixed uses. Indeed, it is generally up to artists to discover uses for their media rather than the other way around. Film-makers discovered the artistic potential of the technology of film; the medium did not come with a set of artmaking instructions

So it is not clear that the tool analogy supports the dicta of medium specificity. Perhaps there is an underlying suspicion that there is something wasteful about using one medium to do what another medium can do. But what exactly was wasted by Chaplin doing the Oceana Roll pantomime on film rather than in the theater — the opportunity to do it in the theater? But what if he had done it onstage and on screen? That neither sounds like something "wasteful," in the ordinary sense of the term, nor does there seem anything else wrong with it. The world would be a richer place for having many performances of the Oceana Roll, even across media.

And, in any event, the notion that waste is to be avoided in art is an odd one. Artists do not eschew procedures because they are too time-consuming, or materials because they are too dear. Efficiency, in short, is not a standard to which we often appeal in art; no one chides James Joyce as a slacker for dragging his pen in the production of *Finnegans Wake*. Excellence of effect is typically all that counts.

In this chapter we have looked at the doctrine of medium specificity. This doctrine grows naturally out of the strategy for establishing the possibility of film art by asserting that the film medium is not a perfect recording mechanism but rather that it deviates from the invisible, mirror-like transmission of images of its referents in ways that make expression possible (and formal invention apparent). For the proponent of medium specificity surmises that film art emerges precisely by exploiting those medium-specific deviations. Historically, the doctrine of medium specificity has been of immense heuristic value, because it urges filmmakers and film viewers to pay very close attention to many of the most important variables whose manipulation have made the cinema such a powerful channel of expression. Medium specificity is the kind of "noble lie" that can get people to see motion pictures with greater accuracy and sensitivity.

But the doctrine of medium specificity is very ambitious. It attempts to advance an a priori account of what will succeed and fail artistically on film. Films that fail to exploit the distinctive — a.k.a. cinematic — potential

his thoughts and feelings about American society. Similarly, the film *The History Boys* is highly theatrical in a way that is appropriate to its subject — acting, performance, and striking the pose in the pursuit of academic achievement.

of the medium, perhaps by being essentially theatrical – are going to be as artistically dismal as the early *films d'art*; on the other hand, films that embrace the distinctive possibilities of the medium, like Godard's *Married Woman*, can enter the charmed circle of winning artworks.

We have attempted to show that the normative reach of the doctrine of medium specificity is indefensible. This is not to deny that an artist should understand her medium and its properties. Indeed, it is precisely because Abbas Kiarostami appreciates the difference between film and video that he can, for expressive purposes, exploit their difference in the contrast he draws between them in the body of *A Taste of Cherry* versus its coda.

Our only intention in this chapter has been to reject the suggestion that these observations in any way provide generalizable, a priori dictates of what the artist should or should not do and/or that one can predict systematically what will fail or succeed as art on the basis of some conception of engaging the distinctive features of the medium of any artform, including, especially, film.

Medium specificity may seem like an old-fashioned idea, one that finds itself at home in the early days of film, but which is unlikely to command much of a following in the era of postmodernism in which boundaries between everything – artforms and their media included – are supposedly evaporating. However, medium specificity is an idea that never goes away and is always standing in the flies ready to make a comeback. That is why it is worth studying at the length we have spent upon it in this chapter. For sometime soon, probably someone will latch on to it in order to defend the possibility of computer art and to recommend the direction it should take. That is, I predict that there is likely to be someone in the near future who will claim that what is distinctive about the medium of computer art is, let's say, interactivity, and that only computer artworks that exploit interactivity will be artistically worthwhile. If a view like this has not already found its way into cyberspace, it will. And at that point we will need to reopen the debate about the intellectual credentials of the doctrine of medium specificity, invoking, it is to be hoped, the case of film as a cautionary tale.

Suggested Reading

For a historical overview of the medium-specificity idea in cinema, see Noël Carroll, *Philosophical Problems of Classical Film Theory* (Princeton, NJ: Princeton University Press, 1988). For summary criticism of the position, see "Forget the

Medium!,'' in *Engaging the Moving Image* by Noël Carroll (New Haven, CT: Yale University Press, 2003).

Of proponents of the medium-specificity view, the most powerful and thoroughly argued statement is Rudolf Arnheim's in his book *Film as Art* (Berkeley, CA: University of California Press, 1956). Most of the other canonical film theorists are also committed to the medium-specificity idea, or a variation thereof. Some classic texts in this tradition include: Hugo Munsterberg, *The Photoplay: A Psychological Study* (New York: Dover, 1916); Béla Balász, *Theory of Film* (New York: Dover, 1952); V. I. Pudovkin, *Film Acting and Film Technique* (London: Vision Press, 1958); Sergei Eisenstein, *Selected Works* (London: BFI Publishing/Indiana University Press, 1988); André Bazin, *What Is Cinema?*, vols. 1 and 2, (Berkeley, CA: University of California Press, 1967); and Siegfried Kracauer, *Theory of Film* (Oxford: Oxford University Press, 1960).

An extremely perceptive survey and sophisticated extension of this viewpoint is Victor Perkins' *Film as Film: Understanding and Judging Movies* (Baltimore, MD: Penguin Books, 1972). This book will be discussed in the final chapter of this text but deserves mention now as one of the most astute accounts of the medium-specificity debates.

Modified defenses of medium specificity can be found in Edward Sankowski, "Uniqueness Arguments and Artist's Actions," *Journal of Aesthetics and Art Criticism* 38:1 (Fall 1979), 61–74, and Donald Crawford, "The Uniqueness of the Medium," *The Personalist* 51 (Autumn 1970), 447–69. Comment upon these articles is offered by Noël Carroll in "Medium Specificity Arguments and the Self-Consciously Invented Arts: Film, Video, and Photography," in his collection *Theorizing the Moving Image* (Cambridge: Cambridge University Press, 1996). Exchanges on the issue of medium specificity can be found in the following: between Alan Goldman and Noël Carroll in *Film and Philosophy* 5–6 (2002), and between Murray Smith and Noël Carroll in *Film Studies* 8 (Summer 2006).

For an excellent, critical review of the film–theater debate, see Susan Sontag, "Film and Theater," in her collection *Styles of Radical Will* (New York: Farrar, Straus & Giroux, 1966).

Chapter Three

What Is Cinema?

The question, "What is cinema?" (which we derive from an unequivocally marvelous collection of essays by the distinguished film theorist and critic André Bazin) is an ontological one. "Ontology" is the study of being. The ontology of cinema is an inquiry into the being of cinema, or, to put it less awkwardly, it is an inquiry into the kind of being, the kind of thing, cinema is. To what category does it belong, or, in other words, under which concept do we classify it?

Asked what iron is, we say "a mineral." That is the category of which it is a member. Likewise, philosophers want to ascertain the concept or concepts under which cinema falls. For instance, is it essentially photography, is it art, is it both, or is it neither? What is the nature of cinema?

The ontology of cinema interrogates the mode of existence of cinema – its manner of existing (of being). It aspires to establish the kind of thing cinema is essentially. Another way of framing the ontologist's question is to ask "What is the essence of cinema?"

The philosophy of any practice attempts to clarify the concepts that are indispensable to carrying on that practice. The notion of a number is fundamental to mathematics; so the philosophy of mathematics tries to define *number*, asking whether a number is something real or only a logical fiction. Similarly, since the concept of a law is the *sine qua non* for the practice of the law, the philosopher of law speculates about the nature of law – is a law essentially merely an injunction promulgated by the appropriate people (such as the members of a parliament) in accordance with the correct procedures (such as voting), or does a genuine law derive from something much deeper, like a universal moral code? Of course, *law* is not the only concept that is essential to the practice of law. Concepts like intention, voluntariness, and guilt are also necessary to our legal practices. Consequently, they too fall under the purview of the philosophy of law.

With regard to the cinema, there are a plethora of concepts that are essential to the practices of making, interpreting, and evaluating motion pictures. We will analyze a number of them in this book. But before plunging ahead, we need first to denominate the boundaries of our investigation. We need to answer the question "What is cinema?"

Defining Cinema

The issue of defining cinema arose within the first two decades of the advent of moving pictures. One reason for this was that cinema was a new thing under the sun and, therefore, it needed to be fitted into our scheme of things – where it is the task of philosophy, in the intellectual division of labor, to situate items in our biggest picture of the way things are.

But there were other reasons why commentators became engaged with defining the essence of cinema. Some, as we saw in chapter 1, believed that a proper analysis of cinema would reveal that it could not be art, properly so called, given its photographic provenance, whereas others were invested in demonstrating that, to the contrary, an accurate analysis of the nature of cinema would show that art was within its reach. Thus, both sides of the debate needed an account of the essence of cinema in order to make their case.

Moreover, as we saw in chapter 2, many of the friends of film – those who characterized cinema as possessing inherent artistic capacities – also thought that their analysis of the film medium would provide them with the wherewithal to tell the good films from the bad ones.

Of course, the pressure to prove that moving pictures can be art is, by now, far behind us. Furthermore, as we saw in the previous chapter, we have reason to believe that a descriptive definition of film will *not* provide us with a reliable set of normative guidelines to the filmically good, the bad, and the ugly. Nevertheless, even if isolating the essence of cinema holds forth no promise of disclosing the secrets of cinematic success, curiosity still lingers about the place of cinema on our overall conceptual map. How does cinema stand in relation to things like theater and painting? We should at least know what we are talking about when we say we are going to the movies, lest we find ourselves at the ballet. For such reasons, we need a definition or analysis of cinema.

When philosophers attempt to produce what they variously call a definition, a theory, or an analysis of *x* (whatever *x* is), they usually have in mind something very specific – what is often called an essential or real definition. What is a real definition? The short answer is: a definition or analysis of some concept in terms of a set of necessary conditions that are conjointly sufficient for the application of said concept. But what are those?

A necessary condition states a property that something must possess in order to be a member of the category under analysis. For example, in order to be a nun in the Roman Catholic Church, one must be a woman. It is a necessary condition or a necessary criterion for the sisterhood that the candidate be a woman. That is, someone is a nun *only if* she is a woman. There are several other necessary conditions for sisterhood, including that one be a Catholic, that one take the requisite vows, and that one be inducted by the proper authorities. Taken together – that is to say conjointly – these necessary conditions are *sufficient* for classifying a candidate as a nun; they add up, so to speak, to counting the woman in question as a sister. That is, *if* someone is a woman, a Catholic, has taken the requisite vows, and has been inducted by the proper authorities *then* she is a nun.

You can usually tell if a philosopher is trying to offer you a real definition by his use of the phrase "if and only if." For example, "*x* is a bachelor if and only if (1) *x* is male and (2) *x* is unmarried" is a real definition, an analysis in terms of two necessary conditions (signaled by the locution "only if") that are conjointly sufficient (signaled by the word "if"). The necessary conditions tell us what properties a candidate must have in order to be an instance of the concept under analysis; the sufficient conditions mark off how members of the relevant class of things differ from the members of other classes – how, for example, bachelors differ from husbands, on the one hand, and spinsters, on the other.

Generally, when asked a question of the form "What is *x*?" the philosopher will initially attempt to provide a conceptual analysis or real definition of *x* in terms of necessary conditions that are conjointly sufficient. In this chapter, we are facing the question "What is cinema?" Let us see whether or not we can answer that question in terms of a real definition.

Seeing *x* Versus Seeing a Motion Picture of *x*

As we have learned, one of the earliest proposals for defining cinema was the idea that cinema is essentially nothing but moving photography, a process of sheer mechanical recording. With this definition comes the prejudice that cinema cannot be art, since the mere mechanical recording of something putatively leaves no opportunity for the artist to add or to express her thoughts and feelings regarding whatever she has filmed.

The suggestion here was that whatever you see on film is exactly what you would see in a face-to-face encounter with the object that stood before the camera. Seeing a motion picture of *x*, say a stone falling, in other words, is, on this conception, putatively exactly like seeing the stone falling in front of you, where your view is not mediated by cinema. Consequently, just as a falling stone in nature literally expresses nothing, so a moving picture image of one expresses nothing. The moving picture image is rather like a mirror – it simply delivers up the way things look and nothing more. What you see on film, what you see in a mirror, and what you see in a close encounter of the third kind with whatever gave rise to the aforesaid cinematic image supposedly are perceptually equivalent. Seeing a cinematic image, according to this theory, is precisely like seeing whatever it is an image of in the pro-filmic world – the world as it is arrayed in front of the camera.

That is, perceiving a cinematic image is virtually the same as seeing its pro-filmic referent; the cinematic image itself is, in a manner of speaking, diaphanous. Thus, what we might call "cinematic seeing" is just like normal perception. The normal perception of something and its perception via cinema are in nowise appreciably different.

This view, as we have already seen, is false. There are quite a few differences between seeing an object in nature and seeing an object on film. For example, for many years, most of the objects seen on film were black and white, whereas their referents were in living color. Undoubtedly, cinematic color is still often perceptually discernible from color in nature. However, perhaps color technology could be improved to the point where any differences in hue that the naked eye might detect could be erased.

Indeed, let us imagine that motion picture technology advances to the point where moving picture images of objects and events are virtually indiscernible by normal viewers from the things of which they are images. Suppose, for instance, that so many scan lines are added to high-definition television images that the unaided eye cannot confidently cut the difference between a medium shot of Samuel L. Jackson and Samuel L. Jackson in the flesh. Imagine, in other words, that the image was as persuasive as a sculpture by Duane Hanson. Is there nevertheless some fundamental or essential difference between seeing a moving picture image of x and a normal perceptual encounter with x in, so to speak, nature?

Detached Displays

One such difference is the fact that in a face-to-face perceptual encounter with an object, I am typically able to orient my body toward that object within the very spatial continuum that I inhabit physically. If I see a

Mercedes Benz parked across the street, I can point my body in its direction and walk to it. Normal perception enables me to navigate my way in the space where I live toward the objects I see in the distance. Normal veridical perception, that is, comes with egocentric information about where I stand in relation to what I see. But this characteristic feature of normal perception contrasts radically with our perceptual encounters with movies.

For when I see an image of the Kremlin in cinema, I cannot, on the basis of the spatial information available intrinsically in that image, orient myself to that precinct of Moscow, nor, if it is a movie set rather than the real thing, can I point myself in the direction of the locale where the motion picture was shot. If we are, in a manner of speaking, attached to the arrays that surround us visually in our lives off screen, then cinematic images are *detached displays* – they display persons, places, things, actions, and events that are phenomenologically detached, in the preceding sense, from the actual space of our bodies.

Suppose that I am watching *Casablanca* and what I see onscreen is Rick's bar. I can, of course, orient myself to the screen; I can point myself in its direction. The screen is part of my phenomenologically attached array. But I cannot, on the basis of the spatial information intrinsic to the shot onscreen, orient myself reliably toward Rick's bar – toward the spatial coordinates of that structure as it existed some time in the early 1940s in California (nor could I point my body, by means of the information in the image, toward or away from the fictional locale of the film in North Africa). Simply by looking at the image on the screen, I would not be able to walk, drive, swim, fly, or otherwise move toward the site of Rick's bar – toward the remnants, if any, of the set on some sound stage in LA. The image itself would not tell me how to get to the set, presuming that part, if any, of it still remains, nor the way in which to get to the place in the world where, if it no longer exists, it once did. For the space, so to say, where the set of Rick's bar is located is disconnected phenomenologically from the space in which I dwell bodily as a physical being.

Some readers might say that when they see a movie image of Big Ben in London, then they are confident that they will be able to point their body in right direction. But if this is so, it is because these viewers already know in which direction London lies. It is not information intrinsic to the image on the screen that gives them their marching orders. It is the extrinsic knowledge of geography which they antecedently possess that sets them straight.

Ordinarily, our sense of where we are depends upon our sense of balance and our kinesthetic feelings. What we see is integrated with these cues in such a way as to yield a sense of where we are situated. But if we call what we see on the silver screen a "view," then it is a disembodied view. When I see a visual expanse, like Rick's bar, onscreen, I have no sense of where the portrayed space really is in relation to my body. It is detached. I cannot relate myself reliably to it spatially; it is not attached spatially to my life-world.

In the past, I think, film theorists have attempted to get at the essence of cinema by talking obscurely about how film engenders a peculiar sort of absence, or even a unique play of presence and absence. For the most part, this way of speaking has been unfortunately vague, even murky. However, perhaps what these theorists were trying to get at by the notion of *absence* is the way in which the cinematic display is discontinuous from the space we inhabit. What is present to us is a display, but the referent of the display is discontinuous with, or detached or absent from, the space in which our eyes can plot the way to our destination. Thus, the play of presence and absence that intrigued film theorists might be better characterized by saying – in a more positive and descriptively substantial way – that, in cinema, the image or image series is a detached display.

This feature of the cinematic image, moreover, appears universal; it pertains to every moving picture representation. There are no exceptions. Therefore, we may begin to answer our animating question – "What is cinema?" – by means of a first approximation: "x is an instance of cinema *only if* it, x, is a detached display (or a series of detached displays)." That is, being a detached display is a necessary condition for being an instance of cinema.

Moving Images

That the cinema is a detached display draws a distinction between cinematic arrays and the normal perception of the visible "attached" arrays that give rise to them. However, it does not draw a distinction between near neighbors of cinema, like painting and photography, on the one hand, and theater, on the other. Quite clearly, these artforms are also detached displays. For neither from a painting of Elsinore nor from a stage set of *Hamlet* can one point one's body toward that castle on the shore of Denmark. So what distinguishes cinema from still pictures and theater? Let's start with still pictures – with paintings, photographs, and the like.

Imagine a painting of a cartoon character, say Manga, by some postmodern artist. Now imagine alongside of it a film loop of the same cartoon character striking precisely the same pose. Like the painting of the cartoon character, the image of Manga on the filmstrip remains frozen. Both images are the same size. The image on the screen is a high-definition one of the most technologically sophisticated sort, and there is no flicker effect. Let us suppose, then, that the two images – the painting and the film image – are indiscernible to the naked eye. No one can see the difference. But is there nevertheless a difference and, if so, what is it?

If you were confronted by these two images and you were told that the one on the left was a film projection and that the one on the right was a painting, it would make sense for you to keep watching the one on the left, at least on first viewing, to see whether the cartoon character ensconced there starts to move, whereas anticipating that Manga might move in the painting would be absurd. For movement is a possibility in movies but not in painting. That is why in ordinary language we call film images *moving* pictures or *motion* pictures. One of the earliest labels for film was *bio* – as in "biograph" – which meant life and signaled animation. On the other hand, paintings, photographs, slides, and so forth are called *still* pictures, pictures which, by definition, do not move – indeed, pictures for which the very possibility of movement is ontologically foreclosed.

The difference between a painting and a cinematic image, then, is *movement*. This much is perhaps already built into common speech in locutions like *the moving picture show*. But we need to be careful about the way in which we exploit this clue from ordinary language. It is not simply the case that cinematic pictures move and still pictures do not. For there are a number of films in which there is no movement, such as Nagisa Oshima's *Band of Ninjas* (a film of a comic strip), Michael Snow's *One Second in Montreal* (a film of photos) and his *So Is This* (a film of sentences), Hollis Frampton's *Poetic Justice* (a film of a shooting script), Godard and Gorin's *Letter to Jane* (another film of photos), and Takahiko Iimura's *1 in 10* (a film of addition and subtraction tables).

A perhaps better-known example than any of these is Chris Marker's *La Jetée*, a film of almost no movement whose time-travel narrative is told primarily through the projection of still photographs. Of course, there is one movement in Marker's film; however, it should be easy for you to imagine a film just like *La Jetée* but with no movement whatsoever.

Thus, it would be wrong to require movement as a necessary condition for membership in the category of cinema, since a film like the reimagined *La Jetée* is indisputably a motion picture. Rather, it is more accurate to propose that something is an instance of cinema only if it belongs to the class of things for which creating the impression of movement is a technical possibility.

However, some might balk at this adjustment, resisting the impulse to accommodate motionless films into the corpus of cinema. It might be charged that the prospect of movies without movement is at least oxymoronic (motionless movies! Holy Cow!), and perhaps even self-contradictory. Such experiments are little more than slide shows mounted on celluloid, maybe merely for the purpose of assuring the most efficient mode of projection.

Yet there is a profound difference between a shot of a character from our imagined movie version of *La Jetée* and a slide image of that character abstracted from the film. For as long as you know that what you are watching is a film, even a film of what appears to be a photograph, it is always justifiable to entertain the possibility that the image *might* move. On the other hand, if you know that you are looking at a slide, then it is categorically impossible that the image might move. If you know that what you are looking at is a slide and you understand what a slide is, then it is irrational to suppose that the image could move because it is conceptually impossible.

Movement in a slide would require a miracle; movement in a cinematic image is an artistic choice which is always technically available. Though most frequently exploited, it can also be forgone for artistic effect. Before *Band of Ninjas* concludes – that is, until the last image flickers through the projection gate – the viewer may reasonably presume, if she knows she is watching a film, that there may yet be movement onscreen. For movement is a permanent possibility in cinema. But if she knows she is looking at a slide, then it would be absurd for her to entertain even the possibility that it might burst into movement. It would be irrational of her to do so, of course, because if it is a slide and she knows what a slide is, then she must know that it is beyond the capacity of a slide to support movement within the boundary of its frame.

Furthermore, the difference between slides and moving images applies across the board to the distinction between every species of still picturing – including paintings, drawings, still photos and the like – and every sort of moving picture – including videos, mutoscopes, movies, computer-generated animation, and so forth. When it comes to still pictures, one commits a category error if one expects movement. It is, by definition, self-contradictory for still pictures to move. That is why they are called *still* pictures. That is why it is conceptually confused to look at what one understands to be a painting with the expectation that it might move. But it is eminently rational – and never unreasonable – to stay on the lookout for movement in a film because of the kind of thing – a motion picture or a *movie* – that a film is. Even with a static film, like *Poetic Justice*, it makes sense to wonder whether there will be movement up until the last inch of film has run its course.

With a film like *Poetic Justice*, it is an intelligible question to ask why the filmmaker, Hollis Frampton, made a static film, since he had movement as a genuine stylistic option at his disposal. But it makes no sense to ask why Holbein forswore literal movement in his painting *The Ambassadors*. Unlike Frampton, he had no other alternative. Asking why Holbein's ambassadors don't move is like asking why spiders don't sing *Tosca*.

Of course, once one has seen a static film from beginning to end, it is no longer justifiable to anticipate possible movement in repeated viewings, unless you suspect that the film has been tampered with since the time of your initial viewing. On first viewing, it is reasonable, or at least not irrational, to be open to the possibility that movement will appear onscreen up until the final credits; on second, third, and subsequent viewings, such anticipation is out of place. However, on first viewings, one can never be sure that the film is entirely still till it is over. And this is what makes it plausible to continue watching for movement throughout the first viewing of static films. But to await movement from what one knows to be a painting or a slide is conceptually absurd.

Why categorize static films as cinema rather than as slides or as some other sort of still picture show? Because, as already suggested, stasis is stylistic choice in static films. It is an option that contributes to the artistic effect of a film. It is something whose significance the audience contemplates when trying to make sense of a film. Encountering *La Jetée*, a natural interpretive question is, "Why did Chris Marker choose to make a *movie* out of still photographs?" Perhaps the answer has to do with his attempt to simulate the fragmentary nature of memory. But, in any event, note that this approach makes sense with a static film, whereas it would not with a slide show, every image of which, of necessity, is a still photograph. That is, one crucial reason to countenance the notion of static films and to modify our definition of cinema to assimilate them is an aesthetic reason, viz., stasis is a cinematic variable of potential significance in our interpretive and appreciative responses to a motion picture, whereas stasis is an unalterable, and therefore mute and meaningless, constant in a slide show.

With an individual shot, such as the one that concludes Lo Wei's movie *The Chinese Connection* and which shows Bruce Lee, frozen mid-air delivering a flying kick, the arrest of movement exercises a cinematic option with expressive potential. In this particular instance, freezing the frame, among other things, serves to memorialize Lee and his character – to turn him into the stuff of legend at the *height* of his prowess and glory. But just as the choice of stasis can have an expressive effect by eschewing motion at the level of the individual shot, so too an entire film may accrue meaning by staying still, whereas a painting or a slide cannot exploit this possibility precisely because its only option is to be motionless.

It is informative to say that a film is static; it alerts a prospective viewer to a pertinent lever of stylistic articulation in the work. Contrariwise, there is no point in saying of a painting that it is a literally still painting. It could not have been otherwise. To call a painting or a slide a still painting or a still slide is redundant.

One can imagine a slide of a procession and a cinematic freeze frame of the exact same moment in a parade. The two images may, in effect, be perceptually indiscernible. And yet they are metaphysically different. Moreover, this difference translates into a difference in the epistemic states of the respective viewers of the slide versus the cinematic freeze frame. With the motion picture, the anticipation that the freeze frame may start to move is reasonable or, at least, conceptually permissible; but with still pictures such as slides it is never conceptually permissible. The reason for this is quite clear. Film belongs to the class of things where movement is a technical possibility while paintings, slides, and the like belong to a class of things that are, by definition, still.

Ordinary language broadly informs us about one of the necessary conditions of cinema by referring to it collectively as "the motion pictures." But the wisdom in this common way of speaking needs to be unpacked a bit. It is not the case that every film or every film image imparts an impression of movement. As we have seen, there are static films. However, static films belong to the class of things where the possibility of movement is always technically available in such a way that *stasis* is a stylistic variable in films in a way that it cannot be with respect to still pictures. Perhaps this is one of the reasons that "moving pictures" or "motion pictures" serve as better labels for the practice of cinema than does "film," since these phrases advertise what may be the most pertinent essential feature of the artform, namely, the possibility of movement.

Of course, the category of *moving pictures* is somewhat broader than that which has traditionally been discussed by film theorists, since it would include such things as video and computer imaging as well as celluloid-based cinematography. Indeed, if we could produce moving images sonographically, those too should count as motion pictures. Moreover, this expansion of the class of objects under consideration to moving pictures in general is, in my opinion, theoretically advisable, since I predict that one day the history of what we now call cinema and the history of video, TV, computer-generated imaging, and whatever comes next will all be thought of as a piece.

That is, by defining cinema as belonging to the class of the moving picture, we are characterizing cinematic artifacts in terms of their function – rather than their physical basis – which function is, in short, to impart the impression of movement. This function can be implemented in an indefinite number of media – celluloid-based *film*, most obviously, but also video, broadcast TV, handmade cartoon flip books, CGI, and, truth be told, who knows what successive generations will invent? Furthermore, the capacity to impart movement to pictures is also connected to an even narrower function that, for many, is the central cultural rationale for cinema – its ability to narrate visually by means of pictures that move.

Nevertheless, there is at least one limitation in calling the relevant artform *moving pictures*. For the term "picture" implies the sort of intentional visual artifact in which one recognizes the depiction of objects, persons, and events simply by looking, rather than by reading or deciphering or decoding. That is, we recognize what pictures are pictures of through the operation of certain subpersonal perceptual routines that are automatic and bred in the bone. But not all of the images found in cinema are of this sort. Many films and videos are abstract or nonfigurative or nonrepresentational. Think of the films of figures like Viking Eggeling, Marcel Duchamp, and some of the work of Stan Brakhage. These works may be comprised of non-recognizable shapes and purely visual structures. Thus, rather than speaking of moving pictures, it may be more advisable to talk of *moving images*. For the term *image* covers both pictures and abstractions – Hokusai and Kandinsky; Zhang Yimou and Jordan Belson. That is, the concept of the moving image – like that of the still image – is more comprehensive than that of the moving or motion picture. For whether the image is pictorial or abstract is less relevant for the purposes of classification than that it is moving imagery in the sense of possessing the technical possibility of movement.

Types, Tokens, and Templates

By adverting to the possibility of movement, we have been able to draw a boundary between cinema, on the one hand, and painting, drawing, still photography, and so forth, on the other hand. And we have added another necessary condition to our characterization of cinema: *x* belongs to the category of cinema (1) only if x is a detached display (or a series of detached displays), and (2) only if x belongs to the class of things from which the impression of movement is technically possible. However, these two conditions are not jointly sufficient to differentiate film from its near neighbor theater.

For a theatrical performance is also a detached display. Watching a theatrical performance of *A Streetcar Named Desire*, we cannot orient our bodies – on the basis of the visual information onstage – in the direction of New Orleans. The space in the play is not the space of my body. It is not true, as I look on, that Julius Caesar dies fifteen feet in front of me, even if I am sitting in the first row. Nor can I point my body toward the forum in ancient Rome on the basis of the information available intrinsically in the theatrical image before me. Moreover, quite clearly, theater, as cinema, affords the possibility of movement.

Cinema and theater are in many ways alike. Cinema, as it is most commonly practiced, is an art of dramatic fiction, telling stories through the play of actors. In many ways, cinema was a successor of theater. Even the language of cinema echoes that of theater. We show movies in "theaters," and movie showings are sometimes still called "performances"; at the turn of the century, motion pictures were called "photoplays." Many movie emporiums were housed in refurbished "legit" theaters where some continued to employ rising and falling curtains to signal the beginning and end of the screening.

Indeed, it is hard to deny that cinema was a rival to live theater, providing a cheap substitute whose economies of scale eventually came to dwarf the grandest spectacles on stage. This rivalry, moreover, as we have seen, fueled some of the earliest debates about film, with the lovers of live theater impugning the artistic credentials of film, calling it nothing but the slavish mechanical reproduction of live dramas.

And even today, when the battle between cinema and theater has abated, the affinities between the two remain deep. Arguably it remains the case that the best training for film actors and film directors is theater. Film acting and directing, of course, involve skills different from live theater. Nevertheless, the basics of building character and orchestrating ensemble playing are still best learnt in drama schools.

Furthermore, in addition to these historical correlations, there is also a deep metaphysical bond between theater and cinema. Both are what philosophers classify as type-artforms or multiple-instance artforms. That is, one possible division amongst the arts is between artforms that involve unique singular objects, like typical, one-of-a-kind paintings, and those arts that involve multiple copies of the same artwork. The novel, for example, is a multiple-instance artform. There are probably millions of copies of the novel *Ivanhoe*.

Multiple-instance artforms, in turn, can be analyzed in terms of the type–token relationship. Just as the dime in my pocket is a token of the type designed by the US Treasury, so my copy of *Ivanhoe* is a token of the type authored by Sir Walter Scott in the nineteenth century. My token of *Ivanhoe* grants me access to the type – the artwork– that Sir Walter Scott created. *Ivanhoe*, moreover, is not an ordinary material object. It is not Scott's original manuscript, which itself is a token of the novel. For the original manuscript could be lost or destroyed and we would still say that *Ivanhoe* exists. In fact, every copy of *Ivanhoe* could be destroyed and it could continue to exist, perhaps as human memory traces – a possibility illustrated by Ray Bradbury's novel *Fahrenheit 451* (which was adapted for the screen by François Truffaut).

Along with novels, plays and films also fall into the category of multiple-instance or type-artforms. Tonight's performance at 8 p.m. of the play *Romance* is a token of the comedy created by David Mamet, just as tonight's performance (showing, screening) at 8 p.m. of *Raging Bull* is a token of the movie-type directed by Martin Scorsese. Thus theater and cinema are brethren ontologically as well as historically.

On the basis of the type/token distinction theatrical performances and movie performances do not look very different. In both cases, the performance in question is a token of a type. Does this imply that there really is no deep difference between theatrical performances and motion picture performances? Does it suggest that there is no significant ontological divide between theater and cinema?

No. For, though the simple type/token distinction is useful as far as it goes, it does not go far enough. Theatrical performances and motion picture performances may, indeed, both justifiably be called tokens; however, the ways in which these tokens are generated from their respective types diverge profoundly. And therein lies a clue to the ontological distinction between theater and cinema. Specifically: live theatrical, token performances are generated by interpretations, whereas token performances of motion pictures are generated by templates.

Moreover, this yields a perhaps unexpected artistic distinction between the two kinds of performance. Theatrical performances are artworks in their own right and, as such, are subject to artistic evaluation, but the performance of a motion picture (a motion picture showing) is neither an artwork nor a reasonable candidate for artistic evaluation.

The motion picture performance – a film showing or screening – is generated from a template. Standardly, this was a film print, but in recent decades it might be a videotape, a laser disk, a DVD, or an instantiated computer program. It is through these templates that we gain access to the original designs of the creators of the motion picture in question.

These templates are tokens. Each one of them can be assigned a location in space and time; each one of them can be destroyed. But the film – say, *Chungking Express* by Wan Gar Wai – is not destroyed when any of the prints are destroyed. One might think that the master or negative is privileged. But the negative of Murnau's *Nosferatu* was destroyed as the result of a court order in response to charges that the film plagiarized *Dracula*, yet *Nosferatu* survives and will continue to do so as long as its design is retrievable either through duplicate prints, DVDs, a collection of photos of all of the frames, or as a digital program on disk, or tape, or paper, or otherwise.

To get to a token performance of a movie – tonight's screening of Ozu's *I Was Born But . . .* – we require a template which is itself a token of the film type. The film performance – the projection or showing of *I Was Born But . . .* – is a token of the type created by Ozu, which token conveys Ozu's masterpiece, the type, to us, the spectators.

This account contrasts sharply with the itinerary from the play type to the token performance of the play. Plays have as tokens both objects (the script) and performances (the enactment of the drama). That is, when considered as a literary work, a token of *The Bacchae* is a graphic text of the same order as my copy of the novel *The Devils*. But considered from the viewpoint of live theater, a token of *The Bacchae* is a performance which occurs at a specific time and place.

Moreover, unlike the movie performance (the performance of the movie), the theatrical performance is not generated by a template. It is generated by an interpretation. For, when considered from the perspective of a live theatrical performance, the play by Euripides is much like a recipe to be filled in by other artists including the director, the actors, the set and lighting designers, the costumers, and so forth.

This interpretation or set of interpretations is a conception of the play and it is this conception of the play that governs its performance from night to night. The interpretation may be performed in different theaters and on different nights. It may be revived after a hiatus. For the interpretation is a type, a type which mediates between the play-text type by Euripides and its token performance at such and such a place and time. Thus, whereas token performances of a motion picture are generated by templates, token performances of a play type are generated by a type – an interpretation of the play type. The connection between the play type and its token performance is negotiated by a conception of the play, itself a type, thereby indicating that an interpretation is a type within a type. What gets us from the play to a token performance is not a template, which is a token, but an interpretation that is a type.

Furthermore, and of the utmost importance: an interpretation is an affair of intentional or mental causation. The token performance of *The Bacchae*, in other words, is mind-generated. The token performance of the movie, on the other hand, is mechanically (and/or electronically) generated; it is the product primarily of physical causation. Perhaps this distinction is already built into the phrase "*live* theater." But it pays to be pedantic here. *Live* theater is to be understood in contrast to *mechanical* movies (cinema) where what makes the former living is that it is the product of mental or intentional mediation via an interpretation or series of interpretations.

So one difference between the performance of a play and the performance of a motion picture is that the former is generated by an interpretation and the latter is generated by a template. Moreover, this difference is connected to another very interesting distinction, namely, that performances of plays are artworks in their own right and can be aesthetically evaluated as such, whereas performances of films and videos are not artworks. Nor does it make sense to evaluate them as such. A film may be projected out of focus or the video tracking may be badly adjusted, but these are not artistic failures. They are mechanical or electrical glitches. That is, a film projectionist may be mechanically challenged but he is not artistically incompetent. Artistic competence does not even enter the picture.

In the theater, the play, the interpretation, and the performance are each discrete arenas of artistic achievement. It is to be hoped, of course, that they will be integrated. And in the best of all cases they are. Nevertheless, we recognize that these are separable strata of artistry. We realize that they can come apart. We often speak of a good play interpreted blandly, of a mediocre play interpreted ingeniously and performed brilliantly, and every other combination thereof. But this manner of speaking, of course, presupposes that we regard the play, the interpretation, and the perform- ance as separate levels of artistic achievement – even where the play is written by someone who directs it and acts in it as well. The play by the playwright is one artwork which is then interpreted like a recipe or set of instructions by a director and others in the process of producing another artwork – the performance of the play.

In this regard, theater, like music and dance, can be called a two-tiered artform. In music, at least since the advent of notation, there is the score – the artwork created by the composer; and then there is also the performance – the score as played by a group of musicians. Similarly, there is the choreography of the dance which is one artwork; and then there is choreography as performed by the troupe which constitutes a discrete artwork. And in theater, there is the play – if not of the well-made sort then, at least, some kind of performance plan – and subsequently its execution (or executions).

But cinema is not a two-tiered artform. There is one, and only one, artwork in cinema – the *finished* film or video. In this regard, though a multiple-instance artwork, a finished film or video is like a painting and unlike a theatrical performance, which, in a manner of speaking, finishes the play-text, or an interpretation thereof, by enacting it. It is that enactment that deserves to be treated as an artwork in its own right.

But the performance of a motion picture – a film showing – is not an artwork in its own right. With two-tiered artforms it makes sense to say that last night's performance was better than tonight's. For example, we might say of a ballet that the corps danced more crisply in yesterday's rendition but is a bit sloppy today. But we cannot talk that way about films. What would we make of someone who said Gregory Peck's portrayal of Atticus Finch in *To Kill a Mockingbird* was riveting last week but a bit shabby last night? The suggestion strains intelligibility.

Our practices with respect to theater and motion pictures are very different. If, in theater, the play-text type is a recipe or sketch that the director and/or the actors interpret, and, furthermore, if the recipe and the interpretation can be regarded as different though related artworks, in motion pictures the recipe and the interpretations are constituents of the self-same integral artwork. When the playwright creates a play, we appreciate it independently of what its theatrical interpreters make of it. We can and should read a play-text as we read a novel.

But in the world of motion pictures, as we know it, scenarios are not read like plays and novels. For example, the voters at the Academy Awards do not read the scripts of nominees when they vote for the best screenplay; they watch the movie in which it is a contributing creative ingredient. The only people who read screenplays, apart from actors and directors, are people who are trying to learn how to write them or the people who teach people to write them or film scholars engaged in historical and/or critical research. In contrast to the theater, where the recipe and the interpretation are two different artworks, in cinema the recipe and its interpretation are presented together in one indissoluble package. The scenarios of most motion pictures, like *Duel*, are not literature, whereas the typical play-text, save perhaps for comedy skits, lays claim to literary status – that is, the status of being an artwork in its own right.

Movie scripts are nothing like the play-text of *Hedda Gabler*. Often, as in the case of *Sunset Boulevard*, shooting begins without a completed script; pages arrive on the set day by day, just in time to start the next scene. Moreover, the script is usually reworked and reworked, often as the movie is being shot, and even after. The director changes it, the actors change it (often simply by paraphrasing the screenwriter's lines their own way), then the writers have second thoughts, and the producer intervenes – sooner or later everyone puts in their two bits, and so on. These are not the products of the uncompromising modernist genius à la Becket. The movie scripts that come to us in published form are not the scripts used during the production process – which were quite frequently being constantly altered as the movie was being made – but are more of the nature of transcriptions or records of the words that finally wound up being said in the finished product. They are not the recipes that were used to launch an interpretation. They are documents of what got made – less recipes, and more parts of the dish that was served. That is, once again, they are ontologically ingredients in the motion pictures with which they are associated rather than being independent artworks.

Let us now also consider another difference between theater and cinema, namely, the putative contrast between how we regard the relation of movie actors to their characters and how we understand the relation of stage actors to theirs. Frequently, people appear to hold the conviction that many different actors can play Khlestakov and the performance will still be a token of the play-type *The Inspector General*, but that it would not be the film-type *Shadow of a Doubt* if someone other than Joseph Cotten played Uncle Charlie. The reason for this is that Joseph Cotten's performance of Uncle Charlie – his interpretation of the role – in concert with the direction of Alfred Hitchcock is ostensibly a non-detachable constituent of the movie. It would not be a screening (a token performance) of *Shadow of a Doubt* if this particular ingredient were missing. Cotten's interpretation of Uncle Charlie has been etched onto celluloid indelibly. That is, speaking less metaphorically, the interpretation by the thespians in the case of film is not separable from the film-type in the way that such interpretations are separable from the play-type. When new actors are cast in what are called movie "remakes," we count the results as a new film-type; but for all the cast changes that *Hamlet* has undergone in the course of history, there is still the one and only play-type, the one created by William Shakespeare.

Whereas film performances – performances of the film – are generated from templates which are tokens, play performances are generated from interpretation types. Thus, where film performances in the relevant sense are counterfactually dependent on certain electrical, chemical, mechanical, and otherwise routine processes and procedures, play performances are counterfactually dependent upon the beliefs, intentions and judgments of people – actors, directors, lighting designers, make-up artists, and so on.

Though, in modern Western theater, there is typically an overarching directorial interpretation of the playwright's recipe, the realization of the token performance on any given night depends on the continuous interpretation of that play, given the special exigencies of the unique performance situation. It is because of the contribution that interpretation qua intentional action makes in the production of the performance that the performance warrants artistic appreciation, whereas the performance of a film – a film showing – warrants no artistic appreciation, since it is simply a function of the physical mechanisms engaging the template in the right way.

A successful motion picture performance – the projection of a film or the running of a videocassette or a DVD – does not command aesthetic appreciation. We do not applaud projectionists as we do violinists or pianists. We are likely to complain and perhaps to demand our money back if the film emulsifies in the projector beam, but that is a technical failure, not an artistic failure. If it were an artistic failure, wouldn't we expect the audience to cheer when the film doesn't burn? But they don't. For the happy motion picture performance merely depends upon operating the apparatus as it was designed to be engaged, and, since that involves no more than often quite minimal mechanical know-how, running the template through the machine is not regarded as an artistic achievement. On the other hand, a successful theatrical performance involves a token interpretation of an interpretation type, and, inasmuch as that depends upon intentional factors, such as artistic understanding and judgment, it is an apposite object of aesthetic appreciation.

Furthermore, if the preceding is correct, then we may conjecture that a major difference between motion picture (or moving image) performances and theatrical performances is that the latter are artworks and the former are not. Thus, performances of motion pictures are not objects of artistic assessment, whereas theatrical performances are. Another way to state this conclusion is that, in one sense, cinema is not a *performing* art – i.e., an artform whose token performances themselves are artworks – in contrast to theater, which is a performing artform in the requisite sense.

This, of course, sounds somewhat counterintuitive. Undoubtedly what is so disturbing about this suggestion is that cinema artists – such as actors – appear to do precisely the same sorts of things that the stage actors, whom we call performing artists, do. Stage actors act; film actors act. If the former are performing artists, so too are the latter. So we seem to be denying the obvious.

Let us grant this much. However, the obvious may be more complex than it appears at first glance. When we go to a performance – a showing – of *Seven Samurai*, we are not viewing *a* performance by Toshiro Mifune. If we say that it is a performance by Mifune that is on the screen, then we must immediately qualify our statement: it is not *a* performance by Mifune, but the one-and-only one; it is the same every night. Mifune's acting is an inseparable element of Kurosawa's *Seven Samurai*. Mifune's acting is not *a* performance out of many in the sense that we can track its vicissitudes from night to night. There can be no variation from showing to showing. A film performer is not a live performer.

As Walter Benjamin pointed out in his often quoted essay, "The Work of Art in the Age of Mechanical Reproduction," the stage actor can adjust his performance to the living audience before him through his interpretation. If the audience seems to appreciate broad humor, she might emphasize the sexual innuendo of certain lines. But the motion picture actor's interpretation is fixed on the template for good.

Returning to the example of Mifune, his artistic contribution is done by the time his acting is stored on the reel of celluloid and shipped off in the film can. Whatever alternative interpretations Mifune essayed in his role in *Seven Samurai* were lost on the cutting-room floor. Mifune's definitive interpretation of his role was invented before the first performance of the film.

Mifune's interpretations of each scene in *Seven Samurai* were integrated and edited into the final product of the motion picture-type before it ever reached any distribution site. By the time those objects reached the movie theaters, there was nothing left for Mifune or any other performing artist to do. It was just a matter of a technician running a template through a machine by, as they say, the numbers.

In sum, there are two striking differences between the performance of a motion picture and the performance of a play. One is that the play performance is generated by an interpretation that is a type, whereas, with respect to movies, the moving image performance is generated by a template that is a token. The second difference is that the performance itself of a play is typically an artwork in its own right, while the token performance of a motion picture is not.

Moreover, the first of these contrasts helps us explain the second. For it is insofar as the performance of the moving image is generated merely by engaging the template mechanically and/or electrically that it is not to be counted as an *artistic* performance, properly so called, whereas a performance generated by an interpretation or a set of interpretations is. These two features of motion pictures are enough to differentiate performances of moving images from performances of plays, and, furthermore, the two differentiae under consideration apply to all films, videos, and the like, whether the types themselves are artworks or not.

Thus far, we have identified four necessary conditions for the moving image. Something x is a moving image only if (1) x is a detached display; (2) x belongs to the class of things from which the promotion of the impression of movement is possible; (3) performance tokens of x are generated by templates that are tokens; and (4) performance tokens of x are not artworks in their own right. Moreover, these criteria supply us with the conceptual wherewithal to discriminate instances of the moving image from its neighbors in the worlds of painting and theater.

Two-Dimensionality

Nevertheless, our formula so far is not completely adequate. For example, it is vulnerable to at least one sort of counterexample. Consider what might be called moving sculptures of the sort that are exemplified by the moving figurines on various antique clocks; as the clock chimes noon, a door swings open and a toy grenadier figure marches across the top of the time piece. Similarly, there are the moving sculptures that one meets at the various Disneylands; such as the mechanical effigies of Abraham Lincoln intoning the Gettysburg Address like, well, clockwork.

Inasmuch as these sorts of figures are multiples, they meet the conditions stated above for membership in the category of the moving image, as do the statuettes of ballerinas that once cavorted on the tops of music boxes. All these examples are detached displays in the same sense that the locale of Burnham Wood on a theater stage is literally discontinuous with the space we inhabit. These ballerinas are not dancing in our space, but some ideal, ethereal space.

Moreover, the aforesaid sculptures, we are assuming, are manufactured from a template and come in multiples. And the mechanical movement in the semblance of a pirouette of the ballerina – her performance, if you will – is not an artwork in its own right. Yet, although she satisfies the criteria, clearly, our ballerina does not seem to be the sort of thing that we have in mind when we speak of motion pictures or the moving image.

In order to exclude cases like this, let us propose a fifth condition for membership in the regime of the moving image. Let us require additionally that, in order to be a moving image, x must also be a two-dimensional array. So x is a moving image only if (5) x is two-dimensional. Perhaps, it might seem unnecessary to supplement the formula above with this emendation, since it might be argued that two-dimensionality is already entailed by the fact that we are talking about motion pictures and moving images which are by definition two-dimensional. However, even if this is true when it comes to pictures, it helps to make it explicit that the pertinent images, when speaking of moving images, are two-dimensional.

Here, it may be fair to ask why two-dimensionality wasn't introduced earlier, since it might appear that that would have given us a neat way in which to cleave motion pictures from theater. But appearances can be deceptive, since there is, in fact, theater that is two-dimensional, for example the shadow-puppet shows of Bali, Java, and China. In order to count them as theater rather than moving pictures, we require recourse to the notion that token performances of motion pictures, in particular, and moving images, more generally, are generated by means of templates that are themselves tokens.

So, x is a moving image if and only if (1) x is a detached display or a series thereof; (2) x belongs to the class of things from which the promotion of the impression of movement is technically possible; (3) performance tokens of x are generated by templates that are themselves tokens; (4) performance tokens of x are not artworks in their own right; and (5) x is two-dimensional. Notice that each of these five conditions is alleged to be necessary and to be conjointly sufficient.

However, as soon as the claim of sufficiency is issued, the worry may arise that the preceding formula is too exclusive. Suppose that it became possible to remake motion pictures, like the HBO television series *Rome*, in the round by means of holography. Imagine that we could project a scene of mortal combat in the Coliseum three-dimensionally with the audience seated around the virtual arena like ancient Romans. Would not such a spectacle be rightfully categorized as a moving image? And yet it will not pass muster according to our definition, since a holographic remake of *Rome* is not two-dimensional: for we can measure our legionnaire-gladiators up, down, and around.

There are at least two strategies for dealing with this case. On the one hand, we may argue that it is an illusion that our holograph is three-dimensional. It is produced by an ensemble of two-dimensional projections, and if you try to strike our legionnaire-gladiators, your hand will pass right through them.

But it is not clear that the three-dimensionality of the holograph is an illusory property rather than an objective, response-dependent property. It is true that, though our legionnaire-gladiators have girth, they have no bulk. They have no weight, but they do have height, width, and depth. But since it is not evident that solidity is really a necessary condition for three-dimensionality, it may not be an option to claim that a holographic *Rome* is actually two-dimensional.

On the other hand, perhaps we should bite the bullet on this one. We can argue that just because the holograph is three-dimensional, it is not a moving *image*. Remember that the criterion of two-dimensionality was introduced precisely in order to distinguish what we call moving images from moving *sculptures*. Sculptures are differentiated from pictures exactly in terms of three-dimensionality versus two-dimensionality. Since the holographic *Rome* is three-dimensional, then, it is natural to classify it as a moving sculpture.

Is this merely an ad hoc solution – one that basically invokes a new category in order to evade an embarrassing theoretical predicament (otherwise known as a counterexample)? Not really. Many classic sculptures have moving parts. Many fountains involve sculptural ensembles, for example, in which moving water stands for moving water – the great rivers of the world, for instance or, less exaltedly, as can be observed in Brussels, urine issuing from a young man. Moreover, there are abstract *moving* sculptures, such as Alexander Calder's mobiles.

Thus, the category of moving sculpture has not been made up on the spot. There are such things. Why should not moving holographs be placed in this category, if they are really three-dimensional? Indeed, for an example of such a sculpture, which I think it is natural to think of as a kind of sculpture, albeit light sculpture, see the interactive holograph of Benjamin Franklin at the Lights of Liberty in Philadelphia, which was designed for the celebration of Franklin's 300th anniversary.

Someone might object to this proposal on the grounds that sculptures are not only three-dimensional, but solid, and our holographs are not. But Robert Morris's sculpture *Steam*, the very name of which tells you what you need to know about it, will no more resist your hand swinging through it than our holographic *Rome*. And, if you maintain that *Steam* still has some particles of substance, whereas our legionnaire-gladiators do not, then recall many of Dan Flavin's sculptural installations, such as *Alternating Pink and Gold*. For these sculptural installations are not only comprised of fluorescent rods but also the light they throw off, and the way it illuminates the surrounding walls. If Flavin can create still sculptures with light, then there should be no objection in principle to moving sculptures concocted of the same stuff.

In addition to the anxiety that our characterization of the moving image is too narrow, there is also the suspicion that it is too broad — that it includes what it should not. For example, photographically mass-produced flip books meet all of our criteria for membership in the category of the moving image. Consider, for instance, the upper right-hand corners of Arlene Croce's wonderful *The Fred Astaire and Ginger Rogers Book*. There you will find still photographs of Astaire and Rogers dancing. If you flick the pages quickly enough, as you are patently intended to do, you can animate the dancers. What is in operation here, of course, is the principle behind a children's flip book. And although the third condition of the preceding theory of the moving image excludes handmade flip books of the kind we once made in grammar school, photographically manufactured or other-wise mechanico-chemically reproduced ones would satisfy that condition; furthermore, if the page-turning were automated, the token performance of the animation would clearly not count as art.

Similarly, Muybridge-type photographs of horses, brought to "life" by the nineteenth-century device known as the zoetrope, fit our formula. But these too are not the sorts of things that people usually have in mind when they talk about motion pictures. If I told you that in repayment for a favor I was going to take you to see a motion picture, and I led you to the library and handed you a flip book, you would probably feel cheated.

Admittedly, neither a zoetrope nor a flip book is a paradigmatic or prototypical instance of our concept of the movies. But I see no reason not to include them in the category of the moving image. Indeed, there are at least two reasons, apart from our theory, to do so. First, the label *moving image*, as understood in ordinary language, suits them perfectly. Whatever else would we call these things but moving pictures or moving images? The name naturally fits them. Furthermore, they rely upon the same principles as do standard film images and, in fact, these phenomena are intimately related historically to the development of the motion picture film images we see projected in our local cineplexes. They were, so to speak, the movies before our prototypical movies. So let us embrace them as instances, albeit non-paradigmatic ones, of the category of the moving image.

What about a Simpler Theory?

Some philosophers will be unhappy with the resolution, arguing that it strays too far away from our ordinary concept of motion pictures as we currently apply it. In order to block the inclusion of flip books, zoetropes, and the like, they may propose that membership in the category requires that the candidate be projected onto a screen. One philosopher, Alan Goldman, for example, defines something as a moving image if and only if it is (1) an image capable of movement (2) that is mechanically projected on a screen. Since this conception of the moving image is far simpler than the one we have been evolving throughout this chapter, we can call it "the simplified definition." Moreover, the second condition of the simplified definition – that a moving image be projected onto a screen – ejects flip books and zoetropes from the realm of the moving image. Shouldn't that count in favor of the simplified view? However, on the down side, it also excludes too many other items that surely belong to the category.

The earliest films produced by the Edison Corporation were not projected onto screens but were viewed as kinetoscopes – that is, not screened but viewed in boxes into which customers peered one at a time and which are sometimes referred to as "peep shows." Often these film shorts were recordings of vaudeville turns, like Annie Oakley's sharp-shooting. It was not until the Lumière Brothers popularized film projection that the screening of films became the order of the day. But these early Edison films were surely moving images, even though they were never screened. A definition that does not classify them as moving images is clearly inadequate. Moreover, these viewing devices remained popular in amusement parks and in adult pornography emporiums until the advent of the videocassette. Like the Edison shorts, these films too were undeniably moving images. Indeed, until quite recently, films were usually cut on machines like movieolas and Steembeck editing tables. That is, editors viewed the raw footage in the same way in which the original audiences viewed the products of the Edison company. But who would deny that these editors were watching moving images? Isn't that what they bequeathed to (movie) theater viewers?

In response to these objections, the proponent of the simplified definition might counter that his definition of the moving image is meant to capture current usage and, therefore, is not threatened by counterexamples from the past. I am not sure that this is a compelling response, since current users will still have to classify things like the Edison productions, and I suspect they will categorize them as moving images, or, at least, as motion pictures. But, in any event, even if it were permissible somehow to bracket all these historical counterexamples, there is a remaining conundrum for the simpli-fied definition, since there are quite a large number of ostensibly legitimate candidates of contemporary vintage for the category of the moving image which the simplified definition simply can't accommodate.

Consider, for example, videocassettes and DVDs. These are not projected onto a screen but, rather, are beamed directly at viewers. By the way, the same is true of everything on television. Aren't all these things moving images? If – since they are not projected – the simplified definition rejects them, then at least two difficulties arise. First, there is the obvious problem that pre-theoretically one is disposed to think that virtually everything on TV should count as belonging to the category of the moving image. But second, denying this leads to inconsistency. If I see *There's Something About Mary* in the movie theater, the simplified definition assigns it to the class of moving images. Yet if I watch it on broadcast TV or a videocassette or a DVD, it is not. Thus, the simplified definition invites paradox and should be discounted for that very reason.

At this point in the debate, the defender of the simplified definition is apt to object that televisions have screens, and, consequently, none of the alleged counterexamples concocted in the preceding paragraph really hit their mark. But this is not true. We look directly into TV images; they are not reflected off a screen. Standardly, scholars distinguish between looking at TV and looking at film in this way. Why would the friend of the simplified view think otherwise?

Perhaps the proponent of the simplified view has in mind what most people refer to as the "TV screen" – the thing that we clean with Windex? But this is somewhat of a misnomer, since the image is projected through this piece of glass and not *onto* it. Moreover, this glass is not a necessary feature of the TV delivery mechanism. You can remove this glass and still receive a moving image. If you don't believe me, try it.

Alternatively, by *screen*, the defender of the simplified view may be thinking of the phosphor screen in the cathode ray tube. This lies between the shadow mask and the front glass of the picture tube. It is coated with a phosphor strip that glows when different colored beams of light hit it. But the phosphor screen is part of the picture tube – which is to say that it is part of the projector mechanism. It is not a screen onto which the image is projected. It is a device for generating the image. It is part of what projects the image – it is part of the picture tube – and not something, such as a screen, that receives the image. For typically there is not screen onto which the picture tube throws the image.

This is not to deny that televisions cannot be outfitted with mechanisms to project their images onto bare walls and screens. But usually they are not so equipped. The possibility of projection onto a screen is not a necessary feature of televisions. In television – whether the image comes to us via a videocassette, a DVD, or a broadcast – we look directly into the projector mechanism rather than at a screen onto which something is projected. A screen is not a necessary condition for a televisual image. Thus, inasmuch as televisual images are paradigmatic instances of the moving image, the simplified definition does not even suit contemporary usage of the concept.

Of course, the defender of the simplified view may claim that all she means by a *screen* is that upon which you see something else or through which you see something else. But this is clearly too broad. For it would fail to exclude certain theatrical inventions from the order of the moving image. There are, of course, the shadow-puppet plays mentioned earlier. And, in addition, if a play-actors stage a scene or an entire play behind a back-lit scrim, that will fall under the simplified definition of the moving image, though this seems to be a deeply counterintuitive result.

Philosophers in general prefer simpler theories over more elaborate ones. That is the attraction of the simplified theory. However, accuracy and comprehensiveness are even more important than simplicity. The simplified definition is not as accurate as its more complex competitor. It errs in excluding too many phenomena – from Edison shorts to DVDs of *The Incredibles* – while also including too much – for example, shadow-puppet plays. Consequently, unless a simplified theory can be crafted to avoid these shortcomings, for the duration we will regard something as an instance of the moving image if and only if (1) it is a detached display or a series thereof; (2) it belongs to the class of things from which the production of the impression of movement is technically possible; (3) performance tokens of it are generated by templates which are tokens; (4) performance tokens of it are not artworks in their own right; and (5) it is a two-dimensional array.

To answer the question with which we began – what is cinema? – we can now say that cinema is, at least, necessarily, the practice of making moving images. Admittedly, that's not, as Descartes might say, the whole ball of wax. But isn't it a pretty helpful start?

Suggested Reading

The quest to define cinema has been a perennial one. All of the film theorists cited at the end of the last chapter have their own version of an answer to the question "What is cinema?" See those references as a guide to reading your way through the maze.

An approximation of the theory offered in this chapter is also available in Noël Carroll, "Defining the Moving Image," in his *Theorizing the Moving Image*

(Cambridge: Cambridge University Press, 1996), though the present version is bolder and better defended than the earlier one.

The idea of detached displays or disembodied arrays benefits greatly from Francis E. Sparshott's speculations, though establishing this condition as a necessary one for cinema is not the primary purpose of Sparshott's article. See Sparshott's "Vision and Dream in the Cinema," *Philosophic Exchange* 1 (Summer 1971), 111–22.

Our emphasis upon *moving* pictures here is very deeply indebted to Arthur Danto's magnificent article, "Moving Pictures," *Quarterly Review of Film Studies* 4:1 (Winter 1979), 1–21.

The discussion of tokens, types, and templates with regard to art begins with Richard Wollheim's *Art and its Objects* (Cambridge: Cambridge University Press, 1980), especially sections 35–8. In this chapter, we are working out of Wollheim's framework.

Walter Benjamin's contrast between film acting and stage acting can be found in his "The Work of Art in the Age of Mechanical Reproduction," in *Illuminations*, edited by Hannah Arendt and translated by Harry Zorn (New York: Schocken Books, 1968).

The simplified definition of motion pictures can be found in Alan Goldman, "Specificity, Popularity, and Engagement in the Moving Image," *Film and Philosophy* 5:6 (2002), 93–9.

Chapter Four

The Moving Picture – the Shot

Movies are typically comprised of a series of moving pictures, called shots, which themselves are animated as a succession of still pictures, called frames, pass before the projector beam. A shot is characteristically an uninterrupted camera take – one with no spatial or temporal discontinuities that are detectable by the human eye.

These shots can be very near to their subjects – as in a close-up of Gong Li's face or of the barrel of a gun – or they can be further away, for example: a medium shot of a man, from the knees up, waiting for a bus; or a long shot of an ocean liner steaming into port; or an overhead shot of chorines distributing their limbs decoratively into kaleidoscopic figures in a musical number by Busby Berkeley. Shots may also involve moving points of view as the camera tracks toward or zooms in on its subject or away from it, or travels next to it, as in an exciting car chase.

These shots are, so to speak, the building blocks of traditional cinema. The question to be pursued in this chapter is how best to understand these moving picture shots, ranging from close shots of Tony Soprano to long shots of the spaceship *Enterprise*. (Note that in this chapter our concern is with moving *pictures* and not with, more broadly, moving *images*. That is, we will not attempt to analyze cinematic abstractions here.)

Motion picture shots are representations – pictorial representations of houses, horses, and Hondas. But how it is it that they succeed in conveying their content to audiences? There seem to be at least these four leading alternatives: (1) moving picture shots are illusions of that of which they are pictures (the illusion thesis); (2) shots are transparencies, providing us with indirect perceptual access to whatever gave rise to them (the transparency thesis); (3) shots are coded symbols, somewhat like words (the code thesis); or (4) shots are recognitional prompts, naturally generative symbols that engage the subpersonal perceptual processes that we employ daily for object recognition in such a way that a motion picture shot of, say, a dog will elicit our apprehension of a dog in the picture without any subtending operations of decoding, reading, or inferring (the recognition thesis).

Let us proceed through these options one by one. However, for the sake of full disclosure, I should say out front that my money is on the recognition thesis.

The Illusion Thesis

The first alternative – that the motion picture shot is an illusion – is probably the best known one; I suspect that most readers have at least heard this idea before. It involves the contention that the image on screen is so convincing that one is seduced or deluded into the illusion that the objects and events that gave rise to it are actually before us. Sometimes this or that cinematic process, like Cinerama or Imax, is promoted by declaring that it delivers the illusion of reality. Or a critic may recommend a motion picture by saying that it makes you feel that you are really *there* – there in the world of the movie.

The notion that the moving picture shot is an illusion appeared early on in the history of cinema. One of the earliest films screened by the Lumière Brothers showed a train arriving at a station. Allegedly, as the image on screen chugged toward the camera recording it, viewers scrambled to get out of the path of the engine. Supposedly they felt in mortal danger. Whether this event ever really happened or is merely the hyperbole of some publicist, we may never know for sure (though I frankly admit that I am very skeptical about the likelihood that this report is accurate). Nevertheless, the mantra that a moving picture is an illusion of reality is often repeated; it was the prevailing article of faith of film theorists in the 1970s and 1980s.

What we may call the illusion thesis can be framed in at least two ways: (1) that the moving image is a cognitive or epistemic illusion; or (2) that it is a perceptual illusion. To say that a moving picture shot is a cognitive or epistemic illusion maintains that it involves the provocation of a *belief* on the part of the viewer. Specifically, it involves engendering a *false* belief in the viewer – namely, that one is literally in the presence of the object or event pictured on screen.

Imagine that the image on screen is Big Jake. According to the cognitive or epistemic version of the illusion thesis, as Big Jake saunters toward the camera, I believe that Big Jake is actually sauntering toward me. If Big Jake reaches for his Winchester and points it in my direction, then I fear for my life. For, putatively, I believe that Big Jake is in the same space that I am in and that his bullets can cut me to the quick.

The perceptual version of the illusion thesis can be illustrated by that perennial philosophical example – the straight stick that appears bent in water. As you know, if you take a straight stick and dip it into a running stream, it will appear bent to you. That is, the stick will *look* bent to you, even though you realize that it is straight. This is what we call an optical illusion. Of course, since you know that the stick is straight, you believe it is straight, despite its bent appearance. You are not deceived by the look of the stick. Unlike a case of cognitive or epistemic illusion, you do not form a false belief about the stick. Nevertheless, it does look perceptually as though it were bent.

Another famous example of a perceptual illusion is the Miller-Lyre Illusion. This involves two lines of equal length. But on the tips of the two ends of the bottom line there are what look like arrowheads pointing away from the line, while on the top line the arrowheads point into the line. The effect of this arrangement is that the top line appears longer than the lower line, though they are both precisely the same length. To prove this you may take a ruler to the two lines. This will establish that they are equal, but still one cannot shake the impression that they *look* to be of different lengths.

Even though you come to believe that the two lines are equal, that belief will not change the way in which the lines appear to you. The perception of the inequality of the lines is what philosophers call cognitively impenetrable – i.e., knowing (and believing) that the lines are equal will not change the fact that they look unequal to you. The perceptual illusion here is impervious to our beliefs. We know cognitively that the lines are the same, but we cannot but see the top line as longer than the bottom line.

Cognitive illusions involve beliefs, indeed false beliefs. We are deceived by cognitive or epistemic illusions. Perceptual illusions need not involve being deceived at all. We may know (and, therefore, believe) that a stick in water is straight and yet it still seems stubbornly bent to us. What we know and believe does not change the perceptual impression the stimulus provokes in us. Believing otherwise – for example, that the two lines in the Miller–Lyre example are equal – has no impact on the fact that to our eyes they remain obdurately unequal.

The cognitive or epistemic version of the illusion thesis is not very promising. On this view, moving picture shots succeed in conveying whatever they are pictures of by instilling the illusion that whatever they represent on screen is literally present to us. We are, for example, while watching *Finding Neverland*, somehow convinced, deceptively, of course, that we are looking on as James Barrie – in the flesh, so to say – composes *Peter Pan*. Sometimes this phenomenon is described as a suspension of disbelief. But this is simply a roundabout way of saying that, since we do not disbelieve Barrie is in front of us, we believe that he is. Yet this hypothesis strains credulity.

Among other things, beliefs are mental states that we posit in order to explain people's behavior. Hortense announces that she is thirsty and she reaches for the refrigerator door. We explain her action of reaching for the door by postulating that Hortense believes that there is thirst-quenching liquid in the refrigerator. Herbert reads his assignment; we explain this by indicating that Herbert believes by reading his assignment, he will pass the test tomorrow. Beliefs are connected to behavior, since beliefs make behaviors happen.

But consider the ramification of this for the cognitive or epistemic version of the illusion theory. Putatively, we believe that the objects and events in the motion picture are present to us. But what if the film is *King Kong*? If we truly believed that a fifty-foot tall, very angry gorilla was within arm's length of us, would we sit by idly and wait for him to wrench us from our seats and do – God knows what – to us? No. If we believed Kong was within stomping distance, we'd start running away from him as quickly as possible. Or imagine that we are watching *The Wild Bunch*. Bullets are flying everywhere. But we are casually munching our cheese nachos. Is that how people behave who believe that they are in the middle of a fire fight?

Or, to consider less violent prospects, let us suppose that we are watching two young lovers in the process of removing their clothes and fondling each other. In real life (as opposed to reel life), if we came upon such a situation and believed we were inadvertent witnesses to a tryst, I suspect most of us would turn away, perhaps in embarrassment. But we look on shamelessly at scenes like this on film. Consequently, how likely is it that we believe that we are actually in the presence of this couple? Not very. For how else would one explain our very different behavior when we do not believe the lovers are only on screen?

These behavioral anomalies imply the overwhelming improbability of the conjecture that we are cognitively deceived into believing we are actually involved in a close encounter of the third kind with the folks pictured in movie shots. Our behavior in the movie theater or, for that matter, in our living rooms, is not the sort we would expect from people who believe that King Kong is in the neighborhood, or that they are pinned down by gunfire, or that they have just blundered into a love nest. Given the connection between beliefs and behavior, our behaviors at the movies indicate that we are not in the thrall of any cognitive or epistemic illusion.

Apart from the aforesaid kinds of behavioral anomalies, there are further aspects of the movie-viewing experience that make it positively unlikely that we are deluded into believing that what is pictured on screen is "in our face." Often we have to see through various surface interferences in order to attend to a movie – we must look past the scratches, the dirt on the filmstrip, and the hair in the projector gate, or we must see past the overexposure of the footage in order to secure visual access to the story. But if we are knowingly "seeing through" the image, we cannot be under the misapprehension that what is pictured is somehow really a living presence that is close up and personal, so to speak. For such a mental state would be self-contradictory.

Likewise, sometimes the screen is soiled. Perhaps an unhappy patron threw a glass of Coke at it eons ago and the negligent theater owner never got around to cleaning it off. That splotch is also something that we need to see through. But how can we see through this surface interference and believe in the reality of what is pictured at the same time? That is, movie viewing appears to involve an awareness of the screen, if we know to "see through" these various surface incongruities. But, at the same time, the cognitive illusion thesis has us disbelieving in the screen and believing in the real presence of what is shown. However, this supposes us to be in a contradictory mental state – simultaneously believing and not believing in the presence of the screen – a mental state that borders dubiously upon psychosis.

Moreover, often when appreciating a motion picture we say "How very lifelike." But we would hardly call a movie life*like*, if we thought it was, as the cognitive illusion thesis requires, real life. Sitting in our office, suffering through our daily grind, we never say "How lifelike." We're more apt to say "That's life."

Similarly, we wouldn't call a movie realistic if we thought it was real. When caught in a traffic jam, we don't say "How realistic." If anything we say "I can't believe this is real (or really happening)." Thus, it seems that certain of the ways in which we articulate our appreciation of cinema entail that we cannot hold the beliefs that the epistemic version of the illusion thesis purports we do.

Furthermore, if we were seduced by these alleged cognitive illusions, we would be hard put to render coherently what we experience under their sway with the rest of our experience. How do I explain to myself when watching *Gandhi* how my home entertainment center in the basement of my condo in Philadelphia now somehow abuts onto the Ganges? When a moving picture shot is taken from the ceiling, am I deluded into believing that I am hanging from the rafters? How did I get there? How do I get down? Or recall my watching *The Wild Bunch*. How is it that I emerged from that welter of whizzing bullets unscathed?

Or, even more unintelligibly, suppose I am watching the episode of *Six Feet Under* in which it is true in the fictional world that he inhabits that Nate buries his wife Lisa in the desert unseen by anyone. Yet, if I am caught in the undertow of a cognitive illusion, don't I believe that I am a witness to the event? So how can I also believe that no one saw the burial? Again, the cognitive illusion theory would seem to have the extremely counter-intuitive consequence of leading normal viewers into webs of belief so contradictory that said viewers would appear to be virtually psychotic.

The cognitive or epistemic variant of the illusion thesis is fraught with problems. But perhaps the perceptual version of illusionism is not so troubled. According to the perceptual illusion thesis, we are not necessarily deceived by what we see on screen. Nevertheless, we find what we see irresistibly, perceptually compelling. We do not believe Big Jake is in front of us; it only seems to be or looks that way. But is it really true that the objects and events pictured in motion pictures strike us perceptually as really being present? If the movie is black and white, how is this possible? People in broad daylight don't look black and white to us. Moreover, the film image is odorless. When we perceive the world, we not only see and hear objects, we also smell them.

Perceiving motion picture images typically diverges in a large number of ways from normal perception; it hardly strikes us as though we are perceiving these cinematic images in exactly the same way we would perceive their referents outside the cinema. It is almost always possible to perceive the difference between a motion picture image of a person and the living, breathing being.

If Big Jake were standing in front of me, and I changed my position relative to him, different aspects of Big Jake would come into view. For example, if I moved to my right, more of his left side would occupy my field of vision than was visible previously, just as more of his right side would become proportionately occluded. Psychologists call these "edge phenomena"; that is, I start to see *around* the edges of things when I alter my perspective. But there are no edge phenomena with respect to a static motion picture shot. The shot is taken from a single point of view or monocular station point. If I move from the right aisle of the movie theater to the opposite aisle, there will be no change in what I see of Big Jake. I will not start to see around his other side. In other words, I will not perceive what I would perceive were I moving relative to a real person who was actually present to me. The perceptual experience will be radically different; it will not feel, even if I am not able to put my finger on why precisely, as though I am seeing someone in the flesh.

Additionally, the muscles in our eyes register a phenomenological difference between the flickering image on the screen as an object that inhabits the same physical space in which we are situated, versus the virtual space portrayed in the picture. So, once again, the film image does not seem – does not even feel – literally co-present to me. My body, so to speak, rejects this impression.

Furthermore, many of the objections brought against the cognitive or epistemic version of illusionism can be recycled against perceptual illusionism. I must see through surface anomalies on the screen; but there are no surface anomalies like that in reality. Reality doesn't look as though it has been scratched. And what of moving picture shots that employ a distorting lens? People's anatomies do not come squashed or elongated as they frequently do in film; nor is soft focus a recurrent feature of our perceptual world.

Those early film theorists, like Rudolf Arnheim, were right about the myriad ways in which film departs from normal perceptual experience. They were also right that filmmakers often use these deviations as opportunities for expression which they justifiably expected viewers to notice or, at least, to sense just because the relevant film images diverge from the way in which things normally look. But if this sort of appreciative response to film is plausible – and it gives every indication that it is – then perceptual illusionism cannot be true. Film shots do not strike us perceptually as though the objects they picture are literally in front of us. Moving picture shots are not perceptual illusions of what they present. They just don't look like the real thing.

Even if at some point in the future it becomes technologically feasible to produce motion picture shots that look just like what they are pictures of, this possibility would not entail that that is how we have typically experienced moving picture shots up until now. For the vast majority of moving picture shots do not look like their referents. They have not fooled and will not fool the eye. Even if, one day, there will be shots of Big Jake that look as though the bruiser is in front of us, we have not met those shots so far. Consequently, what perceptual illusionism offers by way of understanding the operation of moving picture shots fails to characterize shots as we now know them.

Nevertheless, the defender of perceptual illusionism may argue that these objections do not show that there is absolutely no place for the notion of illusion in our account of the moving picture shot. Even if Big Jake does not strike us perceptually as being in front of us in the flesh, there still is an element of the image that is implacably illusory, namely: that something is moving on screen. For, it may be argued, nothing is really moving on screen in the movie theater. That is, the appearance of movement is an illusion – specifically a perceptual illusion.

The impression of movement in film is standardly generated by a succession of still pictures projected, nowadays, typically at the rate of twenty-four per second. These still pictures are frames, and they are said not to move. This is not exactly right, since they do move through the gate of the projector. Of course, we do not perceive these frames or their movement. The projector puts projected images of these frames on the screen for us to look at. These images move too – they move on and off the screen – but that is not something our perceptual apparatus registers. Instead, we perceive shots, not frames, or rather projected shots.

Moreover, these projected shots don't move, in the sense that they don't jump off the screen and fly around the movie theater. Rather, parts of the projected shots – projected people, vehicles, animals, etc. – give the impression of moving. Furthermore, the friend of perceptual illusionism maintains, those impressions are illusions, since what is actually on screen are still images.

That is, what is really on screen is a succession of still pictures; but we cannot help but see movement up there. Movement in film is a perceptual illusion. Therefore, one cannot discount the illusion thesis entirely when it comes to understanding how the *moving* picture shot operates.

Parts of the shot – a car, for example – appear to move. Comparable parts of the frame don't move, or, if they do, because they wobble a bit, this is not usually detectable by the human eye. So, the parts of the frame are still, whereas the corresponding parts of projected shots give the impression of movement, that is, in shots where there is movement (as opposed to freeze frames). Perceptual illusionism says that this impression of movement or apparent motion is an illusion.

I think that, at first blush, perceptual illusionism with respect to motion picture movement appeals to common sense. But might not there be some way in which the movement is not illusory? Or, in other words, might there be a way in which we might be prepared to say that the movement within the shot is real, or, at least, objective?

The argument that so readily convinces common sense that motion picture movement is illusory rests upon setting up a forced choice: either the movement in the motion picture shot is metaphysically real or it is illusory. Here, for something to be metaphysically real means: the way in which things stand from the view from nowhere or, if that notion is oxymoronic, then how ultimate reality appears to an omniscient being, like God, who is not limited to what can be detected by human sensory apparatus. This being sees tables and chairs in their ultimate physical reality as swarms of sub-atomic particles; this being sees film frames click by one at a time. Moreover, if something is not metaphysically real in this sense, then it is illusory.

But are these the only alternatives that we should consider? Insofar as common sense starts with this disjunction, common sense sees no other option but to consign movement within the shot to the rank of an illusion. Yet might we not think differently if there were more options at our disposal? Needless to say, that will depend upon what those alternatives are and how compelling they appear.

One alternative, not canvassed so far, is that the motion is real in the sense that it is real, response-dependent motion. That is, the movement within the shot is an objective appearance. A standard motion picture shot will yield the impression of movement to creatures constituted with perceptual systems like ours. Creatures with our perceptual capabilities, including not only other humans, but the members of other species as well, will unfailingly perceive motion on screen when the pertinent frames are projected at certain speeds. This will not be a subjective matter in the sense that some people will see the motion and others won't, depending upon their taste. The design of the motion picture apparatus engages the "design" of our perceptual apparatus in a way that the detection of movement on screen obtains consistently and regularly for normally sighted, human viewers. That is why we say that the appearance of motion is objective in the sense of being *inter-subjective*; it is uniform across sighted, human percipients. Therefore, it seems very misleading to call it an illusion, since everyone will see it that way. Indeed, if a sighted human being reported sincerely that he did not see movement when exposed to standard motion picture projection, we might suspect him of being the victim of some sort of perceptual malfunction.

Nor is this convergence only observable among humans. There is a 1994 videotape entitled *Kitty Safari* which was produced in order to make household cats purr with delight as they watch assorted birds, squirrels, rats, mice, and guppies cavort before the camera. Humans are not the only animals that see movement in motion pictures; felines do as well. In fact, in one installment of *America's Funniest Videos*, a cat perched on top of a television attempted to snatch the racing automobiles zooming toward the camera as they seemed to converge on lower left-hand corner of the screen. Cats, like humans, perceive movement in motion picture arrays.

Furthermore, the motion effect imparted from movies is so uniform that were someone to deny that they saw movement on screen as the guns of Navarone blow skyward, we would suspect that that person were suffering some sort of delusion – an illusion or hallucination of stillness perhaps.

If it does not make sense to say that what everyone sees is illusory then, equally, it admittedly does not seem right to say that the parts of the shot are literally moving from the perspective of ultimate reality. The movement is not metaphysically (or even physically) real. But it may be real – that is to say *objective* – nevertheless; the movement may be a real, response-dependent property of the shot. But what does that mean?

Color is a real, response-dependent property. A property is a real, response-dependent one if it can be detected by normal viewers in appropriately conditioned circumstances. Color is like this. We say that the American post box really is blue, in the response-dependent sense, if it looks blue to normal viewers in standard lighting; it is not green in standard lighting, nor would we say it was green if we suffused it in a yellow light or if the viewers were jaundiced.

Arguably, cinematic motion is real in a comparable, response-dependent way. That the post box is blue is not an illusion. Blueness is a real, response-dependent property of the mailbox. Analogously, cinematic movement is real – real, response-dependent movement – and not illusory movement. Just as we detect the real, response-dependent property of blueness in the post box, so the movement we detect on screen is real, albeit in a response-dependent way.

Perhaps this position may gain support from considerations like this: if, while watching *To Kill a Mockingbird*, one spectator asks another spectator "Did Atticus Finch just cross the courtroom?" the pertinent answer will be "Yes" rather than "There was no movement, just a succession of projected, still frames"; just as when we are asked "Is the fire engine red?", the answer is "Yes" rather than "No, there are just colorless photons over there." Color and cinematic movement are both objective appearances, i.e., real, response-dependent properties that are inter-subjectively verifiable, though only detectable via certain perceptual systems.

It is not an illusion that the desk upon which I now write is solid. It is true that at the subatomic level there are gaps between the particles that comprise the desk. That may dispose us to say that the desk is not solid – gapless – in the sense of ultimate metaphysical reality. But the solidity of the desk is not illusory. Anyone who thought they could pass their hand through it would be counted as a madman. Rather, the desk appears solid, objectively, for those of us possessed of certain perceptual apparatus.

Similarly, we say that the epidermis of an ant is solid, though under a powerful microscope we would see that it is perforated with numerous spiracles through which it takes in air. It is not illusion to say that the ant's back is solid; it is an objective property of the ant's epidermis detectable by creatures with perceptual apparatuses like ours. So, by analogous argumentation, cinematic movement is not an illusion. It is an objective appearance, inter-subjectively available to anyone constituted perceptually in the way we are. Cinematic movement is a real, response-dependent property of the shot.

That is, our alternatives in this discussion are not limited conceptually to a choice between cinematic movement being metaphysically real and its being illusory. There is also the option that is an objective appearance – real, that is, in a response-dependent way. And if cinematic movement is real in this way, then it is not an illusion.

Nevertheless, this argument against relegating cinematic movement to the status of an illusion may strike some readers as proving far too much. They may fear that this notion of response-dependent reality is far too liberal. It seems to threaten to banish entirely the very category of perceptual illusion. Will we say of the Miller-Lyre Illusion, for example, that it is not an illusion, because the apparently greater length of the top line is objective for creatures with our perceptual capacities – that its apparently greater length is a real, response-dependent property of the line? Or that the bentness of the stick in the stream is a real, response-dependent property of the stick? Or, for a fresh example, that waves have the real, response-dependent property of coming toward us, though speaking in terms of what is happening physically, water molecules are merely being displaced sequentially?

The notion of real, response-dependent properties, it may be argued, will make all these illusions disappear. But we cannot dispense with the category of perceptual illusions, since there are such things under the sun.

The invocation of real, response-dependent properties, however, does not evaporate the category of perceptual illusions. An important distinction between the solidity of the epidermis of the ant and the bentness of the stick in water is that we can discover the illusory nature of the latter by using nothing more than our normal perceptual capacities and ordinary or every-day or conventional procedures, ones readily within our reach without resort to special equipment or tests. That is, we can lift the stick out of the water and, using our ordinary powers of sight, confirm that it is straight; or we can bend down and feel that it is not bent while it is still below the waterline. In other words, we can locate the illusion within the realm of our own senses. On the other hand, in order to see the air holes on the back of an ant, we need special equipment – a high-powered microscope, for example.

So if we can detect the pertinent, deviant phenomena by employing our ordinary perceptual capabilities and conventional means, then it is a perceptual illusion. To determine that the lines are equal in the Miller-Lyre configuration, we need only cover the arrowheads with our hands, or apply some ready-to-hand measuring device, like a piece of string, to the lines. We can establish that the wave is not a single block of water rushing at us by floating something in the water and then noting that it stays bobbing in place when the wave *moves* past it. Thus, these two phenomena are perceptual illusions, as is the bent stick in water. But establishing that the desk is composed of atoms and the void, or that the redness of the fire engine is an affair of colorless photons requires far more extraordinary means.

Given this way of marking off perceptual illusions from real, response-dependent properties, in which category does cinematic motion belong? If it is a perceptual illusion, we should be able to discover this using our normal sensory capabilities and ordinary, household paraphernalia. Can we?

In order to assert that the cinematic movement is an illusion, it will not suffice to take the celluloid filmstrip in your hand and to notice that it is composed of static frames. For it is not the film unengaged by the projector that imparts the impression of movement; you have to be able to detect the static frames on the screen while the filmstrip is moving. How would you do that, and would it involve extraordinary means or not?

It may be suggested that the way to establish that there is no movement on the screen is to slow the projector down to a speed where the spectator sees the projected frames one at a time in all their stillness. But this is not a conventional way of viewing films. Moreover, it turns out that it is not, as a matter of fact, a readily available way. Most projectors do not have the capacity to slow down the projection rate to the point where the spectator can see one frame at a time. In all probability, almost all, if not all, of the extant movie projectors in theaters today lack this capacity. Moreover, the projectors that have the capability to run alternately at silent speed and sound speed do not run slowly enough to extinguish the impression of movement, but only to change the apparent velocity of the moving objects on screen.

Of course, certain projectors have been designed that can exhibit the filmstrip frame by frame – for example, analytic projectors like the Athena of yesteryear. But is resorting to such devices a conventional way of checking the projected film for actual movement? Rather, such projectors seem to be like microscopes – they are ways of going beyond what can be discovered by the naked eye. They are expressly produced to pierce through response-dependent appearances. We would not say that the epidermis of the ant is not solid just because if we put it under a suitably adjusted microscope, we would see air holes. There is a perfectly respectable way in which it is appropriate to say that the ant's body is solid. Shouldn't we adopt the same stance with respect to cinematic movement? Moreover, the same kind of argument might be made if it was suggested that we examine the film on a movieola or and editing table, like a Steembeck; these are specialized instruments, like microscopes, and not the sorts of things to which most viewers have access.

So one reason to deny that the cinematic movement in the film shot is illusory is that it is an objective appearance; the motion, that is, is a real, response-dependent property of the shot. But another reason to deny the illusion thesis is that calling filmic movement illusory invites paradox. Why? Well suppose, *pace* the preceding discussion, that we could slow ordinary *film* projectors down to the point where one could see that the cinematic movement was caused by the passage of still frames through the gate. Imagine we slowed down the projection of *Nashville* in just this way. We could then say that the movement in the *film Nashville* is illusory. But now suppose we transfer *Nashville* to a videocassette or a DVD. These systems do not engender the impression of movement frame by frame, nor can the manner in which they impart motion be decomposed in a way that we can grasp using the naked eye. Consequently, we will be forced to the patently contradictory conclusion that the impression of motion in the *film Nashville* is illusory, but the perceived movement in the videocassette version and the DVD is not.

Also, there is another impression caused by film projection that may be pertinent here. Call it the impression of the continuous image. As each frame is pulled away from the projector lamp and replaced by another, there is an interval of darkness. But on screen we see the shot as a continuous picture, though for every second of screening time there are so many blank screens. Moreover, even if there is some flickering, this impression will not be extinguished by slowing the projector or even moving frame by frame. Given the inextinguishability of the impression of the continuous image in the shot, the proponent of perceptual illusionism will have to accept the impression of continuity in the shot as a real, response-dependent property of the shot. But doesn't consistency then demand that we have the same position with respect to the appearance of movement in the shot that we have with respect to its appearance of continuity?

Undoubtedly one of the reasons that the defender of the perceptual illusion of movement feels compelled to deny that cinematic motion is real is that he presupposes that ordinary real movement from A to B involves passing through every point between them. But as Big Jake makes his way across the screen, he does not move through every point on the streets of Laredo; there are gaps. So the movement is not ordinary movement, but an illusion.

However, is it really the case that ordinary movement must be continuous in this way? Recall the phenomenon of shadows. Positioned appropriately with regard to a light source, we are happy to say that my shadow moves when I move from one side of the courtyard to the other. Now imagine that I pass behind a tree for a moment. My shadow will momentarily cease, only to reappear as I clear the tree. Yet we will regard the movement of my shadow as continuous. We will not say there are two shadows here, each with its own discrete spate of movement. Even though there is a gap in the space the shadow traverses, we do not hesitate to regard the movement as ordinary. Furthermore, when we remember that the film image is in many ways an affair of shadows, we should be ready to treat it on a par with the way we regard the ordinary movement of shadows which, among other things, tolerates gaps. If shadow movement is not necessarily illusory, neither need be cinematic motion.

The Transparency Thesis

We have already encountered the transparency thesis in the first chapter of this book. It is the view that the cinematic image is transparent. Putatively we see through the image to the object of which it is an image. In this regard, the cinematic image is analogous to telescopes, microscopes, periscopes, and to those parking-lot mirrors that enable you to see around corners. When we look through devices like these, we say that we see the objects to which these instruments give us access. We see distant planets through telescopes; molecules through microscopes; oncoming traffic through parking-lot mirrors; and enemy vessels through periscopes. These devices augment our visual powers. They are, in this respect, prosthetic devices. They enable us literally to *see* things we could not see otherwise. Moreover, we do not regard these prosthetic devices as delivering representations of the things they show us; we say that we see the very things themselves when we look into these instruments.

When I am sitting high up in the balcony and I look through my opera glasses at the soprano, I see the soprano, not a representation of the soprano. Devices such as opera glasses, and the instruments mentioned above, enhance the range of my vision. They do not produce representations of what they reveal, but put us in visual contact with the real thing. These devices are not, in principle, different from the corrective lenses that we wear to rectify near-sightedness or far sightedness. They are prostheses. They help us to overcome visual shortcomings and to see what is otherwise visually unavailable.

But if we are willing to speak this way about microscopes and telescopes as prosthetic devices, why not extend this idea to photography and cinematography? Cameras also put us in visual contact with things that are remote – temporally remote that is – things from the past. A snapshot enables me to see my childhood sweetheart; the filmstrip grants me visual access to the performance of a silent film star who died before I was born. The telescope puts us in visual contact with a distant galaxy; a camera does the same thing with respect to the distant past.

The claim that we can see into the past may seem like voodoo to you. But it shouldn't. Since the light from far off galaxies takes so long to reach us, it can be said that some of the stars that we see in the here and now had actually collapsed into black holes centuries ago. As we watch the glow stream out of them, we are quite literally seeing into the past. If we can see into the past with a telescope, there should be no impediment to saying that cameras enable us to do likewise.

The argument for the transparency thesis exploits a slippery slope. If a periscope enables us to see over the wall into the adjacent courtyard, why not say that a video set-up does as well? Here one feels like saying "But we don't actually see the courtyard on the video monitor." But what do we mean by "actually see"?

One thing that it means is that our perception is counterfactually dependent upon the visible properties of the objects of our perception – i.e., had the visible properties of those objects been different, then our perceptions would have been different accordingly. There is a causal chain of physical events between the objects of our perception and our perceptions such that if the starting point in that network were otherwise, then our perceptions would vary in concert. For instance, I see the redness of the tomato because the tomato is red, but had the tomato been a green one, what I would see would be green. And had the object been a tuba, rather than a tomato, then, all things remaining constant, what I would have seen would have been a tuba.

Likewise, when I look through a periscope, what I see is counter-factually dependent upon the objects that give rise to my perception. I see an ocean liner, because that is what occupies the pertinent visual arc; had it been a battle cruiser, a battle cruiser is what the periscope would deliver up to me. It is because devices like periscopes and binoculars preserve this sort of counterfactual dependency that we are prepared to say that we see through them to the very objects to which they grant us visual access.

These instruments boost our visual powers. They are on a continuum with unaided sight, in part because they sustain the same kind of relations of counterfactual dependence with the objects of sight that natural per-ception does. That is, what we see through them would have been different had the visible properties they were aimed at been different. The causal chain of physical events involved in looking through a pair of binoculars may add a step when contrasted to unaided vision. But the step is not one that is different in kind from what one finds in unaugmented perception. It remains a causal process that preserves the relevant visual relations of counterfactual dependency. The prostheses and the perception they abet blend together seamlessly.

But is the situation so different when it comes to cinematography? Cinematic "vision" and unaided vision are as alike as the "vision" available through a pair of binoculars is analogous to unaided perception. Counter-factual dependency obtains equally. We expect a cinematic image of x to present the visible properties of x in such a way that had the visible properties of x been different, the image of x would differ correspondingly. For instance, we expect, all things being equal, the cinematic image of a white church to be white, though if, counterfactually, the church had been black, then we would have expected the cinematic depiction of it to be black.

This, of course, correlates both with prosthetically unassisted vision and with the enhanced vision available through the optical instruments discussed thus far. So if we are comfortable with saying we see through binoculars because of the way in which they preserve the counterfactual dependency of the visual output on the visual input, then why should we balk at saying precisely the same thing about cinematic images which possess comparable powers? Since the same kind of physico-causal processes are involved in seeing through a telescope as are engaged in the delivery of a cinematic image to an auditorium, we have no reason, in principle, to treat the one as different from the other. We see the extinct star through the telescope; we see the assassination of JFK through the Zapruder footage.

In order to "see through" a cinematic shot, it is a necessary condition that the photographic process put us in contact with the object by purely mechanical means of the sort that guarantees the preservation of the pertinent relations of counterfactual dependency. However, the proponent of the transparency thesis does not think that this is enough to establish that the shot is transparent. Why not? Well, imagine a computer that is capable of scanning a visual array of simple geometrical shapes and of then printing out a verbal description of it. When a square appears in the array, the computer prints out "square," and so forth. However, no one supposes that in looking at the word "square" on the printout we are seeing through the paper and ink to the very square that the computer detected. A description is not a transparent picture for the simple reason that it is not a picture at all. So what must be added to the concept of transparency in order to forestall the inclusion of computer-generated descriptions of the previous sort from the category?

One way to begin to do this is to think about the ways in which we might be confused by pictures versus the way in which we can be confused by verbal descriptions. When reading, for example, we might confuse the word *sun* for *son*, since the lettering is so very similar. This kind of error is even more likely if we are reading very quickly. However, when we are out in the world viewing objects in nature it would seem virtually impossible (discounting Apollo) to mistake a male offspring for the celestial body.

On the other hand, when it comes to seeing objects out in the world, it is quite possible to mistake the back of a garage for the back of a house, though even when we are tired or reading quickly, it seems highly improbable that one could mistake the word *garage* for the word *house*. What accounts for these differences?

One very plausible hypothesis is that confusions between objects in the case of seeing in nature are rooted in genuine or real similarities between the objects in question, whereas confusions involving words are caused by similarities in the lettering which, in one sense, are perfectly arbitrary. Consequently, we may hypothesize that seeing through a photographic process obtains only where confusion over the object in the photographic or cinematic image is a function of genuine similarity relations between the

pertinent cinematic referents. Descriptions, even if mechanically generated, do not provoke visual confusion on the basis of the real similarities
between the objects they depict, but only confusion in terms of lettering,
which is arbitrary. Authentic transparent presentations, in contrast, traffic
in real or natural similarities, whereas descriptions do not.

So, x is a transparent image if and only if (1) x puts us in mechanical
contact with its object in such a way that the visible output in x is counterfactually dependent upon its visible input, and (2) x preserves genuine or real
similarity relations between the objects and events presented by it. Furthermore, cinematic images are transparent in this sense. Cinematic images are
like telescopes into the past. We see through them to the sound stages of
yesterday.

The first thing to note about this proposal is that even if we accept the
notion that photographic images are transparent, it would not follow that
all cinematic images are, since, as we have noted earlier, not all cinematic
images are based in photography. Computer-generated mattes, like those
in *Sin City*, and other comparable digital effects have figured increasingly in
recent motion pictures. Because computerization permits greater control
over the image and lower costs when it comes to mounting spectacles, we
are likely to see more and more CGI rather than less. But a great many of
these images cannot be said to be transparent. You cannot see through
many of them to the objects that gave rise to them for the simple reason
that there are no such objects. The images were fabricated entirely within a
computer. Consider the army conjured up by CGI in *The Mummy*. Likewise
much of the background rockface in *300* was built in 3D geometry,
employing Autodesk Maya. So, one objection to the transparency thesis
is that it is not a general account of every cinematic shot, but only of those
created by what we might call *straight* photographic means.

But suppose this much is conceded. The question still remains about
whether the transparency thesis helps us understand all those cinematic
shots that were produced photographically. In all probability, most of the
cinematic shots to date fall into that category. Does the transparency thesis
enhance our understanding of them?

An initial problem with the transparency thesis is that, as it has been
articulated so far, it is not clear that everything that meets the two
conditions stated above is something that we would be prepared to say
we see through to its object. The definition, that is, is not sufficient to pick
out so-called transparent pictures.

Consider a case like this one. Imagine a fully automated, enclosed,
railway yard, one that runs itself and has been insulated from the intrusion

of living creatures. Now suppose we build a point-by-point model of the railway yard that links every square inch of it to a super computer, so that every change in the surface of the railway yard registers a change in the model. If an engine switches tracks in the railway yard, then a facsimile engine switches tracks in exactly the same way in the model. As the original engine rusts, so does its counterpart in the model. And so on. The model, however, is in Argentina, while its source is in Samoa, though looking at the model provides no clue to the location of the original.

Following the preceding account of transparency, we are forced to the bizarre conclusion that the model gives us transparent perceptual access to the railway yard – that we can literally see through the model in Argentina to its source in Samoa. For the model is counterfactually dependent upon the visible properties of the original with which it is in mechanical contact. Every change we observe in the model mirrors precisely comparable changes in the railroad yard in Samoa. Moreover, where we might tend to confuse objects – like water tanks and gasoline tanks – in the original railway yard, we will also tend to confuse objects in the model, because the model preserves real similarity relations between things.

But surely this conclusion is unacceptable. Were we to rebuild the model in Samoa in such a way that it stood between us and the original and thus occluded the original in our visual field, we would not say we saw through it, but rather that it blocked our vision. You can't see through solid objects, can you?

What this example may show is that we do not yet have a full account of what it would take for something to be a transparent presentation of *x*. Therefore, until that uncertainty is resolved, and transparency is adequately defined, we cannot really determine whether we see through, in the requisite sense, photos and cinematic images to their objects.

However, the proponent of the transparency thesis might argue that even if he has not provided a complete definition of *seeing through*, he has brought our attention to a continuum of cases where it seems appropriate, each step of the way, to speak literally of seeing. Thus, he argues, the burden of proof belongs to those of us who find it hard to believe that we see through cinematic shots to their objects.

The transparency theorist starts by comparing ordinary seeing and seeing with a corrective lens. Both strike us unequivocally as seeing. But if seeing through a corrective lens warrants being called *seeing*, why stand on ceremony when it comes to telescopes, binoculars, and microscopes? Moreover, if these prostheses are so regarded, why not also treat peri-scopes and mirrors in the same fashion? And if we see through mirrors, there seems no reason not to speak in the same way about photographic and cinematic images which, in effect, function rather like celluloid mirrors. Putatively, seeing through cinematic images is merely a straightforward expansion of the notion of seeing through binoculars.

That is, starting with ordinary seeing, we seem to encounter no principled difference in kind as we make our way through an inventory of cases all the way to the cinematic image. We find ourselves sliding down the transparency theorist's slippery slope. Is there any way to break our fall? In other words, less metaphorically, can we adduce any principled differences between the items on this apparent continuum such that we can distinguish between ordinary seeing and seeing with certain prostheses, on the one hand, from our perceptual engagement with the contents of cinematic shots on the other? That is the challenge with which the transparency theorist confronts us.

Yet, despite the transparency theorist's suggestion, there is at least one difference between ordinary seeing and certain forms of seeing through prostheses, on the one hand, and the alleged seeing through photographs and cinematic images on the other. We encountered it in the preceding chapter where we noted that something counted as a moving image only if it was a detached display. Moreover, there is a striking disparity between seeing x and seeing a detached display of x. When one sees x, one can point one's body toward x, but in seeing a detached display of x, one cannot. Ordinary perception carries egocentric information about the relation of my body to the object of perception. But photos and cinematic images do not afford comparable egocentric information. Thus, the everyday case of seeing x in front of me and seeing a detached display of x should not be treated as instances of the same kind of perceptual experience. For I can orient myself physically to x in the spatial-temporal continuum I inhabit in cases of ordinary seeing, but not with cases of seeing a detached display of x. If it entered my visual field, I could find my way to that railroad yard in Samoa; but if I saw a detached display of it − like the aforesaid model in Argentina − I would have no clues about which way to turn to get to the original.

Egocentric information about my bodily relation to the objects of perception is also available in many of the cases where I employ prosthetic aids. I can point my body in the direction of the star when I use a telescope; toward the microbes when I look into the microscope; at the parking space, when I peer into the rear-view mirror in my car; at the ingénue when I adjust my opera glasses; at the aircraft carrier when I see through a periscope. And so on. In all of these cases, these prosthetic instruments can direct me to the objects they deliver to us. But I could not hope find my way to the White House by looking at a photographic postcard or a newsreel of it. For they are detached displays and, all things being equal, a detached display does not provide perceptually the sort of egocentric information about its object that I need to get from point A to point B.

If I look through a pair of binoculars at a brace of horses racing furiously, the visual array I obtain, though magnified, is still connected to my own body in such a way that I would be able to walk reliably toward the finish line if asked. When I use the binoculars, I can still point myself accurately toward the finish line. My bodily orientation with respect to the things that I perceive is preserved. But someone who does not already know where St. Petersburg is cannot point themselves reliably in the direction of the Winter Palace by watching Eisenstein's *October*.

Ex hypothesi, we do not literally see *x*, unless we can orient reliably ourselves spatially toward *x* by, for example, turning our body, if asked, in the direction of *x*. We can achieve this in the case of ordinary seeing and in many cases of prosthetically empowered perception. It is not the case that we can do this with respect to cinematic images, save in unusual conditions, as when we view a video in the self-same space the video depicts. The possession of versus the lack of egocentric information is the distinction we need to thwart the slippery slope argument introduced to us by the transparency thesis. Since a cinematic image of Fido lacks egocentric information about the relation of my body to Fido, we do not see Fido through it in the same way in which we see Fido in the flesh when he is prancing before us on the lawn.

The transparency theorist may attempt to meet this challenge with two challenges of his own. First, consider the sight of a rose situated ten miles away but delivered to us by a relay of hundreds of mirrors arranged after the fashion of a labyrinth so complex that, by peering into the mirror in front of us, it is impossible to find our way to the rose reflected in it. Ostensibly we have agreed that we see through mirrors. And yet this particular arrangement of mirrors does not enable us to point our bodies toward the rose. Therefore, the transparency theorist argues, we must agree that the preservation of egocentric information is not a necessary condition for seeing.

Furthermore, the transparency theorist invites us to consider a second case. Again we see a rose before us. But we have also been apprised that it is very likely that it is being presented to us through a maze of mirrors like that described in the previous paragraph. Thus, we may come to doubt that we do know how to find our way to the rose. However, we have been misled. The rose is actually right in front of us. We do not believe that it is in front of us; we doubt we can walk toward it. But surely we are seeing the rose, even if we do not believe we are seeing it. We are seeing it, even if we do not believe that we know how to move in its direction. This too indicates that knowing how to orient one's body toward an object is not a logical requirement for seeing the object.

What both of these examples are supposed to show is that egocentric information is not a genuine criterion for either seeing x or seeing through y to x. Thus, the transparency theorist argues, the putative lack of egocentric information cannot be invoked as the reason why we cannot be said to see through photographic and cinematographic images to the objects at which they are aimed.

However, it is not obvious that we must concede the case of the labyrinth of mirrors to the transparency theorist. If every time I try to walk toward the rose I bump my head against a mirror, it is not evident that I am really seeing the rose. Agreeing that some arrangements of mirrors enable us to see through them does not force us to say that we see through every imaginable relay of mirrors. This position, moreover, is not arbitrary, so long as we have a principled way of distinguishing between the two cases. Do we? Of course – the mirrors we see through are the ones through which we can retrieve reliable egocentric information; the ones we do not see through are the mirror arrangements through which we cannot. There is no inconsistency here. If the transparency theorist alleges that there is, he begs the question.

But what of the second example – the case where the rose that dominates our visual field is really directly in front of us but where we doubt it because we are entertaining the suspicion that a Cartesian-type deceiver has surrounded us with a baroque maze of misleading mirrors? Certainly we are seeing the rose, even though, if asked, we might say we don't *believe* we can point or otherwise orient our bodies toward it.

Nevertheless, it pays to notice that there is a difference between being able reliably to point our bodies toward the rose and *believing* that one can reliably point one's body toward the rose. The transparency theorist's example focuses on the doxastic state (the belief state) of the percipient. But even if, given the peculiar circumstances of the thought experiment, the percipient does not believe that she can reliably point her body toward the rose, she may still be able to do so. I may not think or believe that I can lift a fifty-pound barbell over my head, but I may, in spite of what I believe, be able to do so. Similarly, I may not believe that I can walk reliably toward the rose, but, if instructed to give it my best shot, in the situation as outlined by the transparency theorist, I will be able to do so reliably, because actually directly seeing the rose – the very perceptual state I am in – is one that reliably tracks egocentric information about my spatial relationship to the object of perception.

That is, we can say, along with the transparency theorist, that in his second example the percipient is *seeing* the rose, even if she is not confident about where it is located in space, just because the percipient has access to the kind of egocentric information that, if push comes to shove, will enable her behaviorally to find her way to the rose. Her doxastic state notwithstanding, she is able to do so behaviorally precisely because genuine seeing carries egocentric information. The transparency theorist's case is not a counterexample that refutes the necessity of egocentric information to authentic seeing, but rather an example that reconfirms it. For whether or not the percipient believes she can successfully point her body toward the rose, if she is genuinely seeing it, then she can so orient herself reliably toward it, since genuine perception gives her access, whether she believes it or not, to the pertinent egocentric information.

One objection to the hypothesis that genuine seeing requires the ability to reliably orient oneself spatially in the direction of the object of perception might be that this has the counterintuitive consequence that disabled persons, deprived of the capacity for locomotion cannot see, for they cannot move their bodies in any direction. Consequently, we need to adjust our claim so that we assert that genuine seeing only occurs in persons who, if they either possess or *were to possess* the relevant movement capacities, would be able to reliably orient their bodies in the direction of the relevant objects of perception. Since this criterion is behavioral rather than doxastic, it is not threatened by the transparency theorist's second example.

Genuine seeing, including genuine seeing-through, then, is a process that gives us reliable egocentric information about the relationship of our body to the objects in the space we inhabit. Cinematic shots do not afford this sort of information. Thus, we do not literally see through them. Therefore, the transparency thesis appears unacceptable.

The Code Thesis

In the era of the silent film, cinema was often analogized to language. D. W. Griffith, for example, claimed to derive certain of his techniques from the writing of Charles Dickens. The most ambitious early versions of this kind of claim were undoubtedly articulated by the Soviet montagists.

For example, one of the leading theoreticians and filmmakers of that school of cinema, V. I. Pudovkin, argued that "[Film] editing is the language of the film director. Just as in living speech, so one may say in editing: there is a word – the exposed piece of film, the image; a phrase – the combination of these pieces."

That is, according to Pudovkin, the cinematic shot should be understood as something strictly word-like. Perhaps we see a shot of the muzzle of a cannon; this is equivalent to the word "cannon." Then we are shown a close-up of a fuse being lit; this is equivalent to "_____ fires." The two shots are spliced together and we get "The cannon fires."

But even if this somewhat contrived example seems persuasive, it is hard to imagine this account being extrapolated to the operation of shots in general. For shots do not typically function as words. Characteristically, shots carry an amount of information that it would take sentences and even paragraphs to articulate in language; this is an instance of the old truism that "a picture is worth a thousand words." Indeed, moving pictures are probably most often worth even more words than still pictures. And, in any event, clearly a feature-length film, like *Russian Ark*, composed of a single shot cannot be equated with a word, even if we turned off the voice track.

Except in very special situations, such as those in which shots are being manipulated to advance cinematic similes (e.g., from Eisenstein's *October*: "Kerensky is like Napoleon"), moving picture shots are not the equivalent of words, especially if the test of being word-like is that they be summarizable by means of a single word. It was only for the sake of the example that we "translated" the igniting of the fuse above as "fires." It would be more natural to characterize such a shot with a sentence.

But, be that as it may, the content of most shots cannot be readily captured by one word. So it would appear unlikely that most shots are strictly equivalent or even analogous to words. Moreover, if it is argued that the capacity to be summed up in a word is not the true test of shots being word-like, then the burden of providing a method for ascertaining whether a shot is functioning as a word falls to Pudovkin and his followers. Unfortunately, to date, they have not met this challenge.

In addition, another problem is that words are abstract in a manner quite unlike moving picture shots, which are concrete. The word "cannon" need not call any particular cannon to mind, whereas a shot of a cannon is always of a particular cannon – the 155 mm howitzer with a flat right front tire and the initials "NC" scratched on the inside of its barrel, for example. So, shots are arrestingly different from words given their inevitable concreteness, which property, in turn, is connected to the fact that they are naturally described by many words, not one. Related to this and further supporting the disanalogy between cinematic imagery and language is that the neural bases of imagery and language are different, suggesting that we are dealing with distinct communicative systems.

Furthermore, the relation of a word to its referent is arbitrary. We use the word "dog" in order to denote canines, but it is easy to imagine that we might have introduced the word "cat," had it not been otherwise employed, to do the job. On the other hand, that a well-made shot of a dog depicts a dog is not arbitrary; a competent shot of a cat, all things being equal, cannot represent a dog cinematically. The shot of a dog represents a dog, to a large extent, because of a *nonarbitrary* perceptual relation between certain cinematic processes and certain automatic, human, visual processes – ones to be discussed at greater length anon. But for the moment, suffice it to say that a shot is not a word, nor is it particularly word-like because, among other things, its relation to its referent is not, on the face of it, word-like in terms of arbitrariness. That is, whereas the relation of a word to its referent is conventional, it is not merely a matter of convention that the shots of Lassie in the old TV series depict a dog, indeed a collie (rather than, say, an ostrich).

We have argued that a cinematic shot is not a word because, among other things, it would generally appear to carry more information than a word does. At the very least, it must usually be described by more than one word. Shots do not typically evoke single words, save in certain cases of highly controlled figuration, as one finds most famously in constructivist montages. If shots evoke linguistic responses at all, it is more plausible to predict that they would be descriptions of at least the order of sentences. But it will do no good to attempt to repair the code thesis by saying that a shot is not a word, but rather a sentence.

For cinematic shots are neither sentences nor are they sentence-like. Sentences are composed of atomic particles – words – that are minimal units. But shots cannot be decomposed into minimal units like verbs and nouns. Shots do not have discrete subjects and predicates. In a shot of the cannon firing, which part of the picture is the subject and which part is the predicate?

Shots do not contain grammatical units at all. A shot is not structurally analogous to a sentence such as "This is a tall man." Not only does it lack analogues for "this," "is," and "a," but the subject of the shot is not the result of the law-like combination of the acontextually definably meaningful units "tall" and "man." Rather the shot of a man shows all his properties at once and nondetachably, so to speak. You can't break the down the moving picture of the tall man into its component parts in the way that you can analyze the sentence into minimal units such as "tall" and "man." Moreover, if negation is a natural part of language, then film cannot be a normal specimen of language, since it would appear to lack the means to say "no" in its putative vocabulary. Showing a picture of Napoleon is scarcely the equivalent of saying that "Napoleon is not tall."

There is nothing in the shot that corresponds to words. In sentences, meaning is made by the application of certain recursive rules to the atoms of meaning – the words – that comprise the sentences. That is, sentences abide by grammar in order to be well formed. However, moving picture shots are not grammatical, or even ungrammatical. In part, this is because they are not comprised of minimal units of meaning – like words – that can then be assembled in accordance with certain rules.

But in addition there are no rules about what can be combined with what in a movie shot. Whatever can be represented pictorially is kosher; there are no ungrammatical pictures. There may be pictures of physically impossible objects and events – like Dumbo or Mighty Mouse in flight. However, these are impossible pictures, not ungrammatical ones. Even the picture of a monstrous entity – say a head with an arm sprouting from it, as one might find in a film by Brian Yunza, is only a picture of something biologically ill formed rather than a grammatically ill-formed picture. In this regard, a shot is more like a representational painting than it is like a sentence.

Sentences are meaningful in virtue of being built up, via recursive operations, from acontextually defined, meaningful, detachable units, like nouns and verbs, adjectives and adverbs. But shots lack comparably discrete building blocks. The red hair on screen is not made up of two discrete components *red* and *hair*, combined in virtue of certain semantic rules, but is just red-hair-all-at-once, so to say.

Furthermore, the arm of a woman in a film shot is not like the word "arm" in a sentence, because the word "arm" bears an arbitrary relation to its referent, whereas the arm in a film image does not bear an arbitrary relation to its referent. Nor is the perceived biological relation of the woman's arm to her torso a conventional one in the shot of a film, though the grammatical relation of the word "arm" to the word "torso" in the sentence "The woman's arm was connected to her torso" is utterly conventional, its sense governed by its grammar.

Moving picture shots also lack the panoply of other structures available to natural languages like English. Sentences come in a *variety* of moods, but how, without resort to the soundtrack or titles, does one articulate an interrogative shot? Declarative sentences can be active or passive. They have voice. But was our earlier example of the cannon firing active ("The cannon fires") or passive ("The cannon is being fired")?

Confronted by these sorts of objections, the proponent of the code thesis may be moved to abandon the strong thesis that shots are strict analogues of words or even sentences, but, nevertheless, maintain that they are somewhat language-like in the sense that the communication achieved by means of motion picture shots is dependent on conventional codes. Umberto Eco, a leading semiologist, for example, has suggested that single-shot images – of, say, the Eiffel Tower – are best understood as conventional signs. Commenting upon a shot from Fritz Lang's classic film *M*, Eco says "on the basis of some conventions the addressee [the viewer] understands that those traces upon the screen send us back to the content 'a girl holding a balloon.'"

The idea here seems to be that the relation between a shot and what it is a shot of is analogous to a dictionary-like correlation. In the process of viewing moving pictures, we acquire the vocabulary of cinema piece by piece, correlation by correlation. There is a code here, though unfortunately the associational structure of the code has never been spelt out to any degree by semiologists, nor, for that matter, have they even elaborated adequately their operating conception of a *code*.

For semiologists such as like Eco, understanding images must be learned. What must be learned are conventions that link the image in the shot – "the traces on the screen" – to its referents. Film shots are code-like insofar as they are somehow a matter of conventional associations. Comprehending a shot is allegedly a process of decoding it, though the units of the code and their combinatory principles are lamentably left rather obscure by proponents of the code thesis.

Nevertheless, the code theorist believes that a condition for comprehending what a shot stands for is putatively knowledge of a certain set of codes or conventions, perhaps involving dictionary-like correlations. Moreover, these codes and conventions are said to be culturally specific; they could have been otherwise. Thus, the semiologist alleges that they are arbitrary.

Indeed, on this view comprehending a single shot is akin to reading or, at least, deciphering or decoding. Films are decoded by audiences who have learned the conventions of cinema, including conventions for translating or deciphering a single shot. We identify the shot of the man as such in the same way that we associate or correlate the word "man" with "adult male." We employ a code that we have previously learnt.

But the suggestion that the way in which we learn a language is on a par with the way in which we become conversant with a pictorial idiom is immensely dubious. Suppose we call the ancient Egyptian "frontal eye" approach to pictorial representation a code. If it is a code, then we acquire command of it in a way that is radically different from the way in which we would achieve mastery of spoken Egyptian during the reign of King Tut. Once you encounter one or two pictures in the "frontal eye" style, you can readily recognize the kind of thing represented by any other picture in that tradition. But if we were to learn the meaning of one or two spoken words of ancient Egyptian, we would not be any wiser about the rest of the language.

This is not to say that there are no pictorial conventions in the frontal eye style. That we interpret the fact that the pharaoh is so many times larger than other folk in the picture as a measure of his relative social superiority is a learned convention. However, that we recognize the picture of the pharaoh as a picture of a man is not something we need to learn to do. If we can recognize men "in nature," so to speak, we can recognize pictures of men.

That is, once we see one or two ancient Egyptian pictures, we can then go on to identify what virtually every other Egyptian picture is a picture of – at least with respect to the general kind of thing it is a picture of. But were we to hear one or two ancient Egyptian words and learn what they mean, we would not, on the basis of that experience, be able to grasp the meaning of any other Egyptian words, not even the words that denote different natural kinds.

The way in which we acquire knowledge of a code, like a natural language, and the way in which we acquire mastery of a pictorial system differ extremely. *Ex hypothesi*, the reason is because the underlying processes are different. Arbitrary codes are associational and, therefore, must be acquired correlation by correlation over a protracted period of time, whereas pictorial practices can be grasped almost immediately – or, at least, with astounding alacrity in comparison to language learning – and, in a manner of speaking, "all in one shot." Indeed, the empirical evidence is that the underlying brain-processing systems that negotiate language and pictures *are* different.

This contention is borne out by the research of two psychologists – Julian Hochberg and Virginia Brooks. This couple raised one of their children in an environment effectively devoid of pictures of any sort, including drawings, photographs, and, of course, motion pictures. The child had no picture-books, nor did he have access to television; the labels with visual graphics on them were removed from all the household products in his vicinity. Moreover, the child was never tutored in any way about associations between words and pictures. He was never read a story from a picture-book. And yet at the age of 2 or so, when the child's vocabulary was sufficiently developed, he was exposed to a selection of line drawings and black and white photographs and he was asked to identify what they were pictures of. He succeeded in doing so in most cases. He did so at rates that were scarcely random.

In this case, there was no question of the child's learning or being instructed in codes or conventions for decoding or reading pictorial images, including moving picture shots. The child was able to recognize what the pictures were pictures of simply by looking. The code hypothesis fares badly with a case like this one, since there is virtually no process of learning detectable here.

Picture comprehension, including motion picture comprehension, appears to require no special training or instruction. It seems to come naturally. That is, one hypothesis that is superior to the code hypothesis for explaining the way in which we come to comprehend what a picture is a picture *of* is that this comprehension occurs via the activation a natural recognitional capacity – one that arises in tandem with our capacity to recognize objects but which is also triggered by things that are appreciably similar to the visual properties, such as the outline contours, of said objects.

No special training is required to understand what a picture – including a moving picture shot – pictures, so long as one is already familiar with the kind of thing being depicted by the image in question. One can identify what a typical shot of *x* is a moving picture of by looking, if one can identify *x* in "real life," even if one has never previously seen a shot of *x*. The fact that this can be done without any significant training period indicates that nothing like the acquisition of a code is involved in accessing the meaning of moving picture shots. Indeed, the communication here seems to happen in the absence of a code. Therefore, the thesis that the shot is a coded signal seems unlikely. This is not to say that the shot is not a symbol. Rather it is a symbol that communicates in large measure without reference to a code, a vocabulary, or a set of combinatory conventions.

The Recognitional Prompt Thesis

This hypothesis emerges almost unavoidably from a consideration of the shortcomings of the code hypothesis. The code hypothesis would appear to require a learning period during which the code – whether a natural language or something else – is acquired. This seems to follow from the allegation that the codes relevant to understanding shots are arbitrary. How else would one achieve access to an arbitrary code except by learning its basic elements and rules piece by piece? But *even* if some pictorial styles may require an interval of time upon first exposure in order to be grasped, that interval is infinitesimal compared to the chunk of time required to begin to master a language or similarly complex code.

Moreover, once the percipient has – quite quickly – gotten the hang of a pictorial style through one or a few of its symbols, she can pretty much effortlessly apprehend everything else represented in that style. But from one or a few words, one has hardly started to understand the language. Arbitrary codes, especially ones with large vocabularies, take a long time to learn. The velocity with which we acquire mastery of pictorial styles – such as the Japanese "floating eye" style or that of Renaissance perspective – is astounding compared to the amount of time that we expend in absorbing a complex, arbitrary code. Moving picture shots, like other pictures, are grasped virtually at a glance with little or no tutelage. They are so different from codes that there is no reason to suspect they belong to the same psychological category.

Learning a complex code, like a language, involves an extended period of training. It takes a great deal of instruction, including trial, error, and correction. But the subject in the previously cited experiment by Hochberg and Brooks manifested the capacity for pictorial understanding in "one fell swoop." A child does not assimilate the meaning of a word, let alone a series of words or any other complex code, like that. Thus, it is unlikely that anything akin to learning a code, like a language, is operative in mastering the comprehension of a moving picture shot.

Instead, a more attractive hypothesis, given the data, is that humans acquire the capacity to recognize pictures, including moving pictures, naturally, rather than conventionally, at the same time that they acquire the capacity to recognize the objects that pictures represent. Pictorial recognition, including the recognition of moving picture shots, is not a skill that needs to be taught. Pictorial comprehension is a natural recognitional capacity that comes with object recognition. When we see a picture, including a moving picture, of something with which we are already familiar, the same recognitional processes are thrown in gear as when we see that kind of thing "in the wild." Exactly what convergent features of the objects in the pictures and the corresponding objects outside of the pictures serve to trigger this response is a question for psychological inquiry. Philosophically, it is enough to say that the motion picture shot is a *natural recognitional prompt* – a stimulus that engages something bred in the bone to apprehend what it is a picture of simply by looking.

This, however, is not a reversion to the illusion thesis. The hypothesis is that the stimulus imparted by moving picture shots, taken from typical angles, activates the same recognitional capacities that the objects pictured would engage in everyday, "off-screen" life; but, at the same time, we also, by dint of the same faculties, recognize the screen as an independent object in our environment. That is, we recognize both the objects pictured and the screen. *Pace* the illusion thesis, we do not take the objects pictured in the shot to be objects in the space of our immediate physical environment. Indeed, we detect this difference phenomenologically in our own bodies, inasmuch as the muscles in our eyes register the distance between the location of the picture as the surface of an object – the screen – that inhabits the very physical space in which we are situated, and the objects in the virtual space portrayed inside the moving picture.

Nor is the recognitional prompt thesis the same as the transparency thesis. For on the former view all that is claimed is that we recognize the objects and events in the shot, not that we see through the moving picture to the objects and events that gave rise to them. It is not, in other words, that the original objects are engaging our perceptual systems through a prosthetic device, but rather that there is *something* about the picture that naturally arouses our powers of object recognition in virtue of which we are enabled to identify what the picture is a picture of. What that *something* is, we depend ultimately upon perceptual psychologists to define. But what we can say now is that moving picture shots naturally prompt our perceptual system to recognize in them the kinds of objects and events that we apprehend visually in everyday life.

Like the recognitional prompt thesis, both the illusion thesis and the transparency thesis presuppose that we mobilize, without any appreciable prior training, our ordinary recognitional capacities in order to identify what we see in moving picture shots. In that, the three theses are in agreement. But according the recognitional prompt hypothesis, we do not take what we see to be the very object we recognize either mistakenly, as the illusion thesis would have it, or veridically, as the transparency thesis maintains. Rather, a motion picture shot of a gazelle causes us to see or to recognize a gazelle in it; it naturally generates both the recognition of the screen and of the things depicted by the moving shadows reflected upon it.

The hypothesis that motion picture shots are those whose depicta are recognized naturally by untutored spectators – spectators who have not been trained in some specialized processes of reading, decoding, or inferring – simply by looking also fits nicely with the historical fact of the notably rapid, cross-cultural dissemination of the movies. Motion pictures became the dominant artform of the twentieth century and have evolved into an omnipresent channel of communication worldwide because the basic symbols in the practice – the moving picture shots – are accessible virtually automatically to everyone from urban centers in North America to rural communities in Eurasia.

Undoubtedly, these assertions fly in the face of certain anecdotes, repeated endlessly in anthropology classes, about the incomprehension with which tribal peoples greeted pictures in the Western tradition. However, the first thing to emphasize in this regard is that the systematic evidence about the responses of pictorially inexperienced, tribal peoples to pictures is overwhelmingly on the side of the hypothesis that they do, without instruction, recognize what the pictures which are presented to them depict.

Furthermore, in those cases where subjects manifested some trouble in identifying the referents of the alien pictures, it seems likely that their initial difficulties had more to do with misunderstanding what they were being asked to do, rather than with an inability to recognize the depicta of the relevant pictures. For example, when pictures were presented to the Me'en tribe of Ethiopia, they sniffed them instead of looking at them, because the pictures reminded them of a kind of cloth material with which they were already familiar. They did not look at the pictures at all. However, when their attention was directed to the task of identifying the objects being pictured, the vast majority of the respondents had no problems comprehending the pictures.

That is, their putative inability to understand the pictures had to do with their lack of familiarity with the point of picturing and not with an inability to recognize what the pictures were of, since, once the practice of picturing was explained to them, they had no problems with offering the pertinent identifications. Moreover, since they were able to do so with virtually no preparation, it is not plausible to suppose that they had – on the spot – digested some complex body of conventions.

Recognition rather than convention is the fundamental key to pictorial comprehension. To recognize something, of course, requires that what is presented to us be something or, at least, *a type of something*, with which we are already familiar. It is a matter of re-cognizing. So, pictorial recognition is a process of realizing what is depicted in a picture where it is something – or an instance of a type of thing – that is already known to us simply by looking at (rather than by reading or decoding) the picture.

Moving picture shots are, of course, typically pictures. Thus, these building blocks of movies are such that what they depict is recognized by untutored spectators simply by looking. Spectators do not comprehend the reference of single shots by means of reading, decoding, or inferring from so-called traces – as semiological proponents of the code thesis intimate. Rather, the process proceeds by engaging object-recognitional capacities that are hardwired.

The single shot is the basic unit of film communication in the sense that, without the single shot, other levers of cinematic communication, like film editing, would remain mute. Without single-shot units, there would be no editing. The single shot is typically, in a manner of speaking, the *sine qua non* of filmic communication. Or, in other words, if there were no single shots to be comprehended, there would be nothing for editing to do – nothing for it to organize. So, in this sense, the moving picture shot is the basic element of cinematic communication.

Moreover, the single shot is standardly a picture, and pictures are the sorts of symbol whose depicta are grasped by natural recognitional capacities. That these capacities are natural, of course, implies that they are comprehensible at the level of what they portray to most perceptually competent human beings, virtually automatically. Humans around the world can recognize what a picture – including a motion picture image – is a picture of, simply by looking. And this entails that motion picture shots are accessible to nearly every human being without special training in any code or convention. Needless to say, this is why motion pictures are so eminently exportable globally. This is why motion pictures are everywhere. This is part of the reason that moving pictures are so important.

A benefit of the recognitional prompt theory of the moving picture shot, then, is that it can contribute to an explanation of the widespread success of the motion picture as a means of art and communication. Whereas the code thesis leaves us with the mystery of when spectators ever learned the correlations between Eco's vaguely described traces and their meanings, there is no enigma remaining when we hypothesize that the basic communicative function of shots can be discharged without the mediation of codes or meaning conventions. Of course, the illusion thesis and the transparency thesis also have this advantage over the code thesis. But the recognitional prompt thesis does not have the other liabilities of those alternative conceptions of the motion picture shot.

On the recognitional prompt thesis, we recognize what a shot is a picture of by looking; our inbred capacity for recognizing objects swings into action. Where the image is fictional, we then go on to imagine that the kind of thing we recognize – say, a young man – is an agent, such as the protagonist, in the story. Or maybe we recognize the façade of an ante-bellum mansion in the neoclassical style of the old South and imagine, as the filmmakers mandate we do, that this is Tara. If these images are then dubbed appropriately for the pertinent non-English-speaking audiences, these fictions, all things being equal, will be immediately accessible to audiences everywhere in large part because the pictures that are communicating the story can be recognized by one and all sighted humans.

In this chapter we have reviewed four hypotheses concerning the nature of the moving picture shot – that shots are illusions, transparencies, coded symbols, or natural recognitional prompts. The illusion thesis founders in large measure because we do not behave as though we believe that the events on screen are literally before us; we do not flee, for example, from the onslaught of swarms of raptors. It may even be argued that the movement we detect on screen is objective – in the way that color is objective – rather than illusory.

The transparency thesis proposes that moving picture shots are prosthetic instruments through which we gain perceptual access to objects and events in the past. This cannot be a necessary feature of all motion picture shots, since some shots, such as CGI mattes (which are not produced by means of straight photography) need have no referent from the past to show us. The claim of the transparency thesis that we see through moving picture shots may also be challenged on the grounds that even shots produced by straight photography fail to provide the sort of egocentric information characteristic of genuine seeing and seeing-through.

The code thesis maintains that the moving picture shot is an arbitrary symbol of the sort found in a natural language. But moving picture shots lack the structure of words and/or sentences; nor do we secure our understanding of them as we do when gaining entry to a complex vocabulary of arbitrary symbols. Rather, we appear to get what motion picture shots communicate virtually immediately. This suggests that they trigger some natural recognitional capacity of which the most likely suspect is our inborn capacity for object recognition. Therefore, it seems very probable that the moving picture shot is best conceptualized as a natural recognitional prompt – a stimulus that communicates its content to spectators who apprehend it simply by looking at the moving picture.

The natural recognitional prompt hypothesis, furthermore, has the added attraction of offering an important part of the explanation of the way in which movies managed to become such a widespread and often transcultural form of art, entertainment, and communication. For the basic symbols in the practice – the moving picture shots – can be grasped at a certain level of understanding by everyone with standard-issue human perceptual equipment.

Another advantage of the review of the motion picture shot in this chapter is that often whole conceptions of cinema are based upon extrapolations from analyses of the nature of the shot. From the illusion theory of shots, some have jumped to the illusion theory of cinema – that is, to the theory that whole films are illusions. Some (though not the philosophers who developed the transparency thesis) allege that all mainstream cinema strives to the condition of transparency. And others have claimed that entire films are coded or semiotic systems. One side benefit of this chapter is that some of the premises that ground these larger extrapolations have been undermined.

On the positive side of the ledger, we also have a naturalistic account of the moving picture shot. Let us see if we can develop further theories in this vein for other aspects of motion pictures.

Suggested Reading

The illusion theory undoubtedly derives ultimately from Plato's discussion of pictorial representation in Book X of his *Republic*. That account has been so influential that it has been applied virtually without hesitation to cinema. A great many theorists simply extrapolate, with scant modification, from Plato the view that the motion picture image is an illusion and go on from there. A sophisticated version of the illusion theory, however, can be found in Richard Allen, *Projecting Illusion* (New York: Cambridge University Press, 1995).

The illusion theory is critically discussed in Gregory Currie's fine book *Image and Mind: Film, Philosophy and Cognitive Science* (New York: Cambridge University Press, 1995). Currie, among other things, defends the view that the impression of movement in motion pictures is not illusory. Currie's view, in turn, is rejected by Andrew Kania in "The Illusion of Realism in Film," *British Journal of Aesthetics* 42:3 (July 2002), 243–58.

The transparency theory is suggested, if only obscurely, in André Bazin's *What Is Cinema?*, vol. 1 (Berkeley, CA: University of California Press, 1967). A version also seems to be advanced by Stanley Cavell in *The World Viewed* (New York: Viking, 1972). Recent defenders of transparency with respect to photography include: Kendall Walton, "Transparent Pictures: On the Nature of Photographic Realism," *Critical Inquiry* 11:2 (Dec. 1984), 246–77; and Patrick Maynard, "Drawing and Shooting: Causality in Depiction," *Journal of Aesthetics and Art Criticism* 44:2 (Winter 1985/6), 115–29.

Critics of the transparency theory include: Nigel Warburton, "Seeing Through 'Seeing Through' Photographs," *Ratio* new series 1 (1988), 64–77; Gregory Currie, "Photography, Painting, and Perception," *Journal of Aesthetics and Art Criticism* 49:1 (Winter 1991), 23–9; and Noël Carroll, "Defining the Moving Image," in his *Theorizing the Moving Image* (New York: Cambridge University Press, 1996). Kendall Walton has responded to critics of the transparency theory in his "On Pictures and Photographs," in *Film Theory and Philosophy*, edited by Richard Allen and Murray Smith (Oxford: Oxford University Press, 1997). Recent important articles on the transparency thesis include Aaron Meskin and Jonathan Cohen, "On the Epistemic Value of Photographs," *Journal of Aesthetics and Art Criticism* 62:2 (Spring 2004), 197–210, and Aaron Meskin and Jonathan Cohen, "Photographs as Evidence," in *Photography and Philosophy*, edited by Scott Walden (Oxford: Blackwell Publishing, forthcoming).

Regarding the film-shot-as-linguistic theory, the quotation from V. I. Pudovkin comes from his *Film Technique and Film Acting* (London: Vision Press, 1958). Umberto Eco develops his view of the code thesis in his article, "On the Contribution of Film to Semiotics," in *Film Theory and Film Criticism*, edited by Gerald Mast and Marshall Cohen, 2nd edn. (Oxford: Oxford University Press, 1979). Eco's position is criticized by Gilbert Harmon in his article "Eco-location," in the same volume. See also Sol Worth, "Pictures Can't Say Ain't," in *Film Culture*, edited by Sari Thomas (Meteuchen, NJ: Scarecrow Press, 1982). The code/language thesis is criticized at length in Gregory Currie's superb "The Long Goodbye: The Imaginary Language of Film," *British Journal of Aesthetics* 33:3 (July 1993), 207–19.

The recognitional prompt thesis was introduced by Noël Carroll in his "Address to the Heathen," *October* 23 (Winter 1982/3), 89–163 and "The Power of Movies," *Daedalus* 114:1 (Winter 1985), 79–103. Under the rubric of natural generativity, a similar, more intricately defended view of picturing can be found in Flint Schier's *Deeper Into Pictures* (Cambridge: Cambridge University Press, 1986). In his *Image and Mind*, Gregory Currie also aligns himself with a naturalist account.

For a report of the empirical findings of Julian Hochberg and Virginia Brooks, see their "Pictorial Recognition as an Unlearned Ability?" *American Journal of Psychology* 75:4 (Dec. 1962), 624–8. On cross-cultural pictorial recognition, see Jan B. Deregowski, *Illusions, Patterns, and Pictures: A Cross-Cultural Perspective* (New York: Academic Press, 1980), and Paul Messaris, *Visual Literacy: Image, Mind and Reality* (Boulder, CO: Westview Press, 1994), esp. 60–4.

Chapter Five

Moving Images – Cinematic Sequencing and Narration

In the previous chapter, we discussed the single motion picture shot, with primary emphasis on the single shot as taken from a static camera position. However, most motion pictures are comprised of more than one shot. Typically shots are combined into sequences. They are added together in order to perform certain functions. Paradigmatically, that function has been to narrate a fiction. But there are other possible functions as well, including: to depict an environment, as in a travelogue or a nature film; to make an argument, as in the case of *Fahrenheit 9/11*; to draw a comparison or contrast; to make a comment; to arouse an emotion; and so forth. This list, of course, is not exhaustive, nor are the items on it mutually exclusive.

Cinematic sequences are typically assembled by means of film editing. Discrete shots, taken from different camera positions, are spliced together in order to discharge one or another of the preceding functions. The scene of a man becoming aware that he is surrounded, for example, might be narrated cinematically by taking a close-up of his face, registering the emotion of surprise, and then cutting back to a long shot that reveals him to be surrounded by hostile forces of whom he has just become cognizant.

However, a sequence like this one can also be built up within a single shot via camera movement – the image can go from the close-up to the long shot by moving or tracking the camera backwards, thus achieving an effect that may be functionally equivalent (in terms of the information conveyed) to cutting between two different camera positions, but while continuously recording the space traversed between the view from close up and the more distant one. This is sometimes called a sequence shot.

In editing, the space between the close-up camera position and the long view is excised. Hence, the idea of a "cut": something has been *cut* out. In camera movements, which were once called "traveling shots," the "space between" is exhibited.

Furthermore, the preceding sequence of images – from a close camera view to a far camera view – might be secured by action within the camera, as when one zooms out using a telephoto lens. Whether by editing, camera movement, or lens movement, cinematic sequencing – the coherent shifting of discernibly discrete camera views – is a fundamental feature of most motion pictures, save single-shot films made from a fixed camera position as in the case of many Lumière *actualités*.

This chapter is divided into two parts. First, we will be concerned with understanding cinematic sequencing – that is, with how changing camera positions facilitate motion picture communication. Though editing is a primary example of this, we will also consider the ways in which camera movement and the deployment of various types of camera lenses can also contribute to this effect. Then, after examining how sequences are constructed, in the second part of the chapter we will focus on some of the ways in which sequences are combined, most notably in terms of the most common form of movie narrative.

1   Cinematic Sequencing

Cinematic sequences are composed of views taken from different vantage points whether by means of editing together shots from discrete camera positions or by means of camera movements that shift our perspective on the action, or via the adjustment of camera lenses that have functionally equivalent consequences. By way of sequences, moviemakers communicate action, events, and states of affairs as well as often the attitudes and opinions they take toward the circumstances they portray. But how is communication possible through a disparate array of views?

We have already encountered a putative answer to this question. It is perhaps one of the earliest accounts, one popularized by the Soviet montage school of film theory. We heard a clarion statement of this view in the last chapter where V. I. Pudovkin declared: "[Film] editing is the language of the film director. Just as in living speech, so one may say in editing: there is a word: the exposed piece of film, the image [the shot]; a phrase – the combination of these pieces." Call this the "film language hypothesis." How plausible is it?

The film language hypothesis

Proponents of the film language hypothesis are struck by certain very broad analogies between sentences, on the one hand, and cinematic sequences, especially edited arrays, on the other hand. A sentence is putatively composed word by word, the combination of meaningful units resulting in a larger meaningful complex. Similarly, a shot chain is composed of independently sense-bearing shots which when combined yield larger meanings: the shot of the man, followed by the shot of the barrel of a rifle firing, followed by the shot of the man falling communicates the narrative that the man has been shot. Of course, the story could also be told by moving the camera from the man to the rifle and back, or by zooming, in a comparable manner, between these viewpoints. Thus, it appears that sentences and cinematic sequences communicate – that is, they make sense – by combining smaller, meaningful segments into larger ones.*

Sentences are meaningful in virtue of being built up, via recursive operations, from smaller meaningful units like nouns and verbs. This feature of sentences is called compositionality. Linguistic meaning relies upon syntax, a set of rules for composing meaningful wholes, a.k.a. sentences, out of words. A language has a finite vocabulary of arbitrary symbols that can, in principle, be organized by recursive, grammatical operations into an infinite number of sentences.

But, as we saw in the previous chapter, shots, save in extraordinary circumstances (e.g., shots of street signs), are rarely word-like. Shots may signify, but they are typically nothing like words. There is no vocabulary of cinema; no finite dictionary of motion pictures. There are as many motion pictures as there are things and combinations thereof to photograph from an indefinitely large number of camera positions.

The nose of a woman in a motion picture shot is very different from the word "nose" in a sentence, because the word "nose" bears an arbitrary relation to its referent, whereas the woman's nose in the film has a natural

---

* Though it may be easier to think of the individual shots in edited arrays as discrete units akin to words, it is far more difficult to know how we could parse different moments of a camera movement as discrete units. Perhaps this should count as a reason to abandon the film language hypothesis from the get-go, viz., it cannot handle all cinematic sequences, notably functionally equivalent ones, in the same way. Indeed, maybe it cannot handle some of them at all, specifically camera movements.

relation to its referent. Moreover, the picture of the woman's nose is not decomposable into smaller units as the phrase "the woman's nose" is decomposable into "the," "woman's," "nose." They are all of a piece, so to speak; they are not atomic particles of a larger, recursively assembled meaning-compound, as is a sentence. So a meaningful shot is not constructed or composed in the manner of a meaningful sentence. The shot is not a minimal unit of meaning in the same way that a word is, and, furthermore, for the same reason, neither are strings of shots built up after the fashion of sentences. There are no comparable minimal units of meaning in motion pictures, so cinematic sequences are not of a piece with sentences.

Shots, whether one by one or in combinations, are not appropriately equated with words. Consequently, film lacks the kind of discrete building blocks that make linguistic communication possible. Even if cinema had the kind of recursive rules that languages possess, motion pictures standardly would have nothing for them to operate upon, lacking as they do anything that functions like words. Motion pictures, *pace* Pudovkin, have no proper semantics – no discrete, arbitrary, recombinable, minimal meaningful units – for a syntax to organize. There is no vocabulary of film. So, there is no compositionality.

But not only is there no semantics of cinema; there is no grammar either. Pudovkin seems to think that film is a combinatory system exactly akin to a language. Shots are supposedly assembled by editing in the way words are organized into sentences. This suggests that he thinks film, or at least film editing, possesses something like a grammar, i.e., recursively applicable rules for ascertaining what is and is not well formed. But cinema possesses no such rules. So, in addition to being without anything like a requisitely structured vocabulary, motion pictures, as we know them, are also without syntax.

Film instructors, teaching courses with titles like "The Language of Sight and Sound," or "The Grammar of Cinema," may go on and on about rules – such as "Don't cross the one hundred and eighty degree line" (because it will flip the direction of movement on screen) or "Don't edit together shots from virtually the same but somewhat discernibly different camera positions" (because such a cut, called "a jump cut," will cause the appearance of an abrupt tremor in the image). But, in truth, these are rules of thumb, not grammatical rules. The test of whether a stretch of cinematic sequencing is successful is whether or not it works – whether or not it communicates, whether or not an audience can follow it, whether or not it achieves the effect the image maker intends. For every alleged "grammatical" rule of filmmaking, one can come up with cinematically distinguished counterexamples.

John Ford, for instance, violated the one hundred and eighty degree rule in *Stagecoach* and yet the scene in which this occurs is perfectly intelligible to spectators. No one has ever complained that it was ill formed. They understand that the stagecoach is moving in the same direction after the cut; they do not think it makes a hairpin volte-face. Audiences are able to do this, moreover, because this understanding best coheres with their conception of the rest of the narrative.

Crossing the one hundred and eighty degree line is sometimes used, as David Bordwell points out, to give a movie a realistic, rough-edged look, as in the case of *Homicide: Life on the Street*, or it may be used to arouse a feeling of tumult in audiences, as in the case of *8 Mile*. In *Half Nelson,* the camera crosses the one hundred and eighty degree line when the character Drey is riding her bicycle in order to highlight the dramatic tension and transition she is undergoing. In a film about how opposites bring about change, there is a related scene later in the film where Drey is riding her bike in one screen direction and her teacher is driving in the opposite direction. Though not strictly a matter of crossing the one hundred and eighty degree line, the editing here shows how opposing screen directions can be used to mark thematic points, a potential exploited in the earlier scene just mentioned in which the one hundred and eighty degree line is literally crossed.

Similarly, Jean-Luc Godard employs jump cuts in a number of films, including *Breathless*, where they function as a sort of expressive punctuation, signaling the improvisatory temper of the film and its film-maker. Viewers do not interpret these edits as rents in the fabric of the universe, but as signs of authorial exuberance. The jump cuts are perfectly intelligible to viewers, who understand them as the fingerprints of the auteur. Nor is the jump cut merely the gesture of a single moment of motion picture making. The use of jump cuts for expressive purposes appears in contemporary movies such as Ridley Scott's *Matchstick Man*.

In language, we can distinguish between a string of symbols being intelligible and its being well formed (or grammatical). We can say that we understand a young child's ungrammatical utterances and that we can interpret garbled telephone conversations with missing parts, even if neither consists of complete sentences. For there is a distinction between intelligibility and grammaticality in language. But with motion pictures, intelligibility is the whole story.

Moreover, insofar as cinema is an artform, motion picture makers need not regard any rule as inviolable. In principle, any of the so-called rules of thumb of cinema can be forsaken, so long as the edited array is successful – intelligible to the relevant spectators. Cinematic sequencing, though it possesses certain tried-and-true *strategies*, lacks a specific syntax, and, therefore, there is no grammar of film in the strict sense of the term, despite the fact that you might pick up a book entitled *The Grammar of Film* in a used book store.

Just as we speak of the *art* of poetry rather than the *grammar* of poetry, so we should think of cinematic sequencing more in terms of art rather than syntax. We do not chide a poetic effect if it departs from grammar, so long as it is effective. Think of the work of e. e. cummings. Similarly, when it comes to the art of cinematic sequencing, everything is a matter of artistic effect, since there are no genuine grammatical rules in this vicinity to speak of.

When confronted with an edited array in a movie – say a shot of one man walking, cut against the shot of another man walking – we infer the significance of the shot chain on the basis of what makes sense given the context (which is generally narrative). If we know, given the rest of the story, that the two characters are in different countries, we infer that they are both taking their walks at approximately the same time of day. But, if we know that they are due for a showdown on the streets of Dodge City, then we infer that they are probably in the same locale, heading toward each other. The shot chains may look exactly alike, but we will infer different meanings depending on the best way of making it cohere with whatever else we know about the rest of the fiction.

But, it must be stressed that we have no rules to which to resort in cases like this. Rather, we depend upon holistically interpreting the array of shots in context; we do not *read* the cinematic sequence. The notion of "reading a film" is at best a metaphor, and a misleading one at that. We process the flow of information delivered to us by cinematic sequencing through an iterated series of hypotheses to the best explanation where our abiding concern is the search for coherence. This involves something quite different than the exercise of rudimentary reading skills. Thus, inasmuch as a certain sort of inference, rather than anything resembling basic reading, underwrites cinematic sequencing, and especially editing, cinematic sequencing does not appear to be linguistic. So, once again, as we concluded in the previous chapter, the film language hypothesis is best rejected.

The attention management hypothesis

But if cinematic sequencing does not communicate after the manner of a language, how does it do so? An alternative hypothesis is that it does this by what might be called attention management. Motion picture makers communicate to spectators by controlling their attention. Through cinematic sequencing, the moviemakers select what the viewer sees as well as the order in which she sees it along with the duration of what she sees and its scale. The moving picture maker articulates her own intentions to the audience by guiding our attention. We attend to what the filmmaker displays, from the angle the moviemaker elects, at a screen size proportionate to her choosing, for as long a time – or as short a time – as she deems appropriate. Then we fit these details together with the story (or the argument, etc.) that we have been prompted to construct so far from what we have been shown.

The motion picture maker determines the object, the acuity, and cadence of our attention as well as its precise place in the relevant succession of images. The moviemaker both holds our attention and shapes it by controlling the objects of our perception in addition to the order, pace, and scale at which we peruse them. The constant shifting of camera views draws our attention to the screen insofar as our perceptual system is keyed to change and movement. And once our attention is riveted to the array, the alternative, successive framings of the situation guide us through it in accordance with a highly deliberate pathway.

The motion picture maker communicates with us by means of the aforesaid factors – such as the scale and duration of the camera view – whose modulation not only tells us what it is important to see, but does so in an ordered succession that alerts us contextually to the significance of the relevant items in the emerging configuration, whether the configuration be that of a narrative or an argument or something else. That is, a very fundamental level of cinematic communication involves the motion picture maker articulating her intentions by directing and molding our attention in terms of cinematic sequencing – showing us this rather than that in a certain order, and at a certain velocity and scale.

Needless to say, manipulating just these variables is not the whole story of cinematic communication. There are many other important contributing factors – including, as already noted, the audience's sense of the overarching direction of the motion picture, whether in terms of a story, an argument, or some poetic vision. Undoubtedly, we use our emerging sense of the whole, generally abetted by language (dialogue, voice-over, subtitles, and/or intertitles), to contextualize the array of details that the shifting camera viewpoints in the cinematic sequencing bring to our attention. However, for the narrative or argument to emerge in the course of a motion picture, the audience must typically be shown images in an appropriate order, cadence, and scale, namely ones that are pertinent to the communication that the motion picture maker intends to deliver. Moreover, in general, what the image track brings to the viewer's attention should ideally reinforce or be otherwise coordinate with the dialogue and/or voice-over, unless what is intended is ironic, comic, or a gesture of avant-garde subversion.

The construction of the cinematic sequence – the flow of disparate images (or shifting camera views) – is executed by the movie editor, if it is a matter of cutting, or by the cinematographer, if it is a matter of camera movement or lens movement. Such construction is typically done in conjunction with the motion picture director. Working in concert, the motion picture production team fixes the cinematic sequence, determining what will be shown, in what order, at what pace, and at what screen scale. Where successful, these cinematic sequences strike us as intelligible com-munications not because – as the film language hypothesis would have it – we have learnt some sort of grammar which we use to render them coherent. Rather, to a substantial degree, the cinematic sequencing engages features of our cognitive and perceptual make-up that were already in place before our first exposure to moving pictures and mobilizes them to make sense of the array.

For example, in order to underline the importance of an element in the storyworld – say a gun in a mystery in which it figures as a valuable clue – the filmmaker moves in for a close-up. In this way, we know to look at the gun; indeed, we have no real perceptual alternative. And we know that the gun is important, not as the result of some language-like code, but because (1) it is the only thing to see and (2) its scale has been magnified to the point that it occupies the whole screen; it has been writ large, so to speak. Nor is the emphatic scale of the gun as a signal of its narrative weight an arbitrary association. It is rooted in perception where there is a natural correlation between bigness and importance that can be observed cross-culturally at rates of occurrence that are far from random.

That is, our disposition to look at the gun in the close-up is not something we need to learn. It happens automatically. First, it is the only thing visible. Moreover, that making something large is a signal of importance – a way of visually announcing "Look here now" – is no more of an arbitrary communicative strategy than is raising one's voice for emphasis. We use both techniques in communicating with infants. That these techniques work strongly suggests that humans are innately susceptible to their influence – that we do not acquire them as we do linguistic codes. Indeed, the application of techniques like this would appear prior to the acquisition of any particular language just because they are among the strategies that facilitate language acquisition.

The preceding close shot signals that the gun is important. But why? Perhaps the next shot pulls back to show us a detective and his partner leaning over the gun at a crime scene. This second shot reframes the situation in order to lead us to consider the relevance of the discovery of the gun to the investigation. Reframing the elements of the situation in this way – in this case, by placing the gun in a larger gestalt or narrative configuration – strongly inclines the spectator to ponder and then probably to infer the role of the gun in the larger narrative context. The shifting camera position achieves this by directing one's attention from the gun back to the ongoing investigation. Next, when the detective notes something special about the gun – perhaps the initials on its handle – the camera cuts or otherwise moves in to a closer view in order to fill our attention with this telltale clue.

In this example, the cinematic sequence moves from close shot to broad shot and then back to a closer view, perhaps one taken at a slightly different angle than the first one. By constantly reframing the scene, the filmmakers assure, by exploiting our natural perceptual tendencies, that we will be attending just where we need to be attending in order to follow what is going on – in order to be apprised of the detail or details that we require in order to be prepared to make the inferences necessary to move us forward as the story moves forward. Or at least this is what transpires in the standard case, as opposed to intentionally disjunctive cases, such as *Le Chien Andalou*. That is, typically the filmmaker selects various details and shows them from various angles and distances, choosing camera positions in such a way that the audience member is attending precisely to what she needs to consider so as to keep track of what is happening in the story or the argument. We can call this process variable framing.

Variable framing

Cinematic sequences are built through variable framing which exploits our natural perceptual dispositions in order to guide our attention to where the motion picture maker wants it to be – usually to whatever is important to the unfolding of the action or argument. That is, it is through variable framing that the moviemaker manages the audience's attention.

So far examples of variable framing involve shifting from close shots to broader shots. However, variable framing also occurs when the camera changes its position on the action without changing its distance from it appreciably. For example, in the celebrated mortar sequence in Buster Keaton's *The General*, there is a medium shot of the cannon lowering its muzzle, taken from in front of the artillery piece, and then there is a shot at roughly the same distance from behind the gun, underscoring the importance of this state of affairs in the narrative – namely, that the mortar is aimed dead-on at our hero.

Variable framing is a matter of changing camera positioning in order for the motion picture maker to ensure that the audience is attending to the action exactly in the way the moviemaker intends. This is a lever of control over the audience's attention that has virtually no parallel in theater. In the theater, the audience, for the most part, needs to guide its own attention as to where to look. This is why theatergoing requires the acquisition of certain skills, including disciplined attention, that are virtually unnecessary when encountering the typical movie. In theater, one must finally find one's own way through the spectacle. One must make one's own perceptual pathway through all the finery and the stage flats and the extras milling about, not only to fix on the heroine, but also not to be distracted by everything else there is to see. It takes a deliberate effort, especially for those unaccustomed to theater. In motion pictures, even for neophytes, this generally happens virtually automatically due, in large part, to variable framing.

How does variable framing work?

Variable framing is fundamentally a matter of changing the position of the camera on the action. Typically, changing the position of the camera provides the filmmaker with three distinct levers for directing or influencing the audience's vector of attention. These three levers – the variables of variable framing – can be labeled: indexing, bracketing, scaling.

As we have seen, editing, camera movement, and "lens movement" are the best-known mechanical bases for variable framing (though methods which look just like these can be contrived via animation, whether manual or digital). These techniques, in turn, provide the motion picture team with three formal instruments for influencing or directing the audience's attention. These formal variables, as already noted, can be called *indexing*, *bracketing*, and *scaling* respectively.

Indexing occurs automatically when the camera is brought closer to its subject, whether by means of a camera movement, a cut, or a zoom. It functions like the gesture of pointing. One might think of it as a form of cinematic ostension. When the camera moves, that indicates that the spectator should be looking in the direction the camera is headed, if the camera's movement is being recorded, or in the direction toward which the camera is aimed, if the shot has been presented by means of a cut.

In *Casablanca*, there is a scene where Elsa visits Rick in order to plead with him to sell her a set of exit visas. The relevant shot begins with Rick opening the door to his office screen right, and then the camera pans screen left to show us Elsa by the window. As the camera travels from left to right, our eyes follow it irresistibly. Its movement points us in the direction we should be looking. Indexing is not an arbitrary, language-like convention for where we should look. It is keyed to the way in which our perceptual system works. It is a technique that manages or guides our attention automatically, even naturally.

In addition to indexing, the filmmaker also directs our attention by bracketing what we see. That is, as the camera is moved toward an object, a character or an event, it effectively screens out everything beyond the perimeter of the frame. By moving a camera toward an object, either by means of editing or camera movement, the filmmaker indicates that what is important at this moment is what is on the screen. The frame acts as a bracket. Everything outside the frame has been bracketed from attention.

On the one hand, bracketing is exclusionary. What does not fall inside the cinematic bracket, in effect, should not concern the audience's attention. But bracketing is also inclusive. The bracket indicates that what is important for the audience to consider is what falls inside the bracket – that which is visible within the cinematic frame. Furthermore, that we look inside the bracket, rather than outside it, is hardly an arbitrary, language-like convention. It does not need to be learned. For we have no alternative but to abide by the placement of the bracket. Bracketing is not an unmotivated element in an artificial code. Rather, the technique is tailored by its very nature to compel viewers, endowed with standard-issue perceptual equipment, to attend to just what the director intends, as signaled by variables like bracketing.

In terms of cinematic sequencing, most editing and camera movement function by employing the exclusionary and the inclusive dimensions of bracketing simultaneously – both to eliminate distracting detail and to focalize attention on the center of the bracketed area. Thus, bracketing both filters out irrelevancies and spotlights what is significant.

However, in some cases (indeed, in enough cases that this option should be regarded as a standard deviation), a motion picture maker may deliberately place the bracket in such a way that what may be most significant for the narrative is left offscreen, perhaps in an adjacent space. This is often done for emotional effect. Thus, the approach of the murderer is frequently hinted at onscreen, but the killer is "hidden" outside the bracket, as is the case in early scenes in Fritz Lang's classic *M*. We hear the child-killer, but we don't see him. This raises a certain *frisson* in the spectator and keeps us riveted to the screen in the expectation that sooner or later we will get to see the murderer — that what is offscreen will come onscreen.

Moving the camera forward not only indexes and brackets certain details rather than others. It also changes the scale of what the audience is looking at. In Hitchcock's *Notorious*, there is a famous crane shot that begins on a second-floor landing and edges over behind a chandelier before it swoops down toward the character of Alicia Huberman, finally landing on her hand, where she has secreted the cellar key that she plans to give to the American agent, Devlin. As the camera moves in on Alicia, it not only points to her and removes surrounding, distracting detail from the most significant element of the shot, but it also makes the key larger. That is, the key literally occupies more screen space at the end of the shot than at earlier moments. As it becomes visible, it "grows" in scale, taking up more screen space and more retinal space to boot. Moreover, the increase in scale alerts the audience not only to the presence but also to the importance of the key in the scene.

Although someone might be tempted to say that it is a convention that visual largeness should come to mark importance, it is difficult to agree that this is purely arbitrary. Would it be equally effective psychologically to make what is important in a scene small? But then how could a director be assured that the audience would take note of it? By means of scaling, the director fills the audience's awareness with whatever she deems appropriate. Likewise, scaling enables the director to make what is less significant to the narrative smaller and, therefore, a less likely object of audience attention. This is not merely a matter of marking an item as less important. It is a way of making it less probable that the audience will be looking at it or that they may be able to see it. Scaling may be a "conventional" device in that it is frequently used in film; but it is not conventional in the sense of the arbitrariness that we speak of with relation to language, since, given the human perceptual make-up, it is not arbitrary that we attend to the objects that dominate our visual field nor that we are less likely to attend to objects that are not prominent.

Scaling, bracketing, and indexing are three different ways at the director's disposal to make objects and events, characters, and actions salient to the audience. To a large extent, through these means, the director manages or guides the audience's attention from moment to moment to where it is most appropriately fixated, given the purposes of the ongoing narrative or argument.

Moreover, these devices help the filmmaker modulate the audience's attention over time. First the audience is shown a medium long shot of a scene and then the camera moves in, and, by means of indexing, scaling, and bracketing, certain details are selected out for special attention. Or, the sequence may start with a closer shot and then the shot is changed to a broader view, encouraging the audience to think of the detail presented in the close shot in terms of its relevance to the larger gestalt encompassed by the altered bracket – for example, first we see a close-up of the simmering fuse on the end of a stick of dynamite, indexed, bracketed, and made large-scale, and then we see the larger context – the targeted bridge exploding – in the broader shot that follows.

Constant reframing permits the director to control not only what we see, but when we see it in terms of the sequence of views that is most advantageous for our (usually inferential) processing of the story or the argument that she is developing. Variable framing, that is, is the primary means by which a director directs. And what does a director direct? The audience's attention.

Typically, scaling, bracketing, and indexing come into play whenever the camera is moved. However, they need not always occur coincidentally. One may change the bracket without changing scaling – for example, when a camera follows a character but maintains her screen dimensions. Or one may index a scene by moving the camera forward slightly without appreciably altering the scale or the bracket of the shot. Or one may emphasize the changing bracket in a shot, as in the famous trolley-car ride in *Sunrise*, without indexing anything in particular, or introducing notable scale changes. Nevertheless, scaling, bracketing, and indexing are generally employed in concert and, when so employed, they afford a very powerful means through which the motion picture maker controls the audience's attention, delivering to them with great clarity what they should be thinking about with respect to the larger evolving direction – whether narrative or otherwise – of the motion picture.

In the typical motion picture, these means are placed in the service of the ongoing narrative. Bracketing, scaling, and indexing are generally deployed in such a way that the *first* item or configuration of items in the shot of which the audience is induced to take note is that which is most pertinent to following the story as it is emerging. These devices make certain narrative details – characters, objects, actions and parts thereof – salient; they make us cognizant of what is (ideally) maximally significant for us to attend to in the story at the moment the shot appears. And then we are presented with new narrative information in the next shot, which has also been structured in terms of the principle that the *first* item or group of items that grabs our attention again be the one that is most relevant to tracking the progress of the narrative. Furthermore, as a consequence of this coordination of narrative purposes with visual structure, most typical movies are not only easy to follow; they seem perspicuous through and through.

Of course, for various reasons, a motion picture maker may deviate from the principle that the first item the audience is prompted to see be the one that is the most significant for the narrative. Frequently, a film-maker, perhaps for expressive effect or emotional impact, may lead the audience's eye so that the most significant narrative detail is not evident immediately, but only after a second look. For example, we might see a jittery character first, and, only after first taking him in, are we prompted to notice that in the background there is a man with a knife standing ominously behind him. This kind of standard deviation itself, however, owes much of its forcefulness to the fact that the basic approach to visual narration in motion pictures is to show us the most diegetically significant item in a shot first – that is, to coordinate all the visual strategies available to the director, including bracketing, scaling, and indexing, in such a way that the most important narrative item is the first thing upon which our attention battens. Nor is this principle a grammatical rule, since the art of storytelling is often enhanced by initially diverting the audience's attention.

Furthermore, if the film is not a narrative, but, for example, an argumentative nonfiction film, the same principles of cinematic sequencing generally apply. Even avant-garde films may employ these principles, though it can often be difficult to divine the overarching point of directing our attention to this or that item in motion pictures of this sort. And, of course, some avant-garde films may subvert these principles for the very purpose of drawing our attention to them. Indeed, such exercises may accrue a large portion of their fascination by baring the devices, such as variable framing, that make mainstream motion pictures so accessible to viewers with little or no prior exposure to them.

If we compare the stage drama to the ordinary movie drama, we might say metaphorically, that, in terms of attention, the narrative in the motion picture has been visually predigested for us. In theater, we must ultimately locate and select the objects of our attention; we have to find the objects that are most relevant to the ongoing narrative. But with movies, a great deal more of that work is done for us by the variable framing than is done for us in the staging of the typical play, housed, as it usually is, under the proscenium arch with its rigidly fixed dimensions. Think of how much more difficult it was to take in the first plays you saw in comparison with the first movies you encountered.

With motion pictures, the right standpoint on the action is delivered automatically to the viewer most of the time, especially in those movies made for mass distribution. That is why, as suggested previously, motion picture viewing involves less effort than most theater viewing. It is also why movies may strike viewers with little experience of live theater as more readily intelligible than staged dramas, inasmuch as each cinematic moment is such that it shows in bold relief what is necessary to see in order to grasp the emerging story.

Of course, variable framing does not operate without substantial input from the spectator. Not only must the spectator follow the perceptual trajectory that is mapped out by the variable framing, but she must also assimilate what she sees, in combination with what she knows about the evolving story, in order to make inferences about what is going on. In Fritz Lang's *You Only Live Once*, there is a scene about which the spectator infers that heroine is on the verge of suicide. This is never stated outright. Rather, the viewer has to put together the details – that the variable framing selects out and makes salient – with what is happening in the storyworld. As the clock tells us that the time of her husband's execution is at hand, we ask ourselves why we are being so emphatically shown the wife filling a glass with water and then adding an unidentified white powder to it. Suicide, we surmise. Variable framing leads the viewer by highlighting the ingredients we need to take into account in order to infer what is going on; but generally it remains up to the viewer herself to assemble these cues by making the desired or proponed inferences.

Here we see that although the variable framing makes certain inferences likely – indeed, often virtually unavoidable – it still usually depends upon the viewer to arrive at the hypothesis that completes the thought the filmmaker intends to convey. Furthermore, what is interesting about the way in which the viewer puts this information together is that it does not, for the most part, rely on special cinematic and/or language-like codes and conventions, but instead upon the same sort of inferential and interpretational processes – including abduction, inference to the best explanation, and practical reasoning – that we employ to negotiate situations in everyday life.

Think about what goes on in your mind when you chance upon a crime scene in the course of your daily affairs. First, you begin to notice that there are a number of cops milling about; then you observe other details – police barriers, photographers, and the like. Gradually you colligate these facts under the concept of a crime scene. But isn't it the case that a comparable mode of thinking is thrown into gear when Lang presents the wife's near-suicide to us in *You Only Live Once?*

In order to process a film narrative, our default assumption is that we should fill it in with the kinds of beliefs and inferential strategies that we employ in everyday life. Of course, this is only a default assumption. It may need to be waived under certain conditions. Specific genres, for example, mandate frequent departures from the reality principle in order to make sense of them – for instance, with respect to vampire films, we are meant to assume that something that looks very like a man, such as Count Dracula, is nevertheless impervious to bullets. Or a particular film may stipulate that something that is physically impossible is a fact of life in its storyworld – perhaps that one can travel through a black hole and come out the other side intact and alive.

In other cases, the cultural or historical origins of the motion picture may dispose us to modify our assumptions about the storyworld in order to understand what a motion picture maker, whose beliefs diverge from our own, intends to convey. However, we usually begin computing the narrative of a motion picture by deploying our own working cognitive stock, unless alerted to do otherwise or unless our presumptions are evidently culturally or historically inapposite. Undoubtedly we do this because it is our default assumption in any of our dealings with our conspecifics. And though we often do need to adjust our interpretive assumptions to exceptional circumstances like those just canvassed, it is surprising the extent to which the default assumption is almost as reliable with respect to many, many aspects in movies as it is in life.

That much of the reasoning that we mobilize while following most motion pictures is continuous with ordinary, everyday reasoning – within the context of an ongoing narrative – helps explain how it is possible for films to travel so easily internationally: for *The Last Samurai* to be a hit in Tokyo and for *Fists of Fury* to flourish among audiences from Harlem. For, it is not necessary to learn a special code to follow film narratives. To a large degree, motion pictures can be understood by means of ordinary reasoning and the recruitment of our standing concepts and beliefs, including folk-psychological beliefs about the recurrent scenarios of human motivation and action.

With respect to mass-market movies, the variable framing of cinematic sequencing serves up limpidly the details the audience needs to input into its standing cognitive and emotive routines which we then weave into a coherent fit with what we already know has occurred in the motion picture and perhaps with what we anticipate about the future of the story-world. The variable framing operates automatically as a way of directing our attention to what is pertinent, and then those details are assimilated to what we already know and expect of the narrative primarily by means of engaging cognitive and emotive structures that are already in place.

Cinematic sequencing is a process of attention management that employs variable framing to keep the audience focused upon what it needs to know and when it needs to know it in order to follow the emerging point or points of the motion picture. Where the motion picture is a narrative, the cinematic sequencing feeds the spectator the inputs she needs in order to perform the continuing battery of inferences requisite for tracking the story. On the attention management account, cinematic sequencing relies upon activating innate perceptual responses by means of variable framing, which framing, in turn, governs the flow of attention naturally rather than by way of language-like conventions.

Furthermore, this hypothesis fits remarkably well with our hypothesis in the last chapter regarding the status of the single cinematic image as a natural recognitional prompt instead of as something akin to a linguistic symbol. Earlier we argued that one of the primary advantages of movies as a mass artform derives from the fact that their basic symbol – the cinematic image – is accessible to every cognitively and perceptually competent human being; if, in a close encounter of the third kind, you can recognize at least the type of object that the cinematography portrays, then you will be able, all things being equal, to apprehend what the cinematic image is about. This is an important source of the power of movies. That is, movies are accessible because in large measure they recruit our natural capacities.

But this is true not only of the way in which the cinematic image engages perception; it is also true of how cinematic sequencing, by means of variable framing, shapes our attention. Via variable framing, the cinematic sequencing has us attending precisely, though automatically, to the elements in the motion picture array that the moviemaker intends us to be processing at exactly the moment she ordains. This happens automatically because of the way in which the variable framing naturally orchestrates our attention. Moreover, the fact that the standard usages of variable framing tap into our natural perceptual dispositions accounts for the way in which most people follow the average motion picture with great ease and accuracy. Both with respect to the cinematic image and cinematic sequencing, mass-market motion pictures, on film and TV, are, to an appreciable extent, popular and almost universal in their appeal because they mesh so well with certain human capabilities rather than being dependent primarily upon communication on the basis of completely arbitrary conventions or codes.

2 Cinematic Narration

Cinematic scenes and sequences are parts of larger totalities. These scenes and sequences fit into these larger constellations in terms of the functions they perform for the given motion picture work as a whole. The sequences, that is, are subordinate to the purposes of the overarching work and, therefore, the principles that connect the scenes and sequences therein are likewise dependent upon the superordinate aims of the overall motion picture.

Furthermore, motion pictures, as noted earlier, can have a diversity of agendas. A great many tell stories; some make arguments. Others, such as *Man With a Movie Camera* by Dziga Vertov, are involved in extended explorations of comparisons and contrasts. Still others, such as Cocteau's *Blood of a Poet*, portray the inner life of dreams and visions or seek to shock, as in the case of *L'Age d'or*, the surrealist masterpiece by Buñuel and Dali. With different organizing concerns come different structures for connecting scenes and sequences. What motivates scene linkages in *Anticipation of the Night* is different than what makes the scenes and sequences of *Sorry Wrong Number* hang together.

Needless to say, an introductory book like this one is not the place to pursue all the various structures, relative to the disparate programs, that can be deployed to organize the diverse kinds of motion pictures as internally coherent entities. However, it may be fruitful to look at one kind of structure for coordinating sequences, and the variable framing that organizes them, within certain of the larger structures that render entire motion pictures coherent. The specific larger structure that I have in mind is that which determines the shape of the vast majority of popular, mass-market motion pictures – what many affectionately call movies (whether they appear on screen or on television).

Erotetic narration

This basic structure of movie narration is an instance of what can be called erotetic narration. It will be profitable to examine it at some length for two reasons: first, in order to illustrate how the principles that govern variable framing cohere or segue with the principles that hierarchically control the narrative enterprise at large at the level of the entire individual motion picture work; and second, because the issue of the nature of basic movie narration is of philosophical interest in and of itself.

How does the typical movie tell its story? First, in contrast, for example, to a soap opera, the typical movie tells its story in one uninterrupted sitting. It begins and then comes to an end, usually within two to four or so hours after it begins. On the other hand, it is the fervent wish of the makers of soap operas that their sagas continue on and on. If movies follow Aristotle's advice with respect to having beginnings, middles, and ends, soap operas have, as the critic Dennis Porter nicely remarks, "indefinitely expandable middles."

Moreover, the difference here is not simply that the movie stops somewhere whereas the soap opera, ideally, plows on perpetually. The end of a motion picture narrative has an aura of consummation about it; it yields a quite definite impression of completeness. In contrast, the soap opera is, by its nature, incomplete. Even if *General Hospital* were about to go off the air, it is probably by now practically impossible for a soap opera like this to tie up all of its loose ends – that is, to resolve all of its exfoliating plot lines. But ideally we expect a movie to "wrap everything up." "That's a wrap," the director shouts. In short, a movie is not supposed merely to come to a halt; a movie is meant to have what theorists call closure.

Closure

The notion of closure is connected to the sense of finality with which a piece of music, a poem, a story, or a typical movie concludes. It is the impression that exactly the point where the work does end is just the *right* point. To have gone beyond that point would have been an error. It would have been to have gone too far. But to have stopped before that point would also have been a mistake. It would have been too abrupt. Closure is a matter of concluding rather than simply stopping or ceasing or running out of steam or crashing. When a filmmaker effectuates closure, then we feel that there is nothing remaining for her to do. There is nothing left to recount. Closure involves a feeling of completeness with respect to the motion picture. When the last image flickers off the screen, there is no more of the story to tell, nor has anything that needed to be told been left unsaid. Or that, at least, is what ideally the viewer feels and is intended to feel.

But what accounts for closure? As already observed, we often say with respect to a successful movie narrative that "everything has been wrapped up." But what is meant by saying that a movie has "wrapped things up"? A tantalizing suggestion can be found in David Hume's essay "Of Tragedy," where he points out: "Had you any intention to move a person extremely by the narration of any event, the best method of increasing its effect would be artfully to delay informing him of it, and first to excite his curiosity and impatience before you let him into the secret." For example, when early on the narrator of Martin Amis's novel *House of Meetings* makes a point of saying that he has a letter in his pocket that he hasn't opened for twenty-two years, the reader automatically wants to know why and also what is in the letter, and she is willing to stay with the story until she finds out. Call this Hume's principle. And although Hume is offering this advice to playwrights, it has also become the creed of screenwriters.

On Hume's view, an immensely effective way of holding on to the attention of a viewer involves presenting the audience with a chain of events about whose outcome her curiosity has been perked – about which she wants to know what happens next – but then hold off informing her. For example, arouse in an audience the desire to know whether the secret agent will escape the dungeon and destroy the paralyzing nerve-gas machine, or whether the evil genius will victoriously carry out his plans to enslave the world – and then withhold the answer to that question until the last reel of the film.

One can test the reliability of this technique – as well as the hypothesis that curiosity is the glue that keeps the audience stuck to the screen – by shutting the projector down just before the final reel unravels. The audience will jump to its collective feet and demand to know whether and how the secret agent saved the world. For those are the questions that had been organizing their viewing activity.

What Hume calls a "secret" we may more prosaically refer to as a question or a set of questions to which the audience expects answers. And using this suggestion, we can propose an account of how closure is secured, or, more colloquially, how the filmmaker "wraps things up." To wit: the filmmaker wraps the story up when she has answered all the questions that have stoked the audience's curiosity. Those questions, needless to say, do not come from nowhere. They have been planted by the filmmaker in a way that ideally grabs hold of the attention of the intended audience. These questions won't relax their grip on us as the story moves forward. Closure transpires when all the questions that have been saliently posed by the narrative get answered. It is the point at which the audience can presume that everyone lived happily ever after and leave it at that.

The film *Totosi* revolves around the question of whether the infant who has been accidentally kidnapped by Totosi will be returned to his parents. When we learn the answer to that question, the film is over. We do not ask whether the child got into Harvard, since that is not a question the film encouraged us to ask. The impression of completeness that arrives with closure derives from our sense that all our pressing questions have been answered.

Moreover, this account of closure gives us an important clue to the basics of the way in which plots in movies are constructed. They are constructed by generating questions about the storyworld of the movie which the movie then goes on to answer. At one level, the plot is a network of events and states of affairs held together by the cement of causation. Yet, at another level – namely, the level of rhetorical address – a typical movie narrative is a network of questions and answers, where the questions are self-generated but then finally resolved.

In order to pith the narrative structure of a typical movie, it is useful to begin at the end. Ascertain what questions are being answered at the conclusion of the film, and then work your way backwards to the scenes and sequences where those questions were introduced, partially answered, or otherwise sustained, refined, transformed, mutated, and so forth. What results is the skeleton of the plot with the animating questions functioning rather like the joints.

Some scenes and sequences set out the conditions necessary for certain questions to take hold. These scenes themselves, including most of introductory or establishing scenes in a movie, generally involve answering the standing questions that we have when presented with a description or depiction of any set of circumstances: where the action is set, and when, who these people are and how they are related, what they want, who they are for and against, why they behave thus and such, and so forth.

Some scenes evoke questions; others answer said questions directly. Still other scenes or sequences *sustain* earlier questions: the failure to apprehend the escaped prisoner leaves us still asking whether he will be caught in a subsequent scene. Sometimes our questions are incompletely answered: we learn that the culprit limps, but we still do not know who he is.

One question may be answered in a way that introduces a new question or set of questions. The question of whether or not King Kong can be stopped is answered when he is gassed on Skull Island, but this raises the question of what will happen once he is shipped to New York. Likewise, after the shower scene in *Psycho*, the question of whether Marion can put her life back together is replaced by the questions of whether her murder will be discovered and her murderer apprehended.

Not all the questions and answers that belong in the unifying network of a movie are of the same order. Some questions orchestrate our attention to the emerging story from virtually one end to the other; others organize large parts of the tale, but not the tale in its entirety, and others are of a still smaller gauge. Questions that structure an entire text, or, at least most of it, we can call presiding macro-questions. Two of the presiding macro-questions of *Moby-Dick* are "Will Ahab and his crew ever find the white whale?" and "If they do, will they be able to destroy it?"

When the *Pequod* encounters other ships that have knowledge of the whereabouts of the white whale, those scenes contribute to keeping us bound to the story; they sustain the presiding macro-questions. When we finally are shown the deadly confrontation and see that all of the crew, save one, of the *Pequod* have perished, the story is over, closured. We do not ask whether Ishmael will open a dry goods store in Gloucester, since the film (and the novel) have not encouraged us to ask anything about Ishmael that is not germane to the hunt for the white whale.

Of course, movie narratives are driven from moment to moment by more than just presiding macro-questions. In the pursuit of some over-arching goal, the protagonist may confront a local obstacle – for example, in order to save Christendom from the machinations of Satan, the heroine may have to retrieve a vial of holy water, perched precariously on a ledge in a cavern and protected by gargoyles. Will she be able to reach the perch on which the holy water rests or not? The solution to this problem is connected to the protagonist's larger project as a means to an end. Questions of this scale, which govern the structure of one or two sequences, we may call micro-questions. They are questions whose answer will eventually contribute to answering a presiding macro-question, but which do not, on their own, answer the presiding macro-question directly and completely.

Between the presiding macro-questions and the micro-questions there may be questions that organize large portions of the movie but which do not organize the plot as a whole. Because of their scale we can call them macro-questions, but not *presiding* macro-questions. In *Psycho*, the question of whether Marion will be caught organizes a number of scenes, but it is not ultimately one of the presiding macro-questions of the film.

Clearly, there is a hierarchical relation between the questions posed by an ongoing movie narrative. Micro-questions are generally subordinate to the presiding macro-questions, and closure obtains when all of the presiding macro-questions and all or most of the micro-questions that are relevant to settling the macro-questions have been answered. Moreover, since it is the function of scenes and sequences to keep the audience bound to this circuit of questions and answers, the variable framing in each sequence will generally operate in the typical movie in such a way that the element or elements that first arrest our attention in successive shots are those that are most pertinent to raising, sustaining, refining, transforming, or answering the questions that are driving the scene.

The problems/solutions model

An alternative to the question/answer model for conceptualizing the erotetic narrative invokes the vocabulary of *problems* and *solutions*. Closure, in this way of speaking, occurs when the protagonists have solved all the problems with which the movie has burdened them – for example, when the cowboy in white has gunned down the villain and all his henchmen and, just in the nick of time, swept the heroine off the railroad tracks, thereby saving her from being crushed by the oncoming locomotive. Obviously, the problem/solution model applies to a very large number of cases. Yet, the question/answer model is arguably superior for several reasons.

First, the question/answer framework will apply to every case where the problem/solution model works, since we can always ask: Will the protagonist solve her problems or not? However, there are also cases where the question/answer model fits, but where the problem/solution model seems strained. Does it really make sense to regard the question of whether two people will fall in love a problem? Certainly their falling in love could involve problems – obstacles, like parents and rivals, to be overcome, and so on. But it need not. Though all problems may be translated into questions, it is not evident that all questions can be translated into problems.* Thus, the question/answer model seems more comprehensive than the problem/solution model.

---

* In *Volver*, the neighbor wants to know whether or not her mother is dead. It seems more natural to describe her request for information as a question rather than a problem. Moreover, it becomes a question whose answer we discover is material to securing closure in *Volver*.

Furthermore, is the problem/solution model suited to deal with cases where the problem goes unsolved — where, for example, the aliens do inherit the Earth as in the 1978 remake of *Invasion of the Body Snatchers*? That is, once again, the question/answer model appears more comprehensive than the problem/solution model, and, for that reason, is to be preferred.

Flashbacks and flashforwards

It is a fact about storytelling that the time of the telling need not correspond to the time of the tale. This is as true of movies as it is of any other kind of narrative. Though the story is shown in a linear fashion in real time with the opening credits preceding the end credits, the events that comprise the story need not be ordered consecutively in that way. There can be flashbacks and flashforwards.

The temporal order in which events are disclosed in a movie can diverge from the order in which they occurred in the storyworld. For example, in *Sunset Blvd.* we learn that Joe Gillis has been murdered before we learn who killed him and why. Nevertheless, the temporal ordering of the telling of the tale is generally not divorced from the erotetic structure of the movie. For flashbacks and flashforwards typically play a role in raising, sustaining, or answering questions. The flashback in *Sunset Blvd.* explains how Gillis died. Likewise the flashbacks at the end of *The Illusionist*, intercut with the inspector's realization that he, along with everyone else, has been tricked, answer our questions about how Eisenheim's scam was executed.

Flashforwards also typically fit into the erotetic structure of narration. The burning motorcycle in *Easy Rider* prompts us to ask who has died and how, just as the flashforward in *Don't Look Now* raises the question of whose funeral we are seeing. And these retrospectively directed questions keep us glued to their respective narratives.

How can movies ask questions?

It may seem strange to claim that movie narratives proceed by posing questions. After all, if it makes any sense to attribute grammatical mood to motion picture footage (and it probably doesn't), most motion picture footage, without any further, stipulated conventions, would have to be classified, if at all, as declarative or indicative. Movie footage, minus dialogue or intertitles, does not ask questions or issue commands. So does it make sense to say that movies ask questions?

On behalf of the question/answer model, the first thing to notice is that questions can and quite frequently do arise from declarative sentences. When we are told that the mayor has just eluded abduction, it is normal to ask who attempted to kidnap him and why. Likewise, when we receive information through media other than language, questions frequently ensue. When we see a photograph of our parents standing next to people we don't recognize, we ask who they are.

Question formation on the basis of received information is a *natural thought process*. It plays a role in every kind of inquiry. With respect to erotetic movie narration, we use the questions evoked by the narrative to organize and to keep track of the representations of events and states of affairs that the story presents to us. A young farmer's wife is raped by marauders. He returns home and finds her dead. We ask ourselves what he will do. He takes a fancy pair of revolvers from their hiding place and straps them on. We surmise that he is bent on revenge. And this then arouses the question of whether he will succeed, fail, or possibly relent – questions that structure our viewing of what is to come.

The evocation of such questions is a matter of a natural thought process. Though we are speaking of questions here, we are not reverting to a version of the film language model. As we have already argued strenuously, there is no grammar of film. In ordinary life when we see our front door ajar, we naturally ask who opened it. Similarly, in a movie, when we are shown that the lock on the door of the heroine's house has been forced, we want to know who opened it and for what reason. It is not that the movie has a syntactical structure isomorphic to the inter-rogative in language. It is the narrative that raises the question – not some celluloid sentence. For, narrative events and states of affairs in fictional movies can provoke questions, just as events and states of affairs in everyday life can do so.

In order to understand how the events and states of affairs represented by the scenes and sequences of narrative movies can evoke questions in viewers, it pays to remember that many of these events and states of affairs stand in various causal relations to one another, albeit causal relations of different strengths. Some of the earlier events in the storyworld are only necessary causal conditions to the later developments; so rather than being fully deterministic of future plot developments, they instead open a range of possible outcomes. For example, once the bridge is mined, it either will or will not explode as the enemy crosses it; but we do not know which state will obtain. Thus, we quite naturally come to wonder what will happen.

The very insufficiency of many of the causal connections in most movie narratives incites our curiosity about what will happen. For, though unpredictable, an outcome is presumed to be in the offing. And, it is natural to ask, if only tacitly, what it shall be.

It is primarily the causal inputs, broadly construed, in erotetic narratives that raise the presiding macro-questions and the pressing micro-questions whose answers secure closure in typical movies. A character forms an intention, has a desire, a need, a purpose, a goal, or a plan; or she has a commitment or an ideal, or makes a promise. These motivational states comprise part of the causal conditions of her action. They also generate questions about whether her intentions, desires, motives, purposes, goals and/or plans will be realized. Can she live up to her commitments, ideals, and promises? Certain obstacles, challenges, or problems erupt. These too structure the causal context of her action. Can she meet them or will they defeat her?

A robbery motivates a chase; a kidnap, a rescue attempt; an injury, a desire for revenge. Will the thieves be caught, the abductee recovered, and the insult repaired? Someone finds himself in a desperate financial situation – his bicycle has been stolen and he cannot afford a new one. But he needs a new one in order to find work to support his family. What will he do?

Characters form beliefs about the situations in which they find them-selves. They interpret their circumstances. Othello, egged on by Iago, comes to believe that Desdemona has been unfaithful. Recognizing Othello's belief, we ask: "What will he do?" "Will he kill her?"

So far, these examples have exploited the mental states of fictional characters as the relevant causal inputs that frequently generate the kinds of questions whose answers will eventually bring on closure. However, there is no reason to restrict the pertinent causal inputs to subjective states. In the film *March of the Penguins*, the rapidly falling temperature abets the presiding macro-question of whether the eponymous penguins and their progeny will survive.

Of course, not only causal inputs may raise macro-questions, but also effects. Presented forcefully with certain effects, like the crop circles in *Signs*, we will expect answers about their origins. Thus, in addition to causal inputs, presiding or large-scale macro-questions can be launched by puzzling events. This, of course, is the way of classical detective films; no sooner is the murder discovered than we ask: Whodunit? In short, any question that arises from the causal nexus of the story can function as an ingredient in the erotetic structure of the movie. For example, *Citizen*

Kane begins with the question of what "rosebud" portends, while *Mildred Peirce* starts off with the question of who killed the title character's husband.

Moreover, it is the role of the variable framing from shot to shot to make salient the element or elements in the sequence that animate the network of questions and answers that compel our attention. For example, the close-up toward the end of *The Illusionist* that indexes, scales, and brackets Eisenheim taking the gems from the blade of the Archduke's sword answers our question about the way in which the heir-apparent has been framed. In turn, the sequence in which this scene is embedded functions to answer the lingering question the spectator has about the earlier scene in which Eisenheim and one of his confederates were hatching a plot. Whatever came of that plot? That is what the flashback involving the inspector in the railroad station discloses.

Of course, not all motion pictures are narrated in this manner. Not even all movies are full-fledged, erotetic narratives. For, though they raise questions, the weekly installments of the movie serials of yesteryear and the daily episodes of the soap operas of today studiously refrain from answering all of their presiding macro-questions in order to guarantee that viewers will return for the next round of plotting.

In contrast to American horror movies, which try to tie up all the loose ends (if only with forays into fantastic physics), recent Asian horror flicks – like *Ringu* by Hideo Nakata and *Ju-on* by Takashi Shimizu – leave the supernatural forces not only at large but also scarcely explained – the refusal to answer the viewers' questions thereby engendering a kind of metaphysical unease about the mystery of things that is far more chilling and far less reassuring than Stateside ghost films where the wraiths get sent back to hell in the course of our learning how they came to be here in the first place.

Or, on a higher plane, one might eschew closure for the purpose of scoring a more elevated thematic point, as Kurosawa does in *Rashomon*, where, by not divulging what happened from the vantage of an omniscient narrator, the director encourages the viewer to entertain perspectivism as the best interpretation of the film and, perhaps, of interpersonal relations in general as well. Some films, such as *L'Avventura* by Michelangelo Antonioni, may not answer the questions they put in motion in order to suggest that not all our questions have answers – that existential meaninglessness is a genuine possibility.

Similarly *Nashville* by Robert Altman defies closure – its ending coming from nowhere – in order to suggest the utter unintelligibility of America in the 1970s. That is, narrative incompleteness = chaos.

The scenes in *Satyricon* are not connected by a nexus of questions and answers, but that, of course, is a leading factor in provoking the alien quality that Fellini sought when he created what he called this "science fiction" film of the past. Likewise, Orson Welles's *The Trial* abruptly shifts scenes in order to inflict a sense of arbitrariness on the viewer which is intended to parallel the plight of the protagonist trapped in an incomprehensible legal system.

The question/answer structure, moreover, may not only be loosened for expressive effect. It may also be slackened for the sake of realism. Often realist films, like Fellini's *Amarcord,* are narrated episodically; scenes are not linked erotetically but by principles of rough temporal contiguity and often geographical propinquity. This type of narration often has as its aim the desire to impart a holistic impression of a specific milieu by itemizing or layering details of life in a certain culture or subculture at a given time.

Furthermore, modernist films, such as *Last Year at Marienbad* and *India Song,* literally defy the erotetic model. For they are all questions with no answers. In some cases, it is the very point of avant-garde films like these to lay bare reflexively the structures that make the normal narrative motion picture experience what it is. These moving pictures are examples of meta-cinema; they are films about films. *Last Year at Marienbad,* for instance, provokes a range of questions – such as whether certain of the characters were at Marienbad during the preceding season – but refuses to answer them in order to reveal to the apperceptive viewer the degree to which motion picture narration proceeds by engaging our expectations (a.k.a. questions). That is, by frustrating our expectations in these matters, the plot arouses in the viewer the recognition that we are accustomed to having all of our pressing questions about the storyworld answered before the lights go up in the auditorium. By subverting those expectations, we are brought to an awareness of the way in which these expectations enable us to follow and organize the motion picture as it unfolds.

So again: not all moving pictures, nor even every movie, employ erotetic narration. But a great many do. In fact, I would hazard to guess that by far the vast majority of feature-length, theatrically released motion pictures (not to mention TV dramas and comedies) deploy this form of narration. Indeed, it is probably one of the major calling cards of popular cinema – one of the central factors that make mass-market movies so attractive for so many. For, when erotetic narration is wedded to variable framing in such a way that, in a given shot, the first item or group of items that grabs the viewer's eyes is whatever is relevant to supporting the pertinent question/answer network, the resulting visual narrative has a level of intelligibility and uncluttered clarity rarely rivaled in daily life. Neurologists have begun to establish the brain's preference for clarity. In this regard, movies are appetizing brain food.

The storyworld gives the impression of being significant through and through. From a narrative point of view, everything that is brought to our attention is explained. The fiction has a completeness and comprehensibility that far exceeds ordinary experience. Thus, the wish for the meaningfulness that so often escapes us in life can be recuperated at the movies due to the coordination of the variable framing within sequences with the erotetic narration across sequences.

Moreover, the notion of erotetic narration not only gives us insight into the power of movies to hold mass audiences in their grip. It also may suggest important clues to the operation of other sorts of plot structures.

Recall our previous examination of some of the effects that can be incurred when motion pictures forgo erotetic narration. In some cases, the result involved disposing the audience to embark upon interpretations – thematic interpretations in the case of *Rashomon*; reflexive ones with respect to *Last Year at Marienbad*. It was also noted that loosening the erotetic structure of a motion picture narrative could also result in either expressive or realistic effects.

In these cases, the erotetic structure seems to capture something like one of our default expectations when it comes to narratives of all kinds – that they are underwritten by the promise of answers to our questions, even if those answers are generally unpredictable ones. But when that default expectation is not realized by the story, we are inclined to search for other sources of motivation for the instance at hand, including interpretive, expressive, and realistic significance.

That is, where we have grounds to suspect that the erotetic irregularity in the movie is not a mistake, but is intentional, we treat it as a heuristic invitation or prompt to search for some other-than-narrative significance. In short, the failure to secure erotetic closure is what in certain cases can make other-than-narrative dimensions of signification possible. That is, the erotetic narrative is the plot structure upon which many seemingly more sophisticated narrative structures play their variations and build.

Suggested Reading

Titles claiming that cinema is a kind of language are readily cited. For example, consider Raymond Spottiswode, *A Grammar of the Film: Basic Film Techniques* (London, 1935). And, as indicated in earlier chapters, one source for the idea of a language of film editing is V. I. Pudovkin's *Film Acting and Film Technique* (London: Vision Press, 1958). In order to be fair to Pudovkin, however, it should be acknowledged that he did not work out this proposal in genuine technical detail. His was more of the nature of a programmatic suggestion. Indeed, the same may be said of most of the theorists who have floated this idea, including many semioticians.

Nevertheless, Brian Henderson does appear strictly committed to such a project in his *Critique of Film Theory* (New York: Dutton, 1980). Henderson's approach is criticized by George Wilson in "Morals for Method," in *Philosophy of Film and Motion Pictures*, edited by Noël Carroll and Jinhee Choi (Oxford: Blackwell Publishing, 2006).

John M. Carroll, employing the Chomskyan framework of transformational grammar, has attempted to work out the editing-as-language notion technically. See Carroll, *Towards a Structural Psychology of Cinema* (The Hague: Mouton Publishers, 1980). A speech-act approach to pictures in general (including motion pictures) is suggested in Soren Kjorup, "George Inness and the Battle of Hastings, or Doing Things with Pictures," *The Monist* 58 (Apr. 1974), 216–35, and id., "Pictorial Speech Acts," *Erkenntis* 12:1 (Jan. 1978), 55–71. As the publication dates of the last three items indicate, the cinema-as-language view is not as influential today as it was in the latter part of the twentieth century.

Philosophical criticism of the approach include Gilbert Harman, "Semiotics of the Cinema: Metz and Wollen," *Quarterly Review of Film and Video Studies* 2:1 (1977), 15–24. As mentioned in a previous chapter, Gregory Currie has challenged the cinema/language couplet in his "The Long Goodbye: The Imaginary Language of Film," *British Journal of Aesthetics* 33:3 (July 1993), 207–19.

The approach to cinematic sequencing as a matter of attention management is developed in Noël Carroll, "Film, Attention, Communication: a Naturalistic Approach," in *Engaging the Moving Image* (New Haven: Yale University Press, 2003).

The quotation from David Hume with respect to narrating comes from his "Of Tragedy," in *David Hume: Selected Essays* (Oxford: Oxford University Press, 1993). An impressive overview of narrative structures in the cinema is David Bordwell, *Narration in the Fiction Film* (Madison: University of Wisconsin Press, 1985). A "sequel" to that book – which brings the discussion up to date with an examination of contemporary narrative practices in the commercial cinema – is David Bordwell, *The Way Hollywood Tells It: Story and Style in Modern Movies* (Berkeley, CA: University of California Press, 2006). The notion of erotetic narration is defended at greater length in Noël Carroll, "Narrative Closure," *Philosophical Studies* (forthcoming).

A current topic of very lively philosophical exchange regarding cinematic narration – which is not discussed in this chapter – is whether or not all motion pictures have fictional narrators. The view that all fictions, including motion picture fictions, have fictional narrators is advanced by Seymour Chatman in *Coming to Terms* (Ithaca, NY: Cornell University Press, 1990), and by Kendall Walton in *Mimesis as Make-Believe* (Cambridge, MA: Harvard University Press, 1990). This claim is rejected by David Bordwell in *Narration in the Fiction Film* and by Gregory Currie in his *Image and Mind*.

The debate is deftly summarized by George Wilson in his "*Le Grand Imagier* Steps Out: The Primitive Basis of Film Narration," *Philosophical Topics* 25:1 (Spring 1997), 295–318. Wilson, himself, comes out in favor of the thesis that all fiction motion pictures have fictional narrators. This position is challenged in: Berys Gaut, "The Movies: Cinematic Narration," in *The Blackwell Guide to Aesthetics*, edited by Peter Kivy (Oxford: Blackwell Publishing, 2004); Andrew Kania, "Against the Ubiquity of Fictional Narrators," *Journal of Aesthetics and Art Criticism* 63:1 (Winter 2005), 47–54; and Noël Carroll, "Film Narrative/Narration: Introduction," in *The Philosophy of Film and Motion Pictures*, ed. Carroll and Choi.

Though this particular debate is not canvassed in this book, it is well worth a look. One very exciting place to go in order to continue your exploration of the philosophy of motion pictures, then, might be to start by checking out the references in the preceding two paragraphs.

Chapter Six

Affect and the Moving Image

There is an undeniable relationship between moving images and our affective life – that is, our life of feeling. Many mass-market motion picture genres derive their very labels from the types of affects or feelings they are designed to provoke – suspense, horror, mystery, weepies (a.k.a. tear-jerkers), and thrills (thrillers). In addition to being motion pictures, movies also generally aspire to being e-motion pictures; they not only yield the impression of movement, they also move us.

Indeed, one of the primary reasons that the kind of moving fictions we affectionately call movies are so popular is undoubtedly their potential to arouse us affectively. After a day of numbing routine, we crave some excitement – a jolt of suspense perhaps, or horror, or fear, or a good cry, or maybe some robust laughter. Movie fictions facilitate experiencing these affective conditions imaginatively, that is, without having to pay the price that these states usually exact – as tears of sadness typically require some genuine loss.

Rather, fictional motion pictures give the system a hearty workout – our affects are enlivened – though we are not the worse for it, as we would be if we had to confront the sort of perils that typically engender horror or suspense. Even if there can be motion pictures that do not massage the emotions – such as surveillance footage of empty parking lots – energizing our affective system is so central to the enterprise of the movies that no philosophical account of the moving image would be complete without discussing it.

Of course, motion pictures may not only be valued for the affective calisthenics they promote. Some motion pictures may be esteemed for engendering feelings in us for peoples and causes that heretofore left us unmoved – such as the plight of exploited factory workers in so-called developing countries.* Furthermore, certain motion pictures can even afford us self-knowledge, by awakening feelings in us we never knew we had and enabling us to examine them apperceptively. But whether for the sake of bracing affective stimulation or for the purpose of expanding our emotional reach – either socially or introspectively – the link between the moving image and our affective life is one of its major draws.

However, it is not the case that moving pictures engage our affective reactions in some simple, unitary fashion; motion pictures engender feeling-responses in us in a number of different ways. This is not only because movies possess several different channels of affective address, but also because our repertoire of affective responses is itself variegated. That is, the motion picture can elicit a range of affects not only because it has a battery of diverse triggers at its disposal, but also because there is a multiplicity of affects available for stimulation. These affects include reflexes, phobias, affect programs, cognitive emotions, and moods. "Affect" is our name for this entire domain; others might prefer to call it the "emotions," but for reasons that will emerge in what follows, I reserve that label for only certain species within this genus.

It is the purpose of this chapter to explore, to varying degrees, a diversity of phenomena in the realm of affect in relation to various structures of the moving image. Because there are a number of different affects and a number of different structures at issue, I will attempt to impose some order here by dividing the chapter into two parts. These parts correspond to a crude and ultimately artificial distinction between two levels of motion picture address.

Part 1 pertains to the affective reactions of audiences to the depictive array at large, while part 2 zooms in more specifically upon the range of audience responses to fictional characters, notably to protagonists and antagonists. Or, to put the division more perspicuously, part 2 is about our affective relationships to fictional characters, and part 1 canvasses the broader category of that plus everything else. Part 2 is not opposed to part 1, but rather is more focused on one of the perhaps most important levers movies have upon audience affect.

---

* And, perhaps needless to say, other motion pictures can be particularly dangerous for stoking morally inappropriate hatreds between people.

1   Audience and Affect

The gamut of affect

By "affect," I am referring to felt bodily states – states that involve feelings or sensations. The compass of affect is broad, comprising, among other things, hard-wired reflex reactions, like the startle response, sensations (including pleasure, pain, and sexual arousal), phobias, desires, various occurrent, feeling-toned mental states – such as fear, anger, and jealousy – and moods. Through various strategies and devices, motion pictures possess the capacity to kindle and even to inflame a number of these states. In this section, we will begin to examine a selection of these capacities in relation to the kinds of affective experiences that they are suited to enlist.

Through the manipulation of sound and image, the creators of moving images can induce changes in our bodies. The plummeting camera in *This Is Cinerama* caused roller-coaster chills in the stomachs of audiences, while some of the abrupt cuts in *Bullitt* made our bellies flip. Moreover, moving-image arrays have the power to activate the involuntary and automatic reflexes of audiences at a subcognitive, or cognitively impenetrable, level of response. For example, loud noises – either recorded effects or musical sounds – can elicit instinctual reactions from spectators.

A sudden explosion – even if expected – is apt to make the viewer flinch. The response is cognitively impenetrable in the sense that, despite the fact that you *know* that you are not in danger, your body will respond otherwise and prepare you affectively for flight or some other self-protective behavior. Adrenaline will rush into our veins as we are primed for action. Further- more, this "high" can be enjoyable – can be savored – if there really is no real danger in the vicinity.

This kind of response is called the "startle response." It is an innate feature of the human organism. All things being equal, the adrenaline rush elicited by a fiction is pleasurable – as it is in the case of fireworks (as opposed to battlefield bombardments). This is why so many movies, come seasonal vacation periods, are tantamount to fireworks displays; they literally excite spectators by triggering inborn perceptual/hormonal mechanisms for the purpose of throwing audiences into heightened affective states. So many genres are devoted to this enterprise – from disaster films to war films (whether on earth, or in outer space, or in some fantasy realm, like Narnia, or in the distant future, like *The Time Machine* or *Planet of the Apes*).

These reflex states, of course, are not only tripped by loud noises. Sudden movements toward the camera or of the camera or rapid movements laterally across the screen can put the body on high alert. The maw of the giant shark surges forward and we start backwards. The movie screen is a rich phenomenal field in terms of variables like size, altitude, and speed, which have the capability to draw forth intense, feeling-tuned, automatic responses from the bodies of viewers, as do the variations in the loudness and cadence on the soundtrack.

This is why so many movies are "action-packed." The relentless movement in *movies* provokes a level of inner commotion that is experienced positively. In this way, the movie can keep the audience percolating with affect from the pre-title scene to the end credits. And that is the aspiration of the many summer action spectacles which subscribe, according to some French critics, to the "Boom-Boom" theory of filmmaking.

In addition to reflexes, the standard-issue human organism comes equipped with certain broadly shared phobias. Fear of insects and snakes, for example. Moviemakers exploit these in all sorts of ways; the number of films named after their presiding bug is legion, from *Killer Bees* to *The Spider* (a.k.a. *Earth Versus the Spider*). Ditto snakes – as in the case of *Anaconda*. Sometimes our phobias are titillated by making these creatures enormous – for example, *The Black Scorpion* – but also by marshalling swarming masses of them together as in the case of the army ants in Byron Haskin's *The Naked Jungle*. Or one can have them both larger than life *and* swarming, as Peter Jackson does in the scene in the pit in his remake of *King Kong*

Horror fictions, of course, specialize in phobic creatures. Our instinctual aversion to dead and decaying things is exploited by monsters from A to Z (for zombies). In these examples, we relish the shudder they invite, since we are in no danger of being eaten alive or infected. Again, the heightened affect comes cost-free. But horror fictions are not the only movies that traffic in tantalizing phobic reactions. An instinctual fear of heights plays a role in many action genres; that is probably why so many films feature mountain climbing, airline disasters, roof-top chases, and so on.

Alfred Hitchcock was identified by François Truffaut as a director who overtly strives to tickle phobic responses. In *North by Northwest* he is said to have experimented with agoraphobia (fear of open spaces) in the crop-dusting sequence, while *Vertigo* is, of course, named after a phobia, one which the film attempts to simulate cinematically. The recent film *Snakes on a Plane* exploits several phobias at once by releasing venomous vipers in the cabin of an airplane in flight – thereby racking up fear of reptiles, heights, claustrophobia, and fear of flying in one shot.

Perhaps, little needs to be said about the ways in which motion pictures can arouse sexual feelings; we will leave that research to the reader.

Emotions

The affective responses reviewed so far are somewhat rigid. They are *dedicated* – they issue a fixed response to a very specific kind of stimulus. This is not to discount their importance to either self-preservation or moviegoing. They were evolved to protect us in environments fraught with danger. However, where there is no danger, as is typically the case in most movie theaters, inciting them, as already indicated, can be a source of great pleasure.

However, in addition to these somewhat primitive responses, the body has affective resources that are more discerning – smarter, if you will – in their activation. Whereas the startle response warns the organism on the occasion of a loud noise, these affective systems – which we will call the emotions proper – can detect danger not only in a resounding explosion, but also in a whispered threat or in one's spouse's overly attentive laughter to the attractive stranger.

These resources size up the situations and things that give rise to them and elect differential reactions to the aforesaid stimuli on the basis of antecedent computations, whether immediately prior or after some interval. That is, these computations may occur on contact at the initial level of perception or they may be processed cognitively in the forecourts of the mind, either tacitly or consciously. They may engage the frontal cortex of the brain or they may bypass it and may be relayed directly to our behavioral-response centers. It is the function of these affect systems to evaluate the circumstances before us in terms of certain recurring existential-human themes – like loss – and to prepare us to react appropriately.

For example, if the stimulus is appraised to be harmful, the organism is primed to fight or flee. This response, of course, is what we call fear. Likewise, if the situation that confronts us is one in which we perceive a wrong done to ourselves, or to those we hold near and dear to ourselves, or to our interests, then we are prepared to "get even." This, needless to say, is anger. Other affective responses in this neighborhood include sorrow, pity, indignation, reverence, awe, hatred, love, shame, embarrassment, guilt, humiliation, comic amusement, loyalty, and so forth. This is the realm of the *emotions*.

Emotion is the realm of affect in which differential computational appraisals of stimuli relative to certain interests give rise to visceral feelings which typically prime behavioral tendencies to act. Or, to put the matter graphically, the perception of danger (an appraisal of the large, hulking thing in my vicinity) leads to a chill down my spine (a visceral feeling) which makes me freeze in place (an evasive behavior). Altogether these add up to an instance of the emotional state of fear. Since, as we have seen, there are other sorts of affects, like the startle reflex, which are more primitive structurally, we will reserve the label the "emotions" for only those affects that have the preceding, complex structure that integrates differential computations with feelings.

The emotions are a good thing to possess from an evolutionary stand-point. Compared to processes of conscious, rational deliberation, the emotions are very fast, "down and dirty," decision-making routines. They scope out situations quickly and ready the organism to react, sometimes within the blink of an eye. This is no small advantage in a tight spot. Of course, the emotions are sometimes mistaken. What I may at first size up as a large, potentially dangerous creature standing in the shade may in fact turn out to be nothing but a curiously shaped bush. However, way back when in the environmental circumstances on the African veldt where the emotions first developed, it was better to be safe than sorry.

The emotions were evolved by natural selection in the first instance to respond to percipient's conception of the situation. That is, if the percipient *believed* that the large shape in the shadows was a dangerous creature, then the organism was thrown into a state of fear, even if the stimulus was really only a bush.

Yet if this is how the emotions are supposed to work, it seems to raise a question immediately about how our emotions can – for better or worse – be aroused by fictions, including motion picture fictions. For, with respect to such fictions, the audience clearly knows that the aliens in *War of the Worlds* are made up and that these monsters pose no threat to either the viewers or to anyone they care about. The saga has been concocted from whole cloth. So how is it possible for audiences exercising their natural, selectively given emotional powers to feel fear upon exposure to Steven Spielberg's completely fabricated spectacle? For if they know the film is a fiction, they patently cannot believe that Earth is being invaded from outer space. And the audience must know it's a fiction, since that's what they paid for; no one pays to be shot at by space monsters.

Earlier we hypothesized that experiencing an emotion like fear – where one did not have to pay the usual entrance fee of risking potential danger – could be pleasurable. However, that brings up a prior question, namely: how is it even possible to fear that which one knows does not exist? We calm the upset child by telling him, "There are no such things as ghosts."

So how can we be seized with fear when we know there are no such things as alien invaders?

Indeed, the problem extends to other emotions beyond fear. How can you feel sad about someone's loss of a loved one in a movie melodrama, when you know that there was never a loved one to be lost? And, of course, if you are sitting in a movie theater watching a well-known actress emote, you do know – and therefore believe – that it is "just a story." And yet we cry. Doesn't this defy reason?

Some philosophers have found this phenomenon quite puzzling and have even conjectured that, if movie audiences are emotionally moved by fictions, they must be, at least temporarily, irrational (or, in other words, insane for the duration of the fiction). This conundrum is sometimes called "the paradox of fiction" – the mystery of how one can be emotionally moved (for example, frightened) by something you know does not exist. And yet, on the basis of our understanding of the ways in which the emotions work naturally, it does not appear that we actually are compelled to agree that fearing fictions is in any way paradoxical or self-contradictory, nor must we be forced to such a desperate conclusion as the conjecture that movie viewers must be momentarily deranged.

One consideration against the temporary insanity charge is that, as we have already observed, many emotion-like, affective states – such as reflexes and phobias – can be elicited sans belief. We start at the loud noise – the balloon bursting – even though we know that it is harmless. No one thinks that is irrational. Insofar as emotions are near relations – cousins perhaps – of these more primitive affective states, isn't it possible that they do not require beliefs in order to be launched? And, in any event, since various reflexes, phobias, and affect programs can be set in motion while bypassing the belief-centers of the brain, there would not appear to be a paradox of fiction with respect to affects across the board.

Furthermore, although it is true that an emotional state can, and often is, ignited by a state of belief, this is not the only mental state that can arouse an emotional reaction like fear or anger. We may also simply imagine a state of affairs and then take note of an emotion welling up within us. And there is nothing abnormal or irrational about this.

Consider: we are about to ask our boss for a day off in order to visit a dying relative. We imagine how things might go down. In our mind's eye, he denies our request and makes a characteristically cutting remark. Our ire mounts, though we do not literally believe that our boss has either denied our request or insulted us. We only imagine that he does so, and this is enough to start our emotional engine churning. Or, in a moment of frustration, entertain the idea of saying something hurtful to a person who is mentally disabled, confused, utterly dependent upon you, and who, as well, worships you. A feeling of shame may overcome you, though your lips remain sealed.

Belief – holding the content of proposition x before the mind assertively – can bring forth emotions. But so too can something that has been merely imagined – that is, a propositional content entertained in thought non-assertively. Or, in other words, believing that x and imagining that x – in the appropriate circumstances – are both psychologically empowered to elicit our emotions.

Moreover, it is easy to see the evolutionary advantage to be had in possessing the capacity of the imagination to arouse emotions. For by this means we can enhance the survival prospects of our conspecifics by instilling fear in them with respect to counterfactual states of affairs. In order to warn children off trusting strangers, we may, for instance, tell them tales about what might happen to them if they wander away with just anybody.

Here, of course, we can see an immediate connection between the natural history of our emotions and our emotional responses to fictions. For are not many of the earliest stories that we tell (and show) children counterfactual, cautionary tales – such as what befalls Walt Disney's Pinocchio when he throws in with the fast-talking strangers on his way to school? That is, our capacity to respond to fictions emotionally is rooted in the capacity – endowed by natural selection because of its adaptive advantageousness – of the emotion system to be aroused not only by that which we believe, but also by that which we imagine.*

Motion picture fictions are sense-bearing vehicles that mandate viewers to imagine the states of affairs and events that they depict audiovisually. With respect to *Captain Horatio Hornblower*, we see the actor Gregory Peck

---

* The power of the imagination to engage emotions is also connected to planning. That we can envision alternative futures and gauge what our emotional responses would be to finding ourselves in those states of affairs is clearly extremely advantageous. Imagining how you would feel if your child hurt herself at play may encourage you to baby-proof your house. Human life flourishes in large measure because of our ability to live in the future imaginatively. The emotions, we may hypothesize, are sensitive to imaginings just because they appraise or evaluate those future, possible, counterfactual states of affairs in terms of our abiding interests. Moreover, it does not make much sense to discount this capacity as irrational.

on screen in a three-cornered hat and then imagine that the eponymous naval officer is steering his frigate out of harm's way *because* that is what, given the context of fiction, we realize we are intended to do by the director Raoul Walsh (and his team of fellow fictioneers). In effect, a fictional motion picture instructs its audiences to hold certain propositions before the mind unassertively – for example, to *imagine* that Hornblower is under fire, or to *suppose* that Hornblower is being blasted, or to *entertain the unasserted thought* (rather than the belief) that Hornblower is just barely eluding the enemy attack.

And then, upon entertaining or imagining said state of affairs, we feel suspense for Hornblower and his crew. This is possible precisely because, due to evolution, our emotions are susceptible to imaginings as well as beliefs. The cultural institution of fiction, including the precinct of fictional motion pictures, rests upon our innate capacity to be moved emotionally by representations of counterfactual states of affairs and events. The phenomenon is neither paradoxical nor irrational, but natural.*

Furthermore, emotional states – like fear, pity, levity, anger, sadness, and so forth – can be activated not only by mental occurrences such as believings that x and imaginings that x, but also by nonpropositional states such as patterns of perceptual awareness or attention. That is, upon identifying the animal before me as a people-eating tiger and, thence, believing it to be dangerous, I am reduced to fear and trembling. Likewise, prompted by the visage on screen, I imagine that The Predator exists and then, recognizing all his malignant properties, my flesh crawls with visceral revulsion. But, in addition, an emotional reaction may be thrown into gear before I have fully computed or re-cognized the identity of that which I am in the process of encountering.

For whatever it is may command attention just because it satisfies a very general profile for that which is *potentially harmful*. That is, we may not know what x is specifically, but perception registers that x is large and advancing toward us very quickly. And, as a result, sans conscious identification, our fear-alarms put us on red alert, prior to any further processing. Of course, once we recognize that it is a charging rogue elephant, that then reinforces

---

* But, you may say, what of cases where we quell the child's fear by dispelling his beliefs? Doesn't that establish that emotions require beliefs to take hold? No, for there are also cases on the other side of the ledger. For example, we may overcome our disappointment at failing in some goal today by imagining that we will succeed tomorrow. (I owe this observation to Rianna Oelofson.)

our fright all the more. But the relevant point at this juncture is that there a may be enough information in these very early, very general stages of the tracking process to send the emotion system into a state of terror, even though there is not yet sufficient information to determine the exact nature of the threat.

Emotions can originate near the site of perception and prime the body for action without any further need for computation: the groom slips on a banana peel and we burst into laughter. Or the emotion may arise after being processed cognitively, either tacitly or consciously. Professional envy with regard to your colleague's executive bathroom privileges takes a lot of thinking. Motion pictures, of course, afford opportunities for the emotions to erupt through a variety of routes – some mediated by conscious cognitions, some by tacit ones, and others even more immediately. The quickly moving, dark shadows may send the icy rush of fear down our spine without our apprehension of whatever is casting those shadows. On the other hand, in order to admire the bravery of the hero, we must cognize his actions under the concept of courage and also recognize that that satisfies the pertinent criteria for admiration. Of course, whether a given motion picture involves a greater degree of primarily perceptually motivated emotional states versus ones calling for more cognitive processing can only be determined on a movie-by-movie basis.

Nevertheless, what these emotional states have in common is that they comprise appraisals or evaluations relative to certain recurring human themes, such as personal dignity, which appraisals then engender bodily states of feeling that dispose the organism to behave in certain ways. The samurai, for example, appraises the mud splashed on his brother's sandals as an affront: this causes his blood to boil, and, in consequence, he draws his sword from its scabbard, with lethal consequences. Of course, with respect to motion picture audiences, the behavioral portion of the emotion scenario rarely obtains, since we are only imagining that such-and-such is happening. For example, we are only supposing that someone's sandals have been muddied; thus, even if we are partial to that character, *we* have no reason to act, since, among other things, no one has really been insulted.

It is a remarkable fact about motion pictures that to an arresting extent they are able to elicit – across diversified audiences – roughly the same or converging general emotional responses to the fictions on screen. Suppose, as might happen any day of the week, that an ordinary couple is arguing on a street corner. The affective responses, if any, of real-world passers-by are likely to be all over the map. But, contrariwise, a couple argues onscreen and we all – or nearly all of us – feel indignation at the way in which the heroine is being demeaned. Whether we are in Madras or Manhattan, whether we are Lutheran, Jew, or atheist, Republican or Democrat, any motion picture worth its salt can usually elicit roughly the emotion it intends from its target audience, no matter how far flung, most of the time, its members may be. How is this possible?

To begin to answer this question, first recall that emotions are appraisals – they appraise situations in light of certain interests. The emotion of fear appraises events, objects, and people with respect to concerns for the safety and protection of oneself, one's interests, and the interests of one's confederates foremost in mind. Moreover, these concerns, which we can summarize as a preoccupation with harmfulness, function as the criterion used to appraise or evaluate a predicament as fearsome. That is, emotional appraisals are governed by criteria, as the emotion of fear can only be mobilized upon at least a suggestion of harmfulness.

Upon detecting circumstances that are perceived to be harmful or dangerous, fear takes over. It operates like a searchlight. It directs our attention, organizing the details before us into significant wholes or gestalts. In the first instance, it throws certain of the elements of the situation into bold relief, leading us to attend to the mugger's knife, rather than to the striped design on his tie. Fear then further guides our scansion of the array to pick out further relevant features for notice – for example, that the mugger has several large, equally well-armed companions.

Note here that the presiding emotional state does not batten on these details willy-nilly. They have all been chosen because they are pertinent to alerting us to the level of danger that confronts us. That is, these elements all meet the evaluative criterion of harmfulness. The emotion of fear solves the problem of what we must attend to. It weighs elements of our circumstances in light of our interests, specifically our interests in self-preservation and the avoidance of harm. Fear organizes situations in terms of the evaluative criterion of harmfulness.

Like fear, our other emotions are also criterially governed. In order to be angry, I must believe that me or mine have been wronged. To pity someone, I must believe that they have suffered misfortune. Envy requires that I think that someone else has something I want. And so on. The emotions appraise situations in terms of criteria. The bodily feelings that are then provoked by the emotional state, in turn, bias or organize our apprehension of the eliciting state of affairs in accordance with the criteria that govern the prevailing emotion. Our anger first fixes our attention on the smile of the guy who has just insulted us and then directs us to each of the other laughing faces that surround us.

This is how the emotions work in everyday life. But what does it have to do with viewing motion pictures? In particular, what does it have to do with the way in which moving pictures quite frequently dispose diverse audiences to vent extremely like-minded emotions in response to onscreen fictions – to the degree that all or most of us feel suspense, at the same time, for example, over the issue of whether or not the diminutive protagonist will make the football team of his dreams or whether or not the over-the-hill boxer stands a chance against Apollo Creed?

In life, in contrast to fiction, our emotions have to select the pertinent objects upon which to focus from a plethora of largely unstructured stimuli. But in fictions, including motion picture fictions, things are different. Our emotions are not called upon to organize the situations before us, so to say, *de novo*. To a much greater extent than usually encountered in everyday life, the situations in fictional motion pictures have already been structured for us by the director and his team. We do not typically have to depend, from the first instant, upon our emotions to organize fictional events for us as much as we rely upon the emotions to perform this task for us in the ordinary course of events. For, in the main, the states of affairs and events in motion pictures have been, in a manner of speaking, emotionally *predigested* for us by the creators of the fiction.

That is, the creators of the motion picture have already done much of the work of emotionally sculpting scenes and sequences for us through the ways in which the salient features of the fictional situation have been carefully designed to satisfy the criteria for drawing forth the emotional state intended by the production team. Details that suit the conceptual conditions of the emotional response desired by the moviemakers have been selected, filtered, foregrounded, and emphasized in the narrative, the dialogue, and the composition, and through the camera positioning, the acting, the musical commentary, and so forth.

In contrast to the way that the emotions have to start from scratch when it comes to managing our attention in daily life, when it comes to the general run of motion pictures, the events on screen have been emotively prefocused for us by the creators of the movie. They have selected the elements of the scene or sequence that they think are emotively significant and thrust them, to put it bluntly, in our face. The means to this end at the filmmaker's disposal include: camera position and composition, editing (including the processes of bracketing, scaling, and indexing discussed in the previous chapter), lighting, the use of color, and, of course, musical accompaniment, acting, dialogue, and the very structure of the script or narrative.

Quite frequently in everyday life, when an acquaintance or a colleague slights us – perhaps by a passing remark – we are not immediately angry, even if we are hurt, because we may wonder whether the insult was an intentional wrong rather than merely a thoughtless gaff. But as such remarks recur, anger besets us and inclines us to begin to recognize a discernible pattern of nastiness directed at us. However, in typical movie fictions, we rarely have to waver so long. So often characters wear the meanness of their actions on their sleeve, and if that were not enough, we also have access to the disapproving judgments of the people who surround them in the fiction. From the outset, we not only have a pretty unmistakable gestalt of wrongness served up with arresting clarity, but we also have the reactions of the characters around them to reflect and to reinforce our assessment of the situation.

It is very difficult not to respond negatively to the snarling, arrogant, cruel pronouncements of the dictator in *V for Vendetta*, shot as they are in oppressive close-ups and rasped out with gravelly harshness by the actor John Hurt. The performance is designed to elicit a gut reaction of political defiance, aversion, and even loathing. Generally in fictional motion pictures, the detection work that our emotions need to do for us in daily life is somewhat minimized, since the scenes and characters in these motion pictures have most commonly already been constructed from the vantage of the intended emotional point of view. The aforesaid dictator, for instance, was expressly designed from and for the perspective of loathing. Or, to say it differently, the character was emotively predigested or prefocused for us. And the image was made in such a way that any distracting detail was winnowed or filtered out and features pertinent to the elicitation of the intended emotion were exaggeratedly foregrounded.

But what does it mean for a character, or a scene, or a sequence to be emotively prefocused? Remember: the emotions are governed by criteria. To be happy for my cousin, I must believe that he is doing well. If he is doing poorly, then, all things being equal, happiness would be an odd response to his condition. Moreover, just as the emotions in daily life are governed by certain criteria of appropriateness, so too must the emotions mounted in response to fictions be governed. Thus, a motion picture is emotively prefocused by being *criterially prefocused* – that is, by being so structured that the descriptions and depictions of the pertinent objects of our attention in the movie clearly and decisively satisfy the criteria for the emotional state intended by the creators of the moving picture.

The makers of mummy-monster movies want to put us into the emotional state of horror. Horror is a compound emotion, involving fear and disgust. As we have seen, harmfulness is a criterion for fear. Impurity is a criterion for disgust. Thus, to elicit the horror response from viewers, the makers of a mummy picture will emphasize certain of his properties – namely, those that count as fearsome and those that count as disgusting. His capacity for harmfulness, of course, is satisfied by the lavish attention paid to his killing innocent people, while his impurity is established by elaborating on the fact that his dead body is rotting and badly in need of rejuvenation.

Likewise, suspense is arguably an emotion with two criteria – improbability and the desire that the good shall triumph. When, due to the nefarious plot of some Lex Luthor type, the two trains steam toward each other on a collision course, it is unlikely that disaster can be averted. Moreover, the death of all the nice people on the train is clearly evil. Can even Superman save the day? The narrative and the editing forcefully direct our attention in such a way that it is virtually impossible to miss the unlikelihood that good can come of this state of affairs, and, all things being equal, for the normal viewer the result is suspense.

Once we perceive the objects of our attention under the criterially relevant categories – such as harmfulness *and* disgust with regard to horror fictions or the improbability of the morally correct outcome with respect to suspense – the intended emotion is apt to be raised in us. That is, as a result of entertaining the appropriate appraisals – usually the ones implicated by the criterial prefocusing – we are likely to undergo the bodily responses, such as laughing, crying or squirming in our seat, that the moviemakers have planned.

Of course, not all motion pictures aim at evoking such brash emotional responses as my examples so far might suggest. Some films may aspire to induce more complex, ambiguous, nuanced, and even ambivalent emotional states than horror or suspense movies do. In those instances, however, it is not the case that the process of criterial prefocusing has been retired, but rather that the fictional world may have been constructed so as to satisfy simultaneously the criteria for more than one emotional condition, including possibly even those that conflict. Or, in other instances, the satisfaction of pertinent emotive criteria may only be hinted at subtly; the audience may need to mull over and reflect closely upon the details of the depiction before it arrives at the emotional response the filmmaker intends. For motion pictures may trade in quiet emotions as well as loud ones.

2   Some Affective Relations between Audiences and Characters in Popular Movies

The structure of emotional elicitation that we have called criterial prefocusing can operate with regard to situations either populated by characters or not. Shooting and editing a dark and stormy night can excite apprehension in an audience, since it meets the criteria of a place inhospitable and potentially dangerous for people, even if no people are yet in evidence in the motion picture. However, though affect can be raised in audiences where no characters are in the vicinity, clearly among the most powerful ways for arousing affect and emotion in viewers, particularly in mass-market movies, is through our relation to the fictional characters, notably the protagonists and the antagonists. So in order to round off our introductory and non-exhaustive exploration of some of the modes of affective address employed by the movies, a section about the ties that bind us to fictional characters is in order. But, as was noted in the previous section, there is not just one channel of affective address here, but several. In this part of the chapter, we will first examine a way in which movies may promote our *emotional* connection with characters and then we will conclude by discussing what we call "the mirror reflex," a mode available to audio-visual fictions, but not literary ones.

Identification

A natural place to initiate a discussion about the *emotional* relationship of viewers to fictional movie characters is the notion of identification. There are several reasons for this. First, when asked for an account of our emotive relation to fictional characters, especially the protagonists, most people are likely to invoke some notion of identification. Moreover, identification is probably the oldest account in the Western tradition of our emotional relationship to characters, for it was first propounded by Plato, who feared that the goodly citizens would become possessed by undesirable emotions, such as the fear of death, when exposed to actors shuddering onstage about the prospect of Hades. And this, of course, was hardly a desirable state to incite in potential militiamen.

Today, similar Platonic anxieties are abroad, undoubtedly underlying the recurring suspicion that the representation in the movies of unpalatable sexual feelings and aggressiveness will contaminate the hearts of audiences – most worrisomely, those of impressionable adolescents. But identification is not merely thought of as a source of antisocial tendencies. More often than not, identification is characterized positively as what bonds us to those most upstanding fictional characters, the protagonists.

Typically, it is supposed that to identify emotionally with a character is for one to feel precisely what she feels. By inhabiting the character from the inside, so to speak, her world becomes ours and we embrace her point of view as our own. We grow close to characters – or, at least, to the protagonists – because our hearts beat as one; identification is, in other words, the secret of the bond that we forge with the protagonists. Indeed, a common complaint – though perhaps, as we shall see, an unwarranted one – about popular movies is: "I couldn't identify with the characters."*

Of course, "identification," as it is used in common parlance, is somewhat ambiguous. It can signify a range of things, many of which are completely unobjectionable. However, the version of identification that concerns us is a very specific one. It involves the claim that the audience's affective bond with the pertinent fictional characters is a result of the audience's suffering putatively the self-same, *identical* feelings to the ones the character is undergoing. But, this may not be what people always have in mind when they say they identify with fictional characters.

Sometimes when talking about identification, people make no claim to any sort of identity, affective or otherwise, between the character and themselves. When I say that I identify with Aquaman, I may mean that I wish I were as fearless as he is, but I can't swim and am afraid of the ocean. I make no assumption that Aquaman and I feel the same way about the deep blue sea. I only wish that it were so. Perhaps this shouldn't even be called identification, but rather wishful fantasizing. And, in any event, it is not clear how much of this daydreaming can be indulged while watching a movie flash by without losing track of the story.

Frequently, when folks, especially young folks, say that they identify with a character, they mean nothing more than that they think he's "cool." But you can be a nerd – and know and feel like a nerd – and still think Rico and Sonny are cool. At other times, all people mean when they say they identify with a character is that they've had a similar experience – like the character, they've been laid off, for example. But this really seems to come down to no more than feeling some affinity for the character rather than

* As will become evident after our discussion of sympathy, I think claims like "I couldn't identify with character *x*" should be translated as "I couldn't or didn't care for character *x*." Or, more colloquially, "I couldn't care less about soandso."

endorsing the conviction that one has been infected by the self-same feelings that the onscreen protagonist is now enduring. Might this not be more accurately termed "affiliation" rather than "identification"?

Alternatively, "identification" is often parsed in terms of putting myself in the place of the character. This is not a matter of putting myself in the character's shoes, as they say, but of putting the character in my shoes. But why suppose that this entails that the character and I are in the same affective state? Shouldn't this be called "projection" rather than "identification"?

In what follows, I am presupposing that the core concept of the leading version of identification – and on many accounts, empathy as well – involves the audience member being in the same type-identical emotional state in which the viewer believes the fictional character finds himself. The protagonist is indignant about the treatment of minorities and so are we; the heroine is uplifted by the sight of her Savior, as are we; the hero is terrified of the Alien – us too. However, identity of emotion-types, even if it is necessary, is not enough to constitute identification of the sort we are now considering. Why not?

Consider this: the fans of a certain team at a soccer match may all be in the same emotive state – they all hate the opposing team. Yet we wouldn't call this identification in the relevant sense. For with whom are they identifying? Although they may all be inflamed to the same degree with hatred for the rival team, they are not identifying with each other, since they may not even be aware of the presence of the others, so wrapped up are they in the game that they are witnessing as it unfolds before them. Or imagine each is watching the game alone on television in the solitude of his own den; they have no idea who else is watching; thus, they could not be identifying with all those unknown others.

Nor is it plausible to speculate that these fans are, in the pertinent sense, identifying with any of the soccer players – the players are probably too absorbed in the activity on the field to be emoting anything, and in any event most of them probably don't literally *hate* their opponents. That kind of sports-hatred is for the fans, not for professionals.

But if the sharing of type-identical emotional states is not sufficient for identification, what needs to be added? That the viewers be in the emotional state in question because that is the state they think that the fictional characters are in. That is, putatively, in this sense of identification, I identify with Ann Darrow when I am horrified by King Kong *because* she is – or I imagine her to be – horrified by King Kong. In short, the version of identification on the table maintains: a viewer x identifies with a fictional character y if and only if (1) x is in the same type-identical emotive state as y is in, and (2) because y is in – or x imagines y to be in – that emotive state. To speak metaphorically, the viewer has been "infected" by the ostensible emotive state of the character. For convenience, we can refer to this as the *infection model of identification*.

The infection model of identification

This version of identification, I submit, is the dominant notion that most people today have in mind when they speak of identifying with fictional characters. It is the relationship that many appear to think is their primary bond with fictional characters, notably protagonists, and it is the emotional state that plain viewers and professionals alike think explains why we cheer the protagonists on.

Now I have no reason to believe that something like the phenomenon of affective infection never occurs, especially in *real* life. There is empirical evidence that infants feel distress when they detect distress in their caregivers. But I am not sure that this is a full-blown emotional state, rather than merely a certain kind of affective reflex – called the mirror reflex – which we will discuss at the end of this chapter.

However, that notwithstanding, it is not the sheer possibility of occurrences of the infection model that concerns us. Rather, we want to ask whether the infection model is up to the task for which its proponents recommend it. That is, is it a comprehensive or nearly comprehensive account of our emotional relationship to characters in popular fictions? Does it account for our standard emotive relationships with fictional characters? Is it the emotional bond that typically ties us to them?

Asymmetric emotions

Even a cursory review of cases indicates that the infection model of identification is unlikely to provide anything even approaching a general account of our emotional relationships to the fictional characters in motion pictures. Imagine: the candidate is pumped up by the adulation with which his acceptance speech has been greeted by the adoring crowd; but we know that he is standing in the cross-hairs of the high-powered, laser-guided rifle of a merciless hired assassin. We do not feel the thrill that the candidate does; we feel suspense, even anxiety. Our emotional state is not type-identical with the candidate's. Nor should it be, since the movie mandates that we should fear for the candidate.

Moreover, this species of asymmetry of affect is rife throughout comic fictions. Every time the would-be suitor is discovered in a compromising situation, we are amused, while he is discomfited. Recall, for example, *Meet the Parents*. And with respect to the BBC series *Jeeves and Wooster*, notice that in virtually every situation where Bertie is flustered, we are merry.

Situations in which the emotional states of the characters diverge from those of the audience abound in motion picture fictions of all sorts. In a romance, for example, the wholesome and endearing daughter is head over heels in love with the handsome stranger; but we do not share her joy, since we know that he's a cad. The reason that such situations are so common in motion pictures is that there is generally a significant differential between what we know and what the characters know, and, this, of course, can have a tangibly different impact on what is felt on both sides of the audience/fiction divide. In many cases, we know more than the characters; we tremble for them as they plunge ahead oblivious of peril. Curiosity draws them into the old dark house, into the attic, the basement, the cave, or whatever, though we know better. They haven't got a clue of what awaits them, so they're cool, but we're already shivering with terror. On the other hand, the asymmetry can run in the opposite direction: Sherlock Holmes always knows more than we do, so we never share his aplomb.

Obviously, circumstances like these are not rare. They may even predominate statistically. But, be that as it may, there are more than enough cases of asymmetric affect like these to establish that the infection model of identification cannot be very comprehensive on readily observed empirical grounds. Furthermore, there are also conceptual considerations that invite us to suspect the inadequacy of the infection model. Quite often both the cause and the object of the audience's emotional state differ from those of the protagonist's affective condition. We are presented with a situation in which we learn that Martha's son Henry died last year and we learn that this event is the cause of her grief; the object of her grief is her son, Henry. But the cause of the audience's emotional state is Martha's bereavement and its object is the grieving mother.

Our emotion organizes or gestalts a wider state of affairs than does Martha's, while at the same time also including the object of Martha's grieving as a constitutory component. Moreover, our emotion is pity for the mother, not grief – who is Henry to us? It is the mother with whom we have become acquainted through the movie. In the case we have in mind, Henry has been kept off screen throughout; we only know of him through Martha.

Thus, as the previous example indicates, our emotional states often have different causes and take different objects than the putative mental states of the protagonists. Consequently, the conjecture that our emotions always, or even very frequently, perfectly match those of the pertinent characters is highly dubious. So, again, the infection model looks like it must be abandoned as a comprehensive picture of our emotive relations to movie protagonists.

Indeed, there are certain cases, perhaps many, where the audience member's emotional state can only plausibly be thought to be that of an onlooker rather than one that could correspond to the mental state of its object, the fictional protagonist. When we feel nail-biting suspense as the protagonist claws his way to safety, he is highly unlikely to be feeling suspense or, for that matter, any other emotion. He is probably numb with concentration. He is apt to be so caught up in and focused upon his task that his anxiety is on hold.

In my own experience of extreme situations, such as skidding at high speed on ice in my car, I have noticed that I do not go into an emotional state, like panic, but react very deliberately, as if affectively anesthetized, and do what my driving instructor told me to do decades ago. If I were to respond emotionally – if I were racked with suspense – I'd crash. My passengers can afford suspense, but I can't. Isn't it likely that the same asymmetrical distribution of emotion occurs quite often with respect to motion pictures, particularly action-packed ones?

Nevertheless, the friend of infectious identification may retort that, even if there are many cases where the presumed inner states of audience members and those of the characters diverge, there are also a significant number of cases where the emotive states at issue would appear to be type-identical. The character recoils in contempt at the child molester's ploys; so do we. Emotive symmetry obtains. Therefore, it may be maintained, even if the infection model fails to be applicable across the board, perhaps the argument can be made that it has compelling authority in cases like the preceding one, in which the emotions of the viewers and the protagonists correlate. However, in order to probe this suggestion, we need to introduce a distinction between emotions that are held in common or coincidentally and emotions that are shared due to some intimate causal relation between them.

Coincident versus connected emotional states

American jet bombers have streaked past their fail-safe points and they are winging their way to Beijing. They are freighted with nuclear devices. Atomic warfare looms; millions will die. One of the protagonists, the President of the United States, is stricken with fear; us too. Isn't this a case where the infectious identification holds sway?

No. Why not? Remember that the infection model of identification requires not only that our emotions match those of the protagonists, but also that our emotions be a causal consequence of the protagonists being in precisely the self-same kind of mental state. However, in a great many of the cases in which we find ourselves in the same type of emotive condition as the protagonist, including the preceding example, it is pretty clear that we have gotten there by our own route, so to speak. We are not anxious because the President is anxious. We are anxious because we have been encouraged to imagine that a nuclear armageddon, threatening a catastrophic number of deaths, is in the offing.

Maybe some evidence for this is that the fiction could be told without reference to the President's anxiety and we would still feel anxiety. Were the President made of steel, I speculate that we would still feel suspense. We would feel the same species of consternation precisely because the fictional situation has been structured in a way that makes certain features that are appropriately conducive to the state of fear salient – such as repeated assessments of how much explosive power those jet bombers are carrying, their capacity to evade radar detection, their imperviousness to any and all anti-aircraft defenses, as well as the putatively uneasy diplomatic relations between the United States and China.

In other words, in the vocabulary of the first part of this chapter, the film has been structured emotively in terms of criterial prefocusing. That is, by means of its visual depictions, enactments, and/or verbal descriptions, its circumstances have been organized or filtered in such a way that the features the moviemakers have elected for emphasis are predominantly exactly those suitable for or criterially apposite to the emotional states intended to be excited by the work.

In the Odessa Steps sequence of his film *Potemkin*, the director Sergei Eisenstein selects out of the streaming riot and highlights the callous massacre of old people, a mother and her adolescent son, and then another mother and her infant child – in short, he places brackets around those persons who are culturally figured as harmless and defenseless. His selection of these vignettes for emphasis – rather than shots of the clouds overhead – was designed to activate the viewer's emotions of moral outrage. The sequence was compellingly crafted so that factors that are criterial to moral indignation unavoidably command attention in a way that leads audience members, unless they are Cossacks, to process the episode under the heading of evil and, in consequence, to experience visceral distress.

Most often, I guess-estimate, when the feelings of audience members are congruent with those of the protagonist, it is a result of criterial prefocusing, not infectious identification. The difference is that in the case where criterial prefocusing leads to emotive uptake on the part of viewers, the correspondence between what the audience feels and what the characters are imagined to feel is co-incident or conjoint rather than causal. That is, the audience has been effectively led to the emotional state it is in by a pathway that can be causally independent of what, if anything, the protagonist feels. Thus, cases of congruent emotions between viewers and protagonists, though admittedly quite frequent, are typically not true-blue instances of infectious identification, but are better regarded as cases of coincidentally congruent emotional states engineered by means of criterial prefocusing.

Indeed, it seems to me that postulating infectious identification in most cases is to take on excess theoretical baggage, since typically congruent emotional states, where they occur, can, all things being equal, be adequately explained in terms of criterial prefocusing. For what it is worth, in all the cases that I have examined, criterial prefocusing gives a perfectly acceptable account of the rhyming emotional states. Thus, in the main, talk about infectious identification violates the principle of explanatory parsimony.

Of course, it may be pointed out that often the way in which situations are criterially prefocused in movies tends to parallel the way in which the protagonist sees things. Even if the narration is omniscient and not channeled explicitly through the point of view of the protagonist, movie directors often depict the fictional world from the perspective of leading characters. The gloominess of the portrayal of the environment, for example, may echo the apprehensiveness of the hero as he enters the hiding place of the evil wizard Voldemort.

This is a fair point, yet it does not revive the model of infectious identification. For, on the one hand, the viewer need not be aware that it is the character's viewpoint that he is being invited to take on; rather, he may suppose it to be the perspective of the narrating agency (howsoever he understands that). And, furthermore, the criterial prefocusing here will work in the same way whether or not it is crafted in a manner that reflects the point of view of the protagonist.

Here it is interesting to think about cases where the fiction overtly establishes that the way in which events are criterially prefocused is congruent with the emotive states of the protagonist. Striking examples of this are the use of point-of-view shots in motion picture editing. The character looks offscreen, her face contorted with horror; then there is a shot of what she sees – a shot of a suppurating creature, part reptile, part arachnid, part lawyer, with a maw like a chainsaw – and we are horrified too. Isn't that patently a case of infectious identification?

Again, I think that it is not, for the simple reason that we would probably feel the same level of horror if the sequence were shown without the character looking offscreen. An interesting experiment might be to remove the emotive povs from a movie like *The Descent* in order to assess whether our repulsion at the sight of those slimy, albino cave-dwellers dwindles.

Of course, this leaves open the question of why such point-of-view shots – and other perspective-disclosing devices – are used by fictioneers. The short answer, I think, is that they are a means of priming or preparing or communicating to the audience in a very broad way the general kind of affect (dysphoric or euphoric) that the audience should bring to bear on the objects, persons, situations, and events they are about to encounter. In this way, the point-of-view structures reinforce the affective information available on screen. But I will have more to say about how this communication works in my subsequent remarks about mirror reflexes.

Vectorially converging emotive states

So far the second condition of the model of infectious identification has been hammered on the grounds that, even if the audience is in an emotive state congruent with the imagined mental state of the protagonist, that is generally the result of the viewer having arrived at that state by a process located in his or her own emotive-appraisal system, independently of any necessary causal input involving the fictional character being in the type-identical emotional state. In other words, as those jet bombers race toward Beijing, I fear for humanity, because human life as we know it is endangered in the fiction, and not because the fictional president fears for humanity. My fear is co-incident or conjoint with the protagonist's, while, at the same time, being causally independent from it. Or, at least, this seems to be what is going on by and large in the most significant number of cases.

Nevertheless, it is important not to misinterpret this example. The claim is not that we are never emotively influenced by the emotional states of characters, especially the protagonists and others to whom we have a favorable attitude. For example, at the end of Charlie Chaplin's *The Gold Rush*, the Tramp accidentally meets up with Georgia, the woman of his dreams. The two embrace, they kiss, and they fade out into the land of happily ever after. They are in love, and their successful match gladdens us. Scenes like this happen all the time in popular fictions. Our previous objections to the infection model of identification are not to be taken as an attempt to disavow them. For cases like these should not be taken as cases of infectious identification in the first place.

True, the emotional states of the characters do cause us to be in a euphoric state. But our euphoric state is not precisely the same type of euphoric state that the lovers are in. Their emotional state is infatuation. That is not our condition; we are happy for the couple. I am not in love with Georgia nor am I identifying with that aspect of the Tramp. Were I in love with Georgia, I wouldn't be so happy. I'd be jealous of the Tramp. So I am not in a state of infectious identification.

Yet I am in state of roughly the same emotive valence. They are, let us say, euphoric and I am euphoric as well. Our emotional states converge – they both belong on the positively charged side of the scale of the emotions. We are not in the same emotional states, but our conditions are in broad categorical agreement and we are in that vectorially converging state with the state of the characters because that is the condition in which we imagine them to be.

Contrariwise, when the monster in the concluding scenes of *Bride of Frankenstein* is reviled by his reanimated betrothed, we feel sorry for him. Our emotion does not match his. We do not feel the pain of an unrequited lover. Indeed, I doubt that any viewers, no matter how desperate, harbor any desires for the frizzy-haired, electrified corpse, played by Elsa Lanchester. Yet we do respond to the monster's misery with sorrow. It is in this sense that we share his misery. We are not miserable for being lovelorn, but we do pity the monster.

Both misery and pity, of course, are dysphoric or negative emotions. Both sit on the distressful, discomforting, disturbing, or painful pole of emotional states. Again, our emotions are broadly similar in their general valence. They converge vectorially in their negative directionality. Our emotions are causally coordinated. But this does not count in favor of the model of infectious identification, unless identification means nothing more than a somewhat similarly charged feeling. However, why mobilize the notion of *identity* to describe that?

Simulation theory

We appear to be emotionally tied to movie fictions predominantly through our relations to characters, particularly those called protagonists. But what is the nature of that relation – at least in the largest number of cases? We have just been arguing that the concept of identification does not seem to do it justice. Perhaps the relationship is an instance of what is nowadays called "simulation."

Simulation is a concept from the philosophy of mind that has recently been imported into aesthetics. In the philosophy of mind, the idea is that we understand and explain others, ascertain what they are feeling, identify their intentions, emotions, and motivations, and predict their behavior by simulating them. That is, we input their beliefs and desires into our own off-line cognitive-conative system. Since, *ex hyposthesi*, our cognitive-conative architecture is the same as theirs, if we run their beliefs-desires program on ourselves – using their software on our hardware, so to speak – then we should be able to derive a reasonable fix on what people just like us (folk-psychologically speaking) are likely to think, feel, plan, want, and so forth. That is, we put them into our shoes – or to talk in an equally metaphorical manner, we put their beliefs and desires into the black box that outputs our emotions, decisions, and behaviors – in order to project what they are likely to feel, think, or do. This, moreover, is done on the presupposition that with respect to processing beliefs and desires into emotions, intentions, and deliberations, etc., we are pretty nearly the same structurally.

This theory – called *simulation theory* – is counterposed to another view in the philosophy of mind concerning the way in which we go about understanding others. This alternative view is called the *theory-theory*. This alternative view is the *theory* that we understand what others are about by applying something like a scientific *theory* to their behavior. Simulation is thought to have several advantages over the theory-theory when it comes to reading the minds of others. First, the theoretical framework ostensibly presupposed by the theory-theory would be monumentally complicated – too complex to postulate with any confidence. After all, it would have to be bigger and better than our best existing social scientific theories, since its accuracy would appear to be much greater. Do we really believe that most of us have in our possession such a powerful theory? And if so, why can't our social scientists access it explicitly? That would save them a great deal of effort in the lab.

Second, even if we ordinary folks did have such a mammoth theory at our disposal, if only *sub voce*, it would surely take an immense amount of real time to apply it to particular cases – simply figuring out which laws the case fell under and how the influence of related laws was to be calculated would seem to take forever. But this does not seem to match up to our everyday experience of reading the minds of others. Quite often, we size up people's emotional states and intentions in a blink of the mind; we don't spend hours crunching our way through an elaborate theory. Or so the simulation theorists contend.

But what does all this have to with motion pictures – specifically with the question of our emotional relationship to the protagonists in popular fictions, like movies? In short: putatively our relationship with fictional characters is generally like the relationships we have with other people in the world outside the cinema. The movie fiction invites us to understand them, to apprehend what they are feeling and intending, to speculate about what they will do next, and so forth, just as we must mind-read our conspecifics in everyday life. In order to do so – in order to follow the motion picture fiction (the unfolding of the intentions and feelings of fictional characters) – we simulate them, or at least the leading ones, primarily the protagonists. (Probably it is implausible to suppose that viewers simulate the situations of minor characters, like the plight of the lawyer in the outhouse in the first installment of *Jurassic Park* – or to think that viewers are meant to do so).

When we simulate a character, like Spiderman, we are said to input their beliefs and desires into our cognitive-conative network and thereby to discover what they are thinking and feeling by coming to think and feel broadly similar things as our own system runs through its paces on their steam. On this view, we are engaged emotively with motion picture fictions (as well as other sorts of fiction) by being immersed in a virtually continuous process of replicating the emotions and desires of (especially) the protagonists.

Unlike the proponent of infectious identification, the simulation theorist does not claim that the emotions allegedly reproduced in us are identical, either thoroughly or in part (aspectually), with those attributed to the protagonist. At best, our emotions only approximate those of the characters. However, this still leaves the simulation theorist open to one objection that was leveled at the champions of infectious identification – namely, the charge that simulation theory can be nothing close to a comprehensive theory of our emotional relationships to fictional characters, and this is so because of the indefinitely vast number of cases where the emotions of the audience are and should be different from and sometimes even opposed to those suffered by fictional characters.

This is the asymmetry problem once again. When the protagonist rushes home joyously to tell her spouse that she's been promoted at the same time that we, the audience, know she will open the door only to find her family brutally massacred, our despondent state is nothing like hers. Moreover, if at that moment we were simulating her psychology, we would not be following the story appropriately. We are supposed to be feeling pity. But since similar asymmetries are so often the rule in motion picture fictions, simulation cannot be anything like a comprehensive account of our emotive engagement with the fictional characters in movies.

Of course, as we conceded earlier, sometimes the emotions of the audiences and the characters do converge. Mr. Smith is outraged by corruption in the Senate and so are we. Perhaps simulation explains cases of convergence. But this seems unlikely. Motion pictures proceed at a pace that would seem uncongenial for simulation. Supposedly one of the advantages of the simulation theory over the theory-theory is that simulation is more temporally suited to sussing out the emotive states of our conspecifics. But be that as it may, simulation takes time too and one wonders whether one typically has sufficient breathing space in which to simulate in reaction to a rapidly edited audiovisual array.

Furthermore, another problem with simulation is that it is a firmly established fact that people are notoriously unreliable in identifying their own emotions and intentions. So how likely is it that such unreliable subjects will be able to extrapolate correctly from what they take to be their own case to the case of another?

Moreover, where the other being is a fictional character of the order of a movie hero, the likelihood that we are using simulation to predict their behaviors is especially implausible. Movie heroes don't shirk their duty in the face of overwhelming odds. When surrounded, Rambo lights into his assailants. How many of us – given the black box of our cognitive-conative system – would really reach the same decisions as Rambo does? Given his beliefs that these bruisers are bad guys and his commitment to justice, Rambo goes on the warpath. Wouldn't the rest of us just decide meekly to be arrested? As moviegoers, we probably anticipate that Rambo will not go quietly. But it is improbable that most of us reach this surmise by simulating Rambo, since if we were actually simulating, we would anticipate that he would surrender, wouldn't we?

But an even deeper question of how the simulation account can reach the right answers in cases like these is the question of how often simulation can be supposed to occur in our responses to motion pictures. I contend that, if it ever occurs, it is nevertheless very unlikely that, with respect to popular movies, it is occurring very often. Why?

Simulation theory in the philosophy of mind is advanced as a view about the way in which we go about determining what our conspecifics are thinking and feeling – a way of understanding and predicting their not transparently fathomable behavior in the course of daily affairs. But popular motion picture fictions are not like everyday life. They are expressly designed to be understood – indeed, they are designed to be understood quickly and clearly by untutored audiences.

Needless to say, this aspiration extends to the way in which the fictional characters are constructed. Perhaps in our ordinary experience, our conspecifics strike us as opaque in a way that calls for simulation. I would not say that this never happens, though I am not convinced that it is happening all of the time. Nevertheless, I do contend that the kinds of situations that call for simulation occur rarely with respect to the kind of fictional characters who inhabit movies, because those characters are intentionally fabricated in such a way that they wear their feelings and their thoughts on their sleeves. Thus, there is little or no need to hypothesize the operation of simulation in response to popular motion picture fictions, since we usually know exactly what the fictional characters are feeling and thinking faster than it would take to simulate said fictional beings.

Does it seem impossible that we might penetrate into the heart of a fictional being so easily? To establish that it is not impossible, let us take a brief digression into literary fiction before returning to the case of movies. Most popular literary fictions employ the device of free indirect discourse. This means that the author can narrate what the character is thinking and feeling from both the inside and the outside. We have her context described for us, often in emotionally suggestive terms, her physical states delineated, and we are also made privy to her thoughts. In such circumstances there is no call for simulation. We are just told what the character is feeling and thinking. Perhaps some readers use the text as a script for attempting to raise similar emotions in themselves. I don't, but I wouldn't want to claim that others are like me in this respect. Nevertheless, it should be clear that there is no pressure to mobilize simulation theory in cases like this in order to explain how we come to grasp the feelings and thoughts of the protagonist. We are told them outright.

Of course, this feature of literary fictions is not as common in audiovisual fictions (though there are exceptions, from *Diary of a Country Priest* to *The Twilight Zone*). That is, we do not typically enter the minds of protagonists as frequently in movies and TV as we do in literary fictions. But, on the other hand, it is true that quite often the characters in these artforms do tell us precisely what they are feeling and what they are thinking, often by way of dialogue with interlocutors. And even in those cases where the characters do not explicitly articulate their state of mind, I would still urge that the characters in movies manifest their feelings and thoughts so openly that simulation is effectively beside the point.

How is this possible? Perhaps one way to get at this is to ask whether with respect to everyday experience simulation and the theory-theory exhaust our way of gaining access to the feelings and thoughts of others. Arguably, they do not. Often – in fact, probably most often – we impute thoughts and feelings to others on the basis of schemas, scripts, prototypes, contextual cues, exemplars, and other heuristics, rather than by means of a theory or a simulation. These stratagems, in turn, enable us to infer the inner states of others.

Confronted with a co-worker who has just been fired or a friend who has lost a loved one, we infer on the basis of a culturally shared script that, all things being equal, they are down. If their shoulders are slouched and their eyelids heavy, we recognize these as signs of distress in virtue of our prototype for distress. We have no need to perform a simulation, because, through experience, we have amassed a repertoire of schemas, scripts, prototypes, and contextual and/or recognitional cues, among other heuristics, to key us to the inner states of conspecifics.

When we hear that a relative has secured a long-sought-after job, all things being equal, we suppose that she is happy and we rejoice for her. There is no need for simulation. We have access to a body of prototypes regarding emotional responses in certain contexts as well as recognitional cues, such as facial expressions and postures, which enable us to assess the emotional states of others. These are not theories and they are not applied by subsuming particular situations under nomological generalizations as the theory-theory might have it. Rather, they are prototypes – schemas, scripts, and recognitional cues – employed by *analogy* (analogy rather than subsumption). In daily life, such strategies provide us with reasonably reliable means for tracking the emotional states and thoughts of conspecifics, and I, at least, am pretty confident that we depend on them in everyday life far more than we depend on simulation. For, quite frequently, simulation would just be too time-consuming.

Moreover, if this is right, then it has important ramifications for popular fictions like movies. Inasmuch as popular or mass fictions, like movies, are designed to maximize accessibility, they gravitate naturally toward the use of the schemas, prototypes, exemplars, contextual and/or recognitional cues, and other heuristics that abound in the cultures of their target audiences. Indeed, it is part of the art of designing a character for the purposes of mass consumption that one be able to streamline the details of the character's persona so that it calls forth almost automatically the scripts, schemas, recognitional cues, and other heuristics that are intended to fit it.

In the situation comedy *Sex and the City*, the character Samantha snugly fits the schema of the carnal woman – the sensual woman who loves sex (e.g., the Wife of Bath). When her eyes open wide as a handsome swain glides by, we do not need to simulate Samantha in order to determine her internal state. We can infer it in a split second based on our prototype for carnal women and the recognitional cues that Samantha supplies.

Moreover, with respect to this particular TV series, our surmise will almost always be confirmed when Samantha slyly, albeit redundantly, confides her desires to her friends, Carrie, Miranda, and Charlotte. Nor does this seem to me to be a peculiar example of the way in which characters in popular motion picture fictions function. Instead it appears to be the norm.

Perhaps supporting evidence for this hypothesis can be drawn from our reactions to movie villains. Movie villains, especially very, very evil ones like Michael Meyers, are probably among the most psychologically opaque beings around. By rights, then, we should try to simulate them. But I conjecture that we never do. Why? Because, we render them intelligible by means of our schema for stalker/slashers (though this is a schema that admittedly derives more from the movies than from daily experience – thank God).

The point of emphasizing the operation of recognitional cues and other heuristics in negotiating our emotive relationships to fictional characters in movies, of course, is to show that there is little motivation for hypothesizing the operation of simulation in response to the protagonists in popular motion pictures. For the problem that simulation is supposed to solve with respect to understanding the feelings and thoughts of others in everyday life does not generally arise with regard to popular motion picture fictions because movies intensively exploit the schemas, scripts, prototypes, exemplars, and contextual and recognitional cues that comprise our heuristics for discerning the inner lives of others.

Moviemakers build characters, economically sculpting their features, precisely to trigger quickly and effortlessly the mobilization of those prototypes and heuristics by audiences. Thus, the need to postulate the operation of simulation as the means by which we apprehend the emotions and thoughts of others is largely otiose.

But what, the simulationist might ask, of motion pictures of a more exacting sort – such as the art cinema of the 1960s? Those characters do not show their psychology so unabashedly. Aren't they, at least, ripe for simulation? I suspect not – for the simple reason that most of those characters are simply too opaque to simulate. Their beliefs and desires are often far too murky for us to process through our own cognitive-conative architecture. We don't know what to put into our own off-line system. This is not said to chastise these motion pictures. Often their point is that the human heart is ultimately too mysterious to plumb. Rather, my point is simply that even in these cases, simulation appears irrelevant.

Therefore, once again, the need to posit simulation appears beside the point. But if we are not simulating the emotions of the fictional characters in moving pictures, then it is not the case that were are typically bound emotionally to them by a continuous process of sharing congruent feelings. So what is going on here emotionally?

Sympathy

We are emotionally tied to movies in large measure through our relationship with characters, especially the protagonists. But neither the model of infectious identification nor that of simulation appears to explain satisfactorily the general structure of this relationship in a comprehensive manner. Whether or not infectious identification or simulation ever occur, they occur far more rarely than is often supposed and, therefore, cannot afford a comprehensive account of the emotive address of characters in movies. A problem with the model of infectious identification and simulation theory in this regard is that they postulate a more, rather than less, closely shared emotional state between viewers and characters, whereas, as we have seen, so often the relation is asymmetrical. Consequently, perhaps the place to look for an account of our relation to fictional characters is a condition where what we feel and what the protagonists are thought to feel are categorically different.

An obvious candidate for such a bond is sympathy. Sympathy is not an emotional state that persons bear to themselves. It is, by definition, directed at others. For our purposes, let us construe sympathy broadly as non-fleeting care, concern, or, more widely, a non-passing pro-attitude toward another person (or fictional character, including anthropomorphized beings of all sorts). Sympathy qua emotion is a supportive response. It provides an impulse toward benevolent action with respect to those to whom it is directed, though, of course, that impulse need not and often is not acted upon, frequently because it conflicts with other interests that we might have. And, needless to say, with the fictional characters in movies, the sympathetic impulse cannot be acted upon. Perhaps, one reason why we are so free with our sympathies toward fictional characters is that, since we need not ever act on their behalf, their needs never threaten to fall afoul of our interests. Indeed, it is probably because such sympathies come so cheaply that moralists, such as Augustine and Rousseau, have perennially distrusted the benevolent feelings elicited by fictions.

But, in any case, sympathy, conceived as an emotion, involves visceral feelings of distress when the interests of the objects of our pro-attitude are endangered, and feelings of elation, closure, and/or satisfaction when their welfare is achieved. The emotion in question has as a component the enduring well-being of its object – a desire that things work out well for her. In order to be the object of this pro-attitude, the person in question must be thought to be worthy of our benevolence in light of our interests, projects, values, loyalties, allegiances, and/or moral commitments. When some fictional character so-and-so is appraised to be worthy of our non-passing desire that things go well for her and this is linked to positive feeling tones when gratified and negative ones when frustrated, we are in the emotional state that I am calling sympathy. If "sympathy" strikes you as too saccharin-sounding, then you are welcome to refer to it as "benevolence," or even more aridly as "a pro-attitude."

Though sympathy may initially appear to be just another example of a vectorially converging state, it is important to note that it need not be. For sympathy does not always – and in any event does not necessarily – track, even vectorially, the way in which the character feels. This is due to the fact that sympathy concerns what we believe to be the genuine well-being of the character. Should the heroine fall head over heels for some lounge-lizardly Lothario, she might be in ecstasy, whereas our sympathetic response would be anxiety-ridden, since we surmise that she is headed for trouble. Although, on occasion, sympathy may converge vectorially upon the emotions of the characters we care for, this is not required for the state in question to count as sympathy.

The suggestion that sympathy plays a role in our emotional involvement with fictional characters is fairly unexceptionable. However, what is being claimed now is more than that. I am arguing that sympathy, along with antipathy (which we will discuss presently), constitutes the major emotive cement between audiences and the pertinent movie characters. But why suppose that sympathy holds this place of privilege?

Obviously, during the course of a motion picture, the viewer undergoes many emotional states. One is angry for awhile, then sad, then happy, then gripped with suspense, some laughter erupts, some tears, and then we are happy again. Sometimes sympathy for the protagonist is so strong that you can feel it. At other times, it may appear to take the back seat for an interlude of comic amusement. So why select out of this welter of affects sympathy as the premier emotion?

The first reason might be called its breath. Sympathy for the protagonist is the most pervasive emotion from the beginning to the end of the movie. As soon as sympathy is secured, unless it is later intentionally neutralized by the creator of the motion picture, it stays on the alert, following the protagonist's fortunes throughout, registering distress as they waver, and pleasure as they rise.

Sympathy, once enlisted, is constantly on call throughout the movie. Generally no other emotive stance – save perhaps antipathy toward the villain – is so long-lasting. The indignation we feel toward the surly prison guard who cuffs the hero comes and goes. But our sympathy for the protagonist endures. It provides the emotive optic through which we survey the narrative from one end to the other. Typically, each event in the story is weighed in light of our sympathy for the protagonist; of every event it is pertinent to ask whether it advances or deters her fortunes, even if, in some cases, the answer is neither.

The protagonists in motion pictures have goals and interests that are hard to miss. The narrative trajectory usually involves the accomplishment of these goals and the satisfaction of these interests in the face of various obstacles. We follow this quest from the perspective of sympathy, cheering the protagonists onwards as they advance and feeling consternation when they falter. Of course, as already noted, sometimes our sympathy for the character puts us out of synch with them – as when we believe the person the protagonist trusts to be a scoundrel. But still we track the unfolding narrative in terms of a sympathetic viewpoint, one that disposes us to care about his best interests rather than his subjective assessment of them.

Sympathy is the most persistent emotional bond that we have with respect to the fictional protagonists; in this sense it generally possesses more breadth than other emotions elicited by moving pictures. Furthermore, sympathy also has what might be called special depth. For it is our sympathy toward the protagonist that shapes our overall reception of the action. When we are angered by the way in which the heroine is mistreated, that anger itself is subsidiary to the sympathy that we bear toward her. That sympathy underlies and reinforces our anger. It is our sympathy for the character that disposes us to regard her as inside our network of concern, and, therefore, to assess an injustice done to her as something perpetrated against one of "our own." The negative emotions that we muster in response to the protagonist's setbacks are a function of our sympathy for her. Sympathy is the real foundation here. That is why we say it has depth, even special depth.

Two considerations then can be marshaled to endorse the hypothesis that sympathy is the leading emotional bond between viewers and movie protagonists, namely, that sympathy appears to have greater breath and greater depth than any other competing candidate. The obvious exception here may be the antipathy, distaste, and hatred we often direct to antagonists, a.k.a. movie villains. However, though more needs to be said about this, since antipathy for the bad guys is usually the reverse side of – and, indeed, a function of – the sympathy we feel toward their rival protagonists, the case of antipathy is less of a counterexample to our hypothesis than it is a corollary.

Granting that sympathy is the glue that keeps us connected emotionally to the protagonists, the question remains about the way in which movies are able to recruit our sympathies as effectively as they do. In life outside the movies, our benevolent or altruistic attitudes toward others depend on factors such as kinship, group memberships of all sorts, and group interests. Of course, for both artistic and financial reasons, the creators of movies are aiming at larger audiences than a single extended family and often at audiences that cross regional, ethnic, national, and religious boundaries. And even where their targets are less than global, they must be careful not to trigger the sectarian differences that always exist in virtually every large group. This clearly presents the creators of popular motion pictures with a problem to be solved, namely, how to enlist the care and concern – the sympathetic feelings – for their fictional protagonists from mass audiences of heterogeneous backgrounds and different, often potentially clashing, interests.

That is, if sympathy is the crux of our relationship to the relevant characters in the movies, how is this sympathy mobilized? In everyday life, we extend our sympathies to those with whom we share interests or projects or loyalties, or to those who exemplify values of which we approve, or to those who fall under the protection of certain moral principles. But most of the interests, projects, and loyalties upon which we base many of our quotidian sympathies are highly specific to us. Needless to say, the moviemaker cannot hope to activate on behalf of the protagonists the individualized interests of every viewer. Rather, she must aim at engaging the audience at a fairly generic level of interests, projects, and loyalties. That is, she must find some common ground or touchstone amongst the diverse audience which will encourage us to find the protagonists to be worthy of our good will.

This is a design problem for the popular moviemaker. She must find a way in which to elicit from a disparate audience the converging desire that the protagonists do well – that is, she must elicit our felt conviction that it would be good for the protagonists to do well, or that they deserve to do well. What is the solution to this problem?

As a matter of empirical generalization, I conjecture that the most common answer to this challenge is the creation of protagonists who command the audience's *moral* endorsement. In other words, morality, of an extremely broad cast, provides the moviemaker with an interest, or project, or loyalty upon which viewers of diverse backgrounds can converge.

Moreover, inasmuch as there are certain moral touchstones shared across wide populations, the moviemaker has a lever on their allegiance.

By presenting protagonists who are morally appealing, the moviemaker secures the criterial wherewithal to garner the sympathy that is required for her intended audiences to be absorbed by the story. Such protagonists will meet the criterion of being deserving of our benevolence because they are morally deserving. It is no accident that the protagonists in movies are good guys. Good guys are precisely what the movie doctor calls for – characters likely to engender a pro-attitude from heterogeneous audiences of otherwise varied and often conflicting interests and loyalties. Morality of the fairly generic sort found in movies is just what people from different backgrounds are apt to agree upon, at least roughly. For instance, few would disagree that Maximus is wronged when his family is slaughtered in *Gladiator*, or that Cinderella is badly treated by her stepmother and sisters, or that Superman is a very nice person or that Story in *Lady in the Water* should not be eaten by the Scrunch.

Morality, especially of a fairly widely shared and often nearly universal gauge, supplies the moviemaker with the interests, or projects, or loyalties, or touchstones of affirmation which audiences from similar cultures, and even, frequently, from dissimilar ones, can agree. The protagonists, for example, will typically go out of their way to protect the lame and the halt, the helpless and the sick, the very young, the old, and the defenseless, while simultaneously treating them with dignity and respect. They evince a sense of fairness, justice, loyalty, honor, and honesty, and are altogether pro-social and especially pro-family (in principle, even if they're single), at least where the families in question are portrayed as wholesome ones (as opposed to the Texas Chainsaw Clan). These characters tell the truth and their keep their promises to good people, because they, themselves, are what we call *good people*.

The protagonists in movies are presented as morally righteous. This is undeniable in the greatest number of cases. But even so-called anti-heroes usually oppose some form of compromised moral order in the name of a deeper sense of rectitude. Once you get past their gruff exteriors, hard-boiled detectives always seem to discover that society is even more disreputable than they are. In the end, with respect to his girlfriend, Sam Spade seems almost Kantian in his sense of duty. Likewise, alienated gunslingers protect the little folk against greedy cattle barons, bullying railroad magnates, and, in the case of *The Magnificent Seven*, marauding warlords. Disaffected teenagers, in turn, really care about problems that adult society culpably neglects or misunderstands. And so on. No matter how anti-social the protagonist appears at first glance, he or she is quickly revealed to be pro-social at heart. Moreover, this is how it should be if sympathy is to take hold across a diverse audience whose likeliest point of convergence is apt to be morality, very generously construed.

By "generously construed," I do not simply mean that the audience shares some rough-and-ready principles or rules of thumb, but also a sense of what counts as virtuous. Protagonists win our approval and thence our sympathy, because they are typically portrayed as persons of a variety of virtues. Recognition of these virtues then precipitates in audiences the yearning that the protagonists do well and that their rivals do badly. Our desire is usually so strong that we generally stay to the end of the film just to make sure that things work out this way.

Of course, it must be conceded that it is not always the case that the protagonists with whom we align ourselves are what we would call morally upright; and yet they still get our sympathy. Consider, for example, caper films. However, when one examines the structure of these exercises one notices that the fictional world has been constructed in such a way that the aforesaid protagonists are the most virtuous characters in evidence. The forces of everyday society are either kept off-screen so that their countervailing claims never impinge on our sympathies or they are shown to be venal and/or inexcusably stupid. That is, where the universe in the moving picture is a fallen one, as it is in the TV series *The Sopranos*, a figure like Tony can warrant our sympathies, because, even though he is not moral in any absolute sense, compared to everyone else in the fictional New Jersey where he lives he is the best of a very, very bad lot.

Solidarity

If sympathy is as central to our emotional response to movie protagonists as has been argued, then instances of infectious identification cannot be very common, since sympathetic feelings, conceived as emotions, are not ones that we share with their objects. Sympathy, as mentioned earlier, is, by definition, directed at others. The protagonist does not feel sympathy for himself; were he to do so to any appreciable extent that would probably turn us off. However, though essential to our emotional bonding with protagonists, sympathy pure and simple is usually not the whole story of our emotional connections to protagonists. It is generally supplemented by another emotional state which we may call *solidarity*.

Some fictions have only protagonists. The film *Just My Luck* is an example. There are two major characters – Ashley Albright and Jake

Harden. Their names are clues to their most important attributes. She is always the beneficiary of deliriously good fortune. When she leaves her apartment without an umbrella, it immediately stops raining. When she hails a cab, it arrives from nowhere. And so on. Jake is just the opposite. If he bends down, his pants will split; if he picks up a five-dollar bill, it will be smeared with canine feces. But their luck magically changes hands at a masquerade ball when they kiss, anonymously, while dancing. Now everything Ashley attempts leads to disaster, while Jake becomes a very successful record producer. The rest of the story involves Ashley tracking Jake down in order to reclaim her good fortune with another kiss. However, they fall in love and kiss their way to some kind of providential equilibrium; they will live happily and unhappily ever after in the normal proportions.

What is striking about *Just My Luck* – and this is also true of many other romantic comedies – is that there is no real villain. There are some people who present temporary obstacles to the main characters, but they are not full-fledged antagonists. They are not on the scene long enough for our antipathy toward them to take root, and, anyway, by the end of the film, they all may turn out, by twists of fate, to be nice people after all. With *Just My Luck*, we are encouraged to feel care and concern for Ashley and Jake. But there are no real bad guys.

The majority of movies, however, are not like this. Most pit the protagonists and the other nice people against some adversaries. We are not only prompted emotionally to embrace the good people as members of a generic "Us"; their opponents belong to "Them." Moreover, these "Them" are not just regarded as the opposing team. They are usually presented as people we hate, indeed, often *love* to hate.

If sympathy toward "Us" is characteristically elicited by portraying the protagonists and the other nice people in the fiction as morally good, then the antipathy generated toward "Them" is generally provoked by representing them as morally blemished. Whereas the protagonist is nice to nice people – treating good people with good manners – the villain is at least rude to those he perceives to be his inferiors and very often what he does to them is much worse. The antagonists pillage, cheat, lie, rob, rape, kill, and so on. The hero pets the old sleeping dog on the doorstep; the bad guy kicks it out of his way.

Movies are generally political in the sense defined by the philosopher Carl Schmitt. The fictional population in the motion picture is standardly partitioned into friends and enemies – into Us and Them. Sympathy, motivated by morality, disposes us to assimilate the protagonists into Us.

But that bond is then further strengthened by introducing enemies who, in movies, are customarily marked by being constructed as bad people. As I am now using the concept of "solidarity," it is the name of the complex emotive relation of sympathy-for-the-protagonists *plus* antipathy-for-the-antagonists. This is a psychological condition that most moving pictures strive to raise in audiences. They aspire to dispose the viewer to feel emotionally allied to the protagonist and against the antagonist. The antagonist is designed to instill anger, indignation, hatred, and sometimes moral disgust in us.

Unlike sympathy in everyday life which we tend, all things being equal, to extend quite readily to most of those around us by default, in movies our sympathy must be won. The most efficient way of doing this is to render the relevant characters morally appealing. Our bond with these characters can then be reinforced by setting an array of nemeses against those whom we find repulsive, customarily because their various failings – from petty vices to outright viciousness – are emphatically foregrounded. I suspect that, in most cases, our antipathy for the villains is engendered by their vices, whereas sympathy for the various positive characters is primarily elicited by their superabundantly evident virtues.

However, in some instances, characters may secure our sympathy on the rebound, so to speak. That is, we may be so appalled by the villain that our care and concern goes out to whomever he opposes. In other words, sometimes solidarity in movies may result from the "enemy-of-my-enemy-is-my-friend" phenomenon. This, furthermore, explains why it is that we sometimes find ourselves siding with characters whose morals we do not otherwise share, like Hannibal Lector. We side with Lector in Ridley Scott's *Hannibal*, I suspect, because we find his enemies – those who plan to feed him alive to pigs – to be so much more morally depraved than he is.

Solidarity involves sympathy and antipathy viscerally felt. Though our sympathetic feelings toward the protagonists are not shared by them, our hatred for the villains often is. But we do not hate the villain just because the protagonists do. Rather, we have detected co-incidentally on our own many of the same morally noxious traits of the antagonists that have impressed the protagonists so deeply. Thus, when our hatred is congruent with the protagonist's hatred of the bad guy, the antipathy component of our feelings of solidarity with the hero is essentially conjoint with his. We may air our hatred for the villain at the same time the protagonist does, but primarily as a result of our own process of moral appraisal which has been elicited by criterial prefocusing.

Mirror reflexes

We have been exploring several kinds of emotional relationships between audiences and movie characters. These have included circumstances: (1) where our emotions may be type-identical with those of the protagonists, but due to our own independent appraisal of the relevant situations (in response to criterial prefocusing); (2) where our emotions vectorially converge on the emotional states of characters; (3) where we sympathize with the characters (which, of course, may, but need not, be an instance of a vectorially converging emotion); and (4) where we emote in solidarity with the protagonist (where the antipathy component may be a response congruent with the protagonist's though one we find ourselves in as a result of our own appraisal of the situation). None of these cases corresponds to the popular model of infectious identification which requires that the audience member be in an emotional state that is type-identical with that of the protagonist just because the pertinent character is in that state. But let us conclude by briefly examining a fifth affective relation – one which comes closer to the model of infectious identification, and whose very existence has probably lent some credence to the ubiquitous talk about identification and simulation with movie characters.

What I have in mind here are what may be called *mirror reflexes*. By calling them "reflexes," I mean to signal that they are not full-fledged emotional states. Consequently, the existence of mirror reflexes does not corroborate the model of infectious identification, though it is understandable that some might think it does. But, at the same time, no account of our affective relationship to motion pictures would be adequate without a discussion of mirror reflexes. So, what are mirror reflexes?

Occasionally when speaking to another person, we suddenly realize that we have adopted their facial expression. They are frowning; we start to frown. Or, they are smiling and we find ourselves smiling. We have an unmistakable tendency to ape our interlocutors – to mirror them. This is the case not only with facial expressions, but also with gestures and postures. We tend to fall into step with our companions; when they're walking tall, so are we. If our informant bends toward us conspiratorially, we bend toward them in response. When we watch the outfielder stretch to intercept a fly ball, the muscles in our arm tug slightly in that direction. And so forth. We have an involuntary tendency to mirror automatically the behavior, especially the expressive behavior, of our conspecifics.

Putatively, we do this in order to gain some sense of what they are feeling. By configuring our own facial expression after the fashion of a fellow conversationalist – grimacing when she grimaces – we secure some inkling of her inner state. The feedback from the disposition of our facial muscles buzzes our autonomic nervous system in a way that is presumably isomorphic to what is going on in her system, so long as she is not dissembling. This does not give us full access to her emotional state, but it provides an important clue, since it yields something like a facsimile of the bodily-feeling component of her overall state. It does not tell us her precise appraisal of the object of her state, but it does relay the visceral sensation that goes with that appraisal.

Similarly, gestures and postures are also mimicked – though usually only in a highly truncated manner – in order to gather information about what is percolating inside our conspecifics. If everyone around us starts looking upward, we do too. This mimicry is predominantly automatic, not intentional. It is, in all probability, part of our biological heritage.

Children on their caregiver's knee evince mirror reflexes in abundance. Clearly this behavior is a boon for learning the emotional repertoire – and much else – of one's culture, for it enables the child to discern the situations the caregiver associates with feelings of distress or elation. Among adults, mirror reflexes are also highly adaptive, since they facilitate social communication. Albeit subliminally, one can intuit – at least very broadly – the temperament of a room or the disposition of one's spouse by using one's body as a detector of the kind of internal sensations that are apt to be associated with the manifest expressions of others. These communicative advantages, moreover, are so adaptive that they are probably bred in the bone.

When by mimicry I "catch" the negative vibes or feelings of distress of another, I immediately survey the environment in order to locate the source of his discomfort. His negative affect alerts me in my own musculature to the likelihood that I may soon need to mobilize some vectorially converging emotion, such as fear or possibly anger. Mirror reflexes, which *may* be linked to what neuroscientists call mirror neurons, are not only relevant for gleaning information about what surrounds other people. By relaying to us something of what they are feeling, mirror reflexes help us cope with others. Detecting that one's boss is in a foul mood via mirror reflexes is useful in deciding when to ask him – or not ask him – for a raise. And, in addition, mirror reflexes are immensely functional for coordinating group activities – for getting the troops reeved up as they march off into battle in lock-step camaraderie. In sum, the human capacity for mirror reflexes is, in all likelihood, a stunning asset from the perspective of natural selection, since it is a means for gathering affective information about conspecifics and for synchronizing joint ventures, from face-to-face conversations to cheerleading to military maneuvers.

Aestheticians have been aware of the phenomenon of mirror reflexes at least since the writings of Theodor Lipps. And the filmmaker Sergei Eisenstein explicitly attempted to exploit Lipps' insights not only in his theory of filmmaking, but in his practice as well. Though neither he nor Lipps employed the terminology of mirror reflexes, Eisenstein included close-ups of stereotypical facial expressions and body parts, such as clenched fists, in the hope of inspiring the sort of mimicry in viewers that would prepare them viscerally for the kinds of emotional states that he wished to arouse in them. Less theoretically inclined motion picture makers also discovered the importance of such affective modeling intuitively and it has been a staple of popular cinema since the 1920s. This is a legacy, furthermore, that film has bequeathed to TV. Undoubtedly, a significant amount of the affect stirred up by audiovisual entertainments is connected to the way in which they educe muscular mimicry in their audiences.

Watching a videotape of *Riverdance*, the audience taps its feet, accessing a simulacrum of the spirited pulse of the dancers. As Bruno in Hitchcock's *Strangers on a Train* reaches for the lighter that he has dropped into the sewer, our arm muscles flex, within the circumscribed ambit of our theater seat, in a manner echoing his in order to help us feel his intention within our body. It is not that we identify with Bruno morally or emotionally, but we ape his gesture in order to help us determine a glimmer of what he is feeling. At the conclusion of *Alien Resurrection*, we get a feeling, strangely enough, for the monster's pain that results from his mother's betrayal, not because we identify with Ripley's progeny but because we involuntarily mimic his facial expression.*

And even before we see the monster displayed on screen, the screaming visage of its victim, inscribed with horror and framed in close-up, prompts us to tense up our faces analogously in a way that signals through our muscles that things are about to get unpleasant. The activity on screen primes mimicry of a partial or limited variety which can deliver information about the internal states of characters which we sample in terms of similar sensations in ourselves. Though not full-scale emotions – but only feelings sans objects and, thus, without appraisals thereof – these sensations may nevertheless be a serviceable source of the affective grip such motion pictures have on us in at least two ways.

---

* I owe this example to Amy Coplan.

First, these mirror reflexes contribute to keeping the excitement level in our bodies elevated, thereby realizing one of the abiding promises of popular movies. And second, they may make available information that we can integrate into our more encompassing emotional responses to the characters. The bodily feelings of distress that are imprinted on the contorted features of the protagonist are relayed to us by our selective imitation of his expression so that we can use the dysphoric taste of that sensation as a recognitional cue for the kind of emotion that is appropriate on his behalf – as, for example, sorrow would be appropriate were we to detect by motor mimicry that he is feeling some sort of pain. That is, mirror reflexes may function as sub-routines in the formation of our emotional responses to fictional characters, not only alerting us to the general valence – whether positive or negative – of their mental states, but also calibrating the kind of passion we need to send back their way.

Mirror reflexes are not examples of emotional identification since they do not involve the replication of complete emotional states by only the feeling component and, in fact, they need not duplicate precisely the same feelings, but only vectorially similar ones. Nor are they what are sometimes nowadays called simulations of the emotional states of characters, since they do not employ beliefs and desires. On the other hand, they are important elements of affective address in motion pictures. They can make our bodies vibrate with feeling in the presence of certain characters, and, even more importantly, they can facilitate our recognition of character emotion and modulate our own emotional response to it. In this regard, it would appear that motion pictures, including movies and TV, have resources for exciting the affective reactions of audiences that literary fictions, popular and otherwise, lack.

This capacity is perhaps particularly evident with respect to a structure alluded to several times already in this chapter, namely, point-of-view editing. This figure, at bare minimum, comprises two shots – what have been called the point/glance shot and the point/object shot. The point/glance shot involves a character looking (glancing) offscreen; then the point/object shot shows us what (the object) the character is looking at. The hero in *Rear Window* looks toward the camera – presumably across the courtyard in the world of the fiction; then there is a cut and we see what he sees – a man in an opposite apartment mauling the onlooker's fiancée.

This cinematic figure can be put through its paces either progressively (starting with the point/glance shot) or retrogressively (starting with the point/object shot and backing up to the point/glance shot). The figure can also be iterated; the editor can repeat the figure several times progressively, retrogressively, or in some combination of the two. In early cinema, when filmmakers were somewhat anxious about whether or not people would understand this cinematic figure, it was often reiterated through several cycles. However, today, repetitions are less pronounced, except for dramatic effect.

The comprehensibility of point-of-view editing rests, first and foremost, on certain biological tendencies of the human organism (as well as other mammals) – specifically, the tendency to track the glance of our conspecifics (and, indeed, of other animals) to its target. This is a way in which to derive some insight into what is going on in the minds of others – we follow the gaze of the hostess of the party as she keeps stealing glances at the door and then we speculate that she is expecting someone. This tropism is inborn; a child on his mother's knee naturally follows her eyes wherever they point. When a caregiver introduces a word, the child looks at what mother is looking at, thereby, in the process, being inducted into the conceptual scheme of the culture.

But the point-of-view editing structure does not only exploit our innate tendency to trace the gaze of our conspecifics for the purpose of mind-reading. It also mobilizes the mirror-reflex system for the sake of cinematic communication. For, when the character's face appears in close-up on screen, the viewer has an automatic tendency to imitate her expression, thereby getting an intimation of the range or tenor of her inner state. If mimicking the character's demeanor causes unpleasant turmoil within us, we ready ourselves – we calibrate our expectations – to muster some dysphoric emotion, such as anger, fear, horror, or the like. The character's face in the point/glance shot, in other words, functions as an emotional range-finder, demarcating the valence of the emotions appropriate to the objects we are about to see in the point/object shot and suggesting the approximate scope of the emotions we need to enlist in response. In this way, point-of-view editing capitalizes upon an evolutionary adaptation that took place countless millennia before the birth of cinema.

Although the moving image is a cultural invention, it is useful never to lose sight of the fact that in many ways it succeeds as well as it does because it freely avails itself of our biological heritage. The motion picture is an artform, but, as with art in general, we must not suppose that it is solely an affair of the mind. Motion pictures address our bodies as well. Though we have seen this phenomenon in evidence in other chapters, the way in which moving images interact with our bodies is perhaps never more blatant than with regard to the hold motion pictures can exert over our affective life, including, notably, our emotions, that nexus of mind and body.

Movies can, so to speak, reach under our skin and stir up our feelings. Moviemakers, in this regard as in others, are amateur psychologists, experimenting intuitively with the human sensory apparatus for the purpose of art, fame, and money, but often with results that sometimes reveal how we, as incarnated beings, work. This is not said in order to attempt to reduce the moving image to a repertoire of biomechanical triggers. The moving image is undeniably a cultural creation. But it is important not to lose sight of the fact that culture, including our affective and emotional life, is constructed out of the biological possibilities delivered up by natural selection, often for purposes never dreamt of on the sprawling savannahs where those possibilities took root.

Suggested Reading

The leading volume with respect to motion pictures and the emotions is *Passionate Views*, edited by Carl Plantinga and Gregory Smith (Baltimore, MD: Johns Hopkins University Press, 1999). Though not devoted to affect in motion pictures in particular, but to art and the emotions in general, another very important volume is *Emotion and the Arts*, edited by Mette Hjort and Sue Laver (Oxford: Oxford University Press, 1997). On the range of affect in motion pictures, see Jinhee Choi, "Fits and Startles: Cognitivism Revisited," *Journal of Aesthetics and Art Criticism* 61:2 (Spring 2003), 149–57.

The contemporary discussion of the paradox of fiction was introduced by Colin Radford in "How Can We Be Moved by the Fate of Anna Karenina?," *Proceedings of the Aristotelian Society*, supplement 49 (1975), 67–81. One of the most important attempts to solve the paradox of fiction is Kendall Walton's "Fearing Fictions," *Journal of Philosophy* 75:1 (Jan. 1978), 5–27. Interesting comments on Walton's article include Alex Neill, "Fear, Fiction and Make Believe," *Journal of Aesthetics and Art Criticism* 49:1 (Winter 1991), 47–56, and Richard Moran, "The Expression of Feeling in Imagination," *The Philosophical Review* 103:1 (Jan. 1994), 75–106. Kendall Walton responds to some of his critics in his article in *Emotion and the Arts*.

Concerning the relation of the emotions to movie genres, sources include Flo Leibowitz, "Apt Feelings, or Why 'Women's Films' Aren't Trivial," in *Post-Theory: Reconstructing Film Studies*, edited by David Bordwell and Noël Carroll (Madison: University of Wisconsin Press, 1996), and *The Philosophy of Horror,* by Noël Carroll (New York: Routledge, 1990). Carroll's view is criticized in many places, including Berys Gaut's "The Enjoyment of Horror: A Response to Carroll," *British Journal of Aesthetics* 35:3 (July 1995), 284–9. On suspense, see Noël Carroll, "The

Paradox of Suspense," in his *Beyond Aesthetics: Philosophical Essays* (Cambridge: Cambridge University Press, 2001).

On the issue of identification, see Amy Coplan, "Empathic Engagement in Narrative Fictions," *Journal of Aesthetics and Art Criticism* 62:2 (Spring 2004), 141–52. See also Berys Gaut, "Identification and Emotion in Narrative Film," in *Passionate Views*, ed. Plantinga and Smith. Criticism of Gaut and Coplan can be found in Noël Carroll, "Sympathy for the Devil," in *Philosophy and the Sopranos*, edited by Richard Greene (LaSalle, ILL: Open Court, 2004), and id., "On the Ties that Bind: Characters, the Emotions, and Popular Fictions," in *Philosophy and the Interpretation of Popular Culture*, edited by William Irwin and Jorge Garcia (Lanham, MD: Rowman & Littlefield, 2006).

The most seminal articles regarding simulation theory with respect to aesthetics are Gregory Currie's "The Moral Psychology of Fiction," *Australasian Journal of Philosophy* 73:2 (1995), 250–9, and his "Imagination and Simulation: Aesthetics Meets Cognitive Science," in *Mental Simulation*, edited by Martin Davies and Tony Stone (Oxford: Blackwell Publishing, 1995). Criticism of this view may be found in Aaron Meskin and Jonathan Weinberg, "Emotion, Fiction and Cognitive Architecture," *British Journal of Aesthetics* 43:1 (Jan. 2003), 18–34. See also Carroll, "On the Ties that Bind," and also his "Simulation, Emotions, and Morality" in his *Beyond Aesthetics*. The major book-length study of the emotional relation of audiences and movie characters is Murray Smith, *Engaging Characters* (Oxford: Clarendon Press, 1995).

On mirror reflexes, see Carl Plantinga, "The Scene of Empathy and the Human Face," in *Passionate Views*, ed. Plantinga and Smith. For psychological background on this phenomenon, read Elaine Hatfield, John T. Cacioppo, and Richard L. Rapson, *Emotional Contagion* (Cambridge: Cambridge University Press, 1994), especially chapter 2.

For an up-to-date philosophical discussion of the emotions, see Jesse Prinz, *Gut Reactions* (Oxford: Oxford University Press, 2004). On art and the emotions, see Jenefer Robinson, *Deeper Than Reason* (Oxford: Oxford University Press, 2005).

One aspect of affect not discussed in this chapter is mood. For an introduction to this topic, see Noël Carroll, "Art and Mood," *The Monist* 84:4 (Oct. 2004), 521–55. See also Gregory Smith, *Film Structure and the Emotion System* (Cambridge: Cambridge University Press, 2003).

Chapter Seven

Evaluation

In the preceding chapter, and throughout much of this book, we have been concerned with the relationship between various motion picture structures and the corresponding experiences said structures engender in audiences. Thus, in a manner of speaking, we have stayed inside the movie house. But in this chapter, let us walk outside onto the street and listen to how we talk about moving pictures after we've seen them.

You meet a friend. She says that she has just seen a motion picture – say, *Caché*. What do you say? What do you ask? Supposing that you know that it is a current motion picture, the odds are that you respond with something like: "How was it?" or "Was it any good?" That is, even before you inquire about the specifics of the story, you are likely first to request an evaluation. Moreover, your friend will be happy to gratify you; for evaluating motion pictures is an activity that most people enjoy. We not only engage in moviegoing in anticipation of the experience of it; most of us, in addition, delight in assessing that experience afterwards and then comparing our evaluation of it with those of other viewers.

Perhaps when you first consider the topic of evaluating motion pictures, you are prone initially to think of movie critics. These are people who are in the business of pronouncing upon the value of motion pictures. There are so many movies to see and so little time. Consequently, almost all of us have to fall back on the advice of movie critics from time to time in order to inform our choice of viewing fare.

There are several different ways in which a movie critic may carry out her role. Two of the most common ones are those of the consumer reporter, on the one hand, and the taste-maker, on the other. Consumer reporters try to predict which movies most of their readership will love and which they will hate. For such readers, these critics are consumer guides. Such critics treat themselves as live-detectors, presuming that what they like, their readers will like too. Critics who aspire to the function of consumer reporters speak in the *vox populi*. It is probably the case that most, though not all, journalistic movie critics intend to be of this sort. Or, at least, a great many of their readers expect this of them.

Other critics aim at being taste-makers. They do not attempt to reflect the inclinations of others; instead they hope to shape the taste of their readers. They are always on the lookout for motion pictures that are special, even if – and perhaps sometimes especially if – they are not obviously so; and, in the best of cases, these critics also suggest how the rest of us might learn to go on to appreciate these outstanding motion pictures as well.

The taste-makers and the consumer guides, of course, are often at odds with each other, given their respective aims. What the consumer guide dismisses as boring, the taste-maker may recognize as a deliberate strategy that effectively articulates the theme of the pointlessness of modern life, as in the case of *La Notte* by Michelangelo Antonioni.

Readers who prefer their tastes confirmed will gravitate toward the consumer guides. Those who want their taste expanded are apt to seek and to admire those critics who are able to pick out singular cinematic achievements and to contextualize and explain them.

However, though the role of the movie critic commands an important position in cultures like ours that are awash with movies 24/7 (in movie theaters, on television, on videocassettes, DVDs, personal computers, and even cellphones), as hinted earlier, it would be a grave mistake to think of moving picture evaluation as exclusively a professional affair. Evaluating movies is something that we all do all of the time.

Nor do I mean by this merely that we automatically form preferences for some of the movies we see over others and rank some of them as better than the rest. As humans, we naturally tend to do this with most of our experiences. But with regard to moviegoing, this is not something that simply happens to us automatically. It is, as already remarked, an activity that we avidly pursue. Think about it: when we talk about motion pictures with others, most people spend most of their time airing their evaluation of the movie rather than summarizing, let alone analyzing, it.

And when we converse back and forth with acquaintances about moving pictures we've all seen, most of our energy is devoted to trading evaluations, comparing them, sometimes sharing them, and often arguing about them. Mary says that so-and-so's performance was great; Marty responds "If that's an Irish accent, I'll eat my shillelagh." Indeed, we frequently read critics after we have seen a motion picture in order to enter into imaginary conversations with them, sometimes agreeing with them (and congratulating them on their extraordinary intelligence and sensitivity), though also often wondering aloud what galaxy they come from.

Moviegoing is frequently portrayed as a solitary transaction in which each individual spectator communes with the brightened screen in a darkened room. But moviegoing, as a folkway of contemporary life, is more sociable than this sketch allows. Moviegoing is part of our social life. After we have seen a motion picture, we want to talk about it with others. We want to tell them what we have seen, to exchange ideas with others who have seen the same movies, and to discuss our reactions and theirs. Moviegoing is a fixture of everyday conversation; it is a virtually natural pretext for sociability. On occasion, we may even swap opinions about movies with strangers. And, as a moment's reflection should reveal, evaluation is at the crux of this very elemental form of social exchange and consolidation. It is through such encounters that many of us express and develop ourselves as cultural beings.

This is all highly abstract. But what I have in mind can be clarified by recalling a very common experience. You attend a moving picture with some friends. Afterwards, as often happens, you go out for tea and coffee, or sweets, or a drink. You talk about the motion picture that you have just seen, remarking upon the parts you liked or disliked. But, of course, quite often the conversation does not just end with a summary of personal preferences. The discussion may often turn to whether or not the motion picture is good or whether it worked. That is, there is an almost ineluctable tendency for the conversation to drift from reports of subjective enjoyment or lethargy to questions of objective evaluation.

Experiences like these are part of the typical life of moviegoing – which is to say that evaluation is near the heart of this practice for most of us. It adds zest to the activity. It is something that ordinary moving picture audiences care about deeply. It is something that viewers want to do and are interested in doing well. That too is one of the reasons that audiences read motion picture critics – not simply for advice about what to see, but also for models of how to talk about and to conceptualize what they see.

And yet this is an aspect of the practice of motion pictures about which contemporary philosophers and theorists of cinema are virtually silent. So, in this last chapter, let us join the moviegoing audience where they live and speak of evaluating moving pictures.

Movie Evaluation as a Philosophical Problem

Thus far, I have alleged that evaluating motion pictures is something that we come to almost naturally. So, you might ask, what business does philosophy have here? "Bug off philosophy!" you might be tempted to say.

In order to motivate philosophy's intrusion into the discussion, let us return to the conversation between you and your friends that we inaugurated two paragraphs ago.

Imagine that we have just seen a movie together – for example, Spike Lee's *Inside Man*. You like it; I don't. As often as not, the colloquy will not stop there, as it probably would if we were comparing our preferences in condiments – with me voting loudly for mustard and you plumping enthusiastically for ketchup. Rather, you are liable to press further and to defend your liking of *Inside Man* on the grounds that it is good – asserting, in other words, that your liking of it is justified.

I reply that I do not deny that you liked the motion picture – I concede that this is a psychological fact about you. I take your word for it. I grant your authority in the matter of your likes and dislikes. But I add that your liking of it does not prove that *Inside Man* is a good movie. For, it is eminently consistent for someone to like a fiction and for the fiction in question to be bad, even abominable, at the same time. For example, I've always had a soft spot in my heart for the novels of Edgar Rice Burroughs, yet, *entre nous*, most of them are god-awful.

There is no logically reliable connection between a person's liking of *x* and *x*'s prospective goodness. The correlation between what is liked by people and what is objectively worthwhile is radically contingent. Many love fast food that is nutritionally compromised. So, I accept that your liking of *Inside Man* is sincere, but then retort that this is perfectly compatible with *Inside Man* being a bad movie. Indeed, I up the ante; I contend that *Inside Man* is actually flawed, in fact, irreparably so.

Yet, at this point in our dialogue, take notice that we have left off talking simply about our likes and our dislikes. We are speaking in the idiom of good and bad. Consequently, we have entered the realm of objective evaluation. In effect, you are claiming that any reasonable, informed, and suitably backgrounded viewer ought to regard *Inside Man* as a good film, whereas I am denying precisely that.

Of utmost importance, observe: we are *arguing*. There would no point in our arguing about what we like. You like ketchup; I like mustard. That's it. Period. Full stop. We accept each other's preferences as facts; I don't suppose that it makes much sense to attempt to argue you out of your relish for ketchup. Indeed, what sorts of reasons might I bring to bear?

However, in stark contrast, we are *arguing* about *Inside Man*. And that entails, furthermore, that our discussion revolves around coming up with *reasons* that we believe should sway or even compel others to accept our viewpoint. It is just this – our implicit appeal to third parties and their standards of evidence and inference – that marks our interchange as objective. For we intend to be playing by the inter-subjective rules, or, at least, various ascertainable protocols of rationality.

As has already been stressed amply, a subjective report of a like or a dislike is a psychological fact about us. There is no disputing your likes, even if they are unusual, such as a taste for extremely charred toast. For the expression of a preference of this kind does not, on the face of it, aspire to command the agreement of others. If you dislike broccoli that is not a reason for me to dislike broccoli, since reasons – as opposed to sheer likings – are objective.

Reasons are offered to others with an implicit claim upon their assent. Thus, if you provide a reason for saying that *Inside Man* is a good film and if that reason is relevant and acceptable, then you expect, with sound warrant, that others should concur with your assessment. In our discussion of *Inside Man,* our behavior – our exchange of putative reasons – gives every appearance of being committed to objectivity. You do not, red-faced, pound the table and shout "But I like it!" Instead, you try to find objective reasons that will convince others, notably me, that your assessment is *correct*.

Therefore, you have exited the domain of psychology and embraced normativity. In the face of disagreement, you are now conversationally implicated in establishing that *Inside Man* is a good movie, for *anyone* with functioning eyes to see, ears to hear, and a mind, suitably prepared, to appreciate it. However, as all of us have experienced, our reasons do not always dissolve disagreements about movies as easily as a dehumidifier dispels dampness. So, how are such disputes to be resolved?

Here in a nutshell, then, is one particularly nettlesome problem. The very possibility of the objectivity of motion picture evaluation (as a sub-species of artistic evaluation in general) is a conceptual challenge which invites, indeed beckons, philosophy onto the scene. For it falls to philosophy to engage with and to relieve the seemingly intractably stubborn fact of such disagreement. That is, we not only diverge in our preferences for movies. We think that these divergences, at least in important cases, can be negotiated, at least some of the time, in terms of objective evaluations. But how is this feasible? It the task of the philosophy of motion pictures, since it is a precinct, as established in the first chapter of this book, of the philosophy of art, to address questions like this.

We believe that our contrasting opinions can ultimately be backed up with reasons that others – in fact, nearly all of the relevant others – ought to find probative. We do not think that we are merely airing personal whims or confessing guilty pleasures when we say that Jean Renoir's *Rules of the Game* is a better film than Stanley Kramer's *Guess Who's Coming to Dinner*. We think that a disagreement like this one can be resolved rationally – that is, with reasons. *Reasons*, properly so called, portend objectivity. Nevertheless, where do these reasons come from and what grounds them? Inquiring minds would like to know; and they are surely not perverse in this desire. Clearly, it is the responsibility of philosophy to speak to this urgent issue – the question of the adjudication of apparently relentless disagreement.

In order to get a handle on how such seemingly immovable disagreements might be negotiated rationally, let us follow our earlier, imaginary dispute about *Inside Man* just a little bit further. You say *Inside Man* is good; I say it is bad. What happens next? Very often we start mentioning other movies. You refer to comparable suspense films (with hostage-taking), such as, for instance, William Wyler's *The Desperate Hours* and/or Sidney Lumet's *Dog Day Afternoon* or F. Gary Gray's *The Negotiator*. Your purpose here might be to get me to agree that these are good films; since, if I agree that they are good films, then you will argue that consistency (a fundamental test for rational objectivity) requires that I admit that *Inside Man* is also good. For, once granting the premise – that *Inside Man* shares essential features with these other suspense thrillers which I supposedly have already accepted to be good – I am bound by logical analogy to judge *Inside Man* to be good as well.

At this point, the debate could go in several directions. I might deny that *Inside Man* is really analogous to the three exemplars of suspense thrillers that you have adduced, or I might reject the attribution of goodness to any of the suspense thrillers that you recommend as paradigmatic ones. If I take the first option, I must show that the analogies which you are attempting to enlist are either insubstantial or implausible; this will, perforce, be a matter of close analysis.

But let us imagine that I accept your analogies and, instead, that I go for the second option: I deny that any of the analogues that you have dragooned on behalf of *Inside Man* are themselves good films. Therefore, even if *Inside Man* is strictly analogous in essential respects to your hypothetical paradigms, that premise affords no support in our debate for your contention that *Inside Man* is good, since, by my book, none of the other films cited have anything going for them either. So the fact that *Inside Man* is analogous to them counts for nothing.

However, if I reject all of your paradigms at this juncture, then you certainly have the right to demand that I produce one of my own. What exactly, you ask, is an example by my lights of a good motion picture? Imagine I say *Fast, Cheap & Out of Control* by Errol Morris.

Undoubtedly, you will be taken aback. For, though you agree that *Fast, Cheap & Out of Control* is a good film, you cannot help feeling that somehow I have missed the point. Why? Because that is not the kind of motion picture that *Inside Man* is. *Fast, Cheap & Out of Control* is an essayistic film – an open-textured documentary that encourages the viewer to contemplate the thin line between genius and loony obsession as well as that between the appearance of intelligence and massive parallel processing. What possible relevance can a meditative nonfiction film like *Fast, Cheap & Out of Control* have to gauging the quality of a fictional exercise in thriller suspense such as *Inside Man*? *Inside Man* and *Fast, Cheap & Out of Control* belong to very different categories – they have different purposes, and, consequently, they mandate different standards of evaluation. Isn't it as they say – apples and oranges? Surely, to devalue *Inside Man* because it is not like *Fast, Cheap & Out of Control* strikes most of us as a gross non sequitur.

One feature of evaluation that the preceding debate illustrates is the degree to which our assessment of the merits of a motion picture depends upon placing the movie in question in a certain category. For example, we situate *Inside Man* in the category of the suspense thriller in order to assay its value. It is a psychological fact about human beings that we think this way – to evaluate, we categorize. The rationale for this is that categories are generally connected to acknowledged purposes which, in turn, provide standards of evaluation. For instance, when we classify a piece of cutlery as a steak knife, we identify that its purpose is to slice cleanly through thick pieces of beef, and, consequently, that a good-making feature of such an implement is its sharpness. Sharpness, in other words, is a standard of goodness in steak knives because it is in virtue of its sharpness that a steak knife can discharge its purpose. In this way, categories, purposes, and standards of evaluation form a matrix.

When we view a moving picture, we also – as a matter of our psychological make-up – put it in a category, and this shapes our expectations and, thereby, recruits a certain set of standards. Our disagreement about *Inside Man* at the present juncture turns upon the fact that you have situated *Inside Man* in one category or comparison class and it seems very likely that I have located it in another.

That evaluation is tied to categorization is, as already indicated, a matter of psychology, not logic. Thus, we do not resolve the question of whether or not *Inside Man* is good by merely citing the different categories into which we are disposed to slot it. That may clarify our differences by pinpointing precisely why we hold such different views, but it does not settle our dispute. For our debate will not be adjudicated rationally until we are able to determine which of our competing categories is the *correct* one (or, at least, the more correct one). To decide who is right on the issue of the quality of *Inside Man*, we need to establish who has accessed the right (or the predominantly right) category.

Note that our disagreement about the goodness or badness of *Inside Man* has escalated, in a manner of speaking, into a debate about categories. Which category or categories is/are appropriate or correct in this instance? So, our dispute, then, looks like it can be brought to a reasonable conclusion just in case we can prove which category is the apposite one to bring to bear on *Inside Man*.

Indeed, a great many problems with respect to movie evaluation – though not every one of them – could be solved, if only we had a way to fix the correct category or categories for weighing the moving picture in question. But how does one find the correct category? That is the million-dollar question. For without an answer to that question, it appears that our dispute over the right way to classify *Inside Man* is as rationally intransigent as the issue of whether or not *Inside Man* is good.

The Classical Solution

As we have just seen, one of the central philosophical problems of motion picture evaluation is what we can call "the problem of the correct category." Though this is not a problem that has preoccupied many contemporary theorists of the moving image, it was a matter of overriding concern for what might be called "classical film theory" – that is, roughly speaking, film theory before the advent of semiotics and post-structuralism. This is the kind of theory we encountered previously in the chapter on medium specificity. Figures such as Rudolf Arnheim and the Soviet montagists are representatives of what might be thought of as the first generation of film theorists, whilst realists, such as André Bazin and Siegfried Kracauer, belong to a second generation.

One way of characterizing classical film theory is to identify it as centrally preoccupied with isolating the essence of cinema, which, as discussed in chapter 2, is what many conveniently label as the *cinematic*. The *cinematic*, as we saw earlier, was believed to be that which differentiated film from other artforms, such as theater and painting. Moreover, classical film theorists were not simply interested in finding which property or properties in fact distinguished film from other artforms. The differentiae they sought were also often assumed to have normative implications. That is, classical film theorists were hunting for the way in which film *should* distinguish itself from the other arts.

Speaking summarily, the classical film theorists maintained that cinema, which, for them, meant *film*, should be cinematic. Of course, the various classical film theorists defined what they took to be cinematic in different, even conflicting ways. However, in the main, each had a conception of what counted as cinematic, and they generally also agreed that films ought to aspire to be as cinematic as possible. For the classical theorist, the failure of a film to be cinematic, however that was to be construed, is a defect.

But what does this talk of the cinematic have to do with the problem of the correct category? Simply this: in effect, for the classical film theorist, *all films* – or, at least, all the films we would want to talk about from the artistic point of view – belong in a single category, which we might tag with the label of *film as film*. Therefore, debates about the goodness or badness of a given movie can be referred back to the question of whether or not the specimen under examination is cinematic – that is, whether or not it is a proper instance of the category of film as film. Thus, in order to determine whether *Inside Man* is a good film, we would have to demonstrate that it is cinematic.

One obvious advantage of the classical approach to the problem of the correct category is that it makes the evaluation of moving pictures an extremely unified practice. The notion of the cinematic, in the hands of a given classical theorist, provides a single scale upon which all motion pictures can be weighed and compared. Whether or not a movie is good (relative to the category of film as film) can be ascertained by showing that it is cinematic, while exactly how good it is can be gauged in virtue of how cinematic it is. Likewise, one can say that a motion picture is bad if it fails to be cinematic, or that it is blemished to the degree that uncinematic elements intrude into its style. Moreover, moving pictures can be compared and even ranked as good, bad, better, and worse in accordance with a single measure – their degree of cinematicity.

Undoubtedly, this is a very tidy program. It would provide a way of rationally brokering all disagreements about evaluating moving pictures just in case we are able satisfactorily to characterize what constitutes the cinematic. But there is a fly in the ointment. For, as is well known, different classical film theorists tended to argue for different and often conflicting (or non-converging) conceptions of the cinematic, no version of which, truth be told, has survived unscathed.

Early film theorists, particularly those associated with silent film, for example, tended to locate the cinematic in terms of two contrasts – that which differentiated motion pictures from theater, on the one hand, and that which differentiated film from the slavish recording of reality, on the other hand. As we saw in our opening chapter, they stressed the difference between film, properly so called, and mere recording, in order to establish the credentials of the motion picture as an artform – that is, as something that did not simply duplicate reality but that could reconstitute it expressively, formally, and/or creatively.

But the early film theorists also desired to differentiate the moving picture from theater. The point here was to demonstrate that cinema was a *unique* artform, an artistic category unto itself – film as film. Thus, these film theorists, of whom Arnheim is a leading example, argued that film, properly so called, was neither an imitation of nature nor an imitation of any other artform, notably theater.

Whereas theater narration typically relies upon words, cinematic narration, it was asserted, could and should emphasize movement, image, action, and rapidly changing points of view. If theater is primarily verbal in its typical mode of address, cinema, ideally, is primarily visual. Similarly, cinema has resources, particularly editing, that enable moviemakers to manipulate spatial and temporal transitions with more fluidity than is customary in theater. Thus, editing, or montage, was generally celebrated as the most important, essential characteristic of cinema. On this view, the moving image is essentially visual, its natural subject of representation is highly animated action, and its primary means of expression is editing or montage.

Other techniques were also regarded as cinematic – including close-ups, assertive camera angulation, trick photography, visual devices such as fades, wipes, and superimposition, camera movement, and the like. As with editing, these techniques were prized because they both declared the difference between film and theater (inasmuch as the effects available through these procedures were not easily achievable in theater) and also departed from the "straight" shooting of reality. In other words, the use of these devices standardly indicated that film differed from theater and from what was thought of as the merely mechanical recording of reality (which was sometimes equated, oddly enough, with something called "normal perception"). These techniques, in other words, displayed film as a unique artistic category – film as film.

A feature of a film was cinematic, then, so long as it deployed techniques that underscored the putatively unique capacities of cinema. Stylistic features that failed to do this – such as the use of extended dialogue or stolid tableaux shots – were uncinematic. Excessive reliance on words at the expense of animated action, or of a single camera position to record the declamation of speech-ridden dialogue (rather than exploiting the powers of editing) was not only uncinematic, but downright theatrical. And to be *theatrical*, a.k.a. uncinematic, flew in the face of the canonical standards of film as film. Theatrical or uncinematic films were bad films, inappropriate or defective examples of the category of film as film.

A movie such as *Inside Man* does nicely on this conception of cinema. Dialogue here is primarily in the service of action – of which there is a goodly amount – which, in turn, is nicely articulated through editing. The camera shifts its perspective often and there are no visual dead spots. On the other hand, *Fast, Cheap & Out of Control* would not fare so well because much of its screen time is simply a matter of straightforward interviewing. Thus, this approach to motion picture evaluation could settle our earlier dispute in short order, if only its account of the essence of cinema is found to be compelling.

But this conception of cinema is hardly incontestable. In fact, it was challenged by subsequent theorists in the classical tradition, of whom Bazin and Kracauer are noteworthy examples. These theorists were often called realists because they thought that the essential feature of cinema is photography (cinematography) and that this feature committed cinema to meeting certain standards that emphasized the recording and disclosure of reality.

So, where earlier classical theorists, like Arnheim, thought that the capacity of film to diverge from the recording of reality implied that cinema should employ assertive devices such as editing to reconstitute reality, realist theorists, like Kracauer, looked more favorably on cinema's provenance in photography and inferred that this argued for the realistic usage of film. Indeed, the realist Bazin even argued that the putatively realist origin of cinema in photography privileged certain techniques like the multiplanar, depth-of-field, sequence shot later embraced by directors like Hou Hsiao-Hsien over the rapid montage championed by Soviet film-makers of the 1920s like Alexander Dovzhenko.

As so often occurs in debates like this, the "repressed" of the first generation of theorists, not only returns but is valorized by the next wave of thinkers. Nevertheless, both waves – as represented by Arnheim and the Soviets, on the one hand, and Kracauer and Bazin, on the other – were classical film theorists, since both groups believed in the *cinematic*. However, they disagreed about what constituted that category and, consequently, they disagreed about what standards were suitable to bring to bear on evaluating films as films.

In fact, their theories led them in opposite directions. Highly stylized films, like *The Last Laugh*, *Variety*, and *The Docks of New York*, of the sort favored by Arnheim's theory were likely to be castigated by the lights of second-generation film theorists because of their disregard for the canons of realism.

And in any event, from Kracauer's perspective, a film like *Inside Man* would be criticized as uncinematic because of the various ways in which it violates Kracauer's conception of the (normative) essence of cinema. For instance, Kracauer thinks that cinematic realism mandates a disposition toward the use of open-ended narrative structures, whereas the storyworld of *Inside Man*, with its tricky plot turns, is what he would disparage as "closed" and, therefore, as unrealistically contrived; *Inside Man*, that is, is the kind of suspense thriller that comes with a high quotient of mystery – not of the whodunit variety, but of the "How did they do it and why?" brand – whose neat, "last-minute" answers are just too convenient. Indeed, the movies that employ closure, as discussed in chapter 5, are generically uncinematic, according to Siegfried Kracauer. On the other hand, if only because it is a documentary, *Fast, Cheap & Out of Control* would probably get far better marks from Siegfried.

In the debate over the cinematic, proponents of the earlier view – that film should reconstitute reality – and champions of the later view – the realists – could both score points against each other. Each side could argue that the other team failed as a comprehensive theory of the nature of the moving image, because each side believed that the other was blind to certain kinds of cinematic achievement. The defender of realism could claim that theorists such as Arnheim ignored the accomplishments of films whose style gravitated more toward recording, such as the work of the Italian neo-realists (whose aspiration, of course, could be elegantly explained from a realist point of view).

On the other hand, those who favored assertive stylization and editing could account for many avant-garde experiments which were anything but realistic. Each side pretended to be a comprehensive theory of the nature of film, but opponents of either side could point out that the other side neglected or attempted to sublate, in an extremely high-handed and ad hoc manner, massive amounts of the data of film history.

Furthermore, it did not appear possible to patch up this problem by merely combining the two schools of thought of classical film theory, because, in important respects, they contradicted each other. Adding the two lines of theory together would not lead to a more comprehensive theory, but only to an inconsistent one.

An explanation of why these two strands of classical film theory failed to deliver the goods is that, though each side presented itself as a comprehensive theory of all motion pictures, this was not, in actuality, what either of these theoretical approaches was about. Both were really critical characterizations – couched as theory – of different stylistic tendencies that had crystallized at different points in the history of the moving picture. Theorists such as Arnheim and the Soviet montagists, like V. I. Pudovkin and Lev Kuleshov, were particularly sensitive to stylistic developments in the period of silent filmmaking, whereas realist theorists – notably Bazin and Kracauer – were especially attuned to stylistic developments in the sound film of the 1940s and the early 1950s.

Both sides, in other words, mistook certain period-specific developments in motion picture history to reveal the essence of cinema. This is why their theories were suited to certain bodies of work, while, at the same time, being doggedly undiscerning with regard to the accomplishments of other stylistic traditions. Whereas a theory of the nature of the movies should apply to motion pictures of all styles, these theories inadvertently privileged certain styles over others – to the extent that certain avenues of cinematic achievement were deprecated by them as uncinematic. Thus, their theories failed to be comprehensive because they were biased or stylistically partisan.

Undoubtedly, another – logically less flattering – way to put the matter is to observe that these theorists proposed to demonstrate that certain options of film stylization were uncinematic by deducing the essence of cinema; but, in fact, what they did was to allow their stylistic preferences to shape – indeed, to infect – their conception of the essence of cinema. Kracauer asserts that photography is *the* essential feature of cinema. But how does he know that photography rather than, say, editing is the essential property? The actual answer is because he already presumes that realist filmmaking demarcates the recognized body of achievement in the medium which a theory, like his, needs to track. That is, his "data" have been gerrymandered to elicit his conclusion. But this, of course, begs the question, since Kracauer has already "selected" the "evidence" that *induces* his "conclusion."

Of course, the same kind of interrogation could be aimed at Kuleshov. How does he know editing is the essential feature of cinema? Indeed, Kuleshov's position is almost blatantly the mirror image of certain realist positions. Kuleshov begs the question no less than Kracauer. Moreover, this is the sort of specious reasoning that runs rampant throughout the corpus of classical film theorizing.

One very ingenious attempt to reconcile the differences between the different schools of classical film theory can be found in Victor Perkins's brilliant book *Film as Film*. This is an especially interesting text for us, given the concerns of this chapter, because it is one of the only explicit efforts to provide a rational foundation for film evaluation. Although Perkins would probably bridle at this suggestion, his book is an example of classical film theory, as his title – *Film as Film* – indicates. Like other classical theorists, Perkins tries to develop a unified canon of movie evaluation for all motion pictures, irrespective of genre and period.

Perkins evolves his canon of the evaluation of motion pictures by combining in a logically scrupulous way some of the insights – such as those of the montagist Arnheim and the realist Kracauer – into a single, non-contradictory formula. On Perkins's account, in order to be good, a moving picture must abide by certain realist standards of verisimilitude. In this way, Perkins pays tribute to the theoretical tradition of people like Kracauer and Bazin. But Perkins also pays his respects to the tradition of assertive stylization in classical film theory. For he maintains that the extra credit that a movie accrues (over and above the minimal accreditation as good that it receives for being realistic) is to be added to the movie's account in terms of the extent to which it is stylized – via editing, set design, camera angulation, camera movement, costume, and so on – just so long as this stylization is articulated within the bounds of realism.

That is, a film as film is good *simpliciter*, if it plays by the rules of realism, as set forth by Perkins. How good – or how much better – it is, then, is a matter of how artfully stylized it is, so long as that stylization is constrained realistically. For example, a film such as *Elmer Gantry* can employ hyperactive montage metaphors and still win Perkins's applause for doing so, because those metaphors are motivated realistically within the world of the fiction.

In Perkins's theory, realism and stylization do not contradict each other, but can coexist peacefully, where the two tendencies cooperate in accordance with the principle that realism constrains the legitimate compass of stylization. That is, realism and stylization are coordinated by a rule that says a good film contains both, but is only good to the degree that the stylization conforms to the discipline of realism. In *Elmer Gantry*, figuratively expressive cutting between a swelling fire and the uncontrolled delivery of a "hell and brimstone" sermon is commendable cinematically because the fire that comments upon the frenzied preaching is of a piece with the naturalist settings and narration of the fictional world. It is, so to say, motivated from within the storyworld of *Elmer Gantry*.

In *Elmer Gantry*, the story establishes that the fire started literally backstage, in the same locale as the pulpit; a workman threw a butt on a flammable heap which smolders as the rhetoric mounts. So the fire is given as something that happened in the fiction world; it is not sheerly a comment from an authorial elsewhere. This use of editing putatively contrasts favorably with those Eisensteinian montage-sequences which resort to similes that intrude upon the decoupage from outside the setting of the fiction. That is, when in *October*, for example, Eisenstein compares Kerensky with a peacock, he does not establish that the peacock, as an actual artifact, dwells in the same palace or even the same storyworld that Kerensky does.

By requiring that stylization be constrained by realism, Perkins proposes a principled way for films to exploit both of the tendencies advocated by the conflicting strands of classical film theory. Perkins's offers an immensely intellectually seductive and thoughtful compromise solution to settle the differences between the two opposing camps of classical film theory, camps which, it should be acknowledged, have advanced the very best thinking about the moving image produced to date. In this way, Perkins's approach appears to realize the dream of classical film theory – to solve the problem of the correct category by discovering a standard of evaluation that is applicable to all motion pictures.

Nevertheless, if Perkins's approach represents one of the highest points in classical film theory, it is also unfortunately (I mean that, I really wish it were otherwise) vulnerable to some of the same criticisms that we have seen plagued earlier forms of this kind of theory. We have already observed that a recurrent failing of classical film theorists involved their hypostatization of certain period-specific film styles – their tendency to mistake these styles for the very essence of cinema itself. Ironically, a similar problem besets Perkins's project.

Perkins takes the exploration of stylization within the bounds of realism to be the quiddity of film as film. By why suppose that this tendency is any more representative of the essence of film than experiments in avant-garde irrealism? That is, why think that Otto Preminger's *Carmen Jones* is more cinematic than Jean-Luc Godard's *One Plus One* or his *One or Two Things I Know About Her*?

Yet, when we scrutinize the database of Perkins's theory, an explanation of his assignment of Preminger's position in the cinematic pantheon readily suggests itself. For the examples that bolster Perkins's theory predominantly come from Hollywood movies of the 1950s and 1960s. During that period, constraining stylization within the bounds of realism was, so to say, a rule of the practice or the ongoing game, which we might even call expressive realism. But in this respect, what Perkins has done, like Arnheim, the Soviets, Kracauer, and Bazin before him, has been to misconstrue an essential (or fundamental) feature of a period-specific stylistic practice for the essence of cinema as a whole. That is, Perkins's preference for a certain kind of filmmaking has biased his account of the nature of, as he himself calls it, *film as film*.

One of the greatest promises of classical film theory was that it would solve the problem of the correct category. For, if we could make classical film theory work, we would have the one and only category we need for evaluating all films. By identifying an essence of film – one with normative impact – we would have a standard that could be brought to bear in order to resolve rationally most disagreements about the quality of given movies. But, as we have seen, the search for this kind of essence – call it the philosopher's stone of film theory – has proven as chimerical as the original philosopher's stone.

In most cases, classical theorists have proceeded by begging the question. They have built in their stylistic preferences as premises in their alleged deductions of stylistic imperatives and cinematic standards. This is rather like the magician who puts the rabbit in the hat and then draws it out. But what is not really magic is not logic either.

Sadly, this sort of error recurs throughout the body of classical film theory, even in the work of its most sophisticated practitioners, such as Perkins. Thus, if and until this failing is repaired, the prospects for solving the problem of the correct category by means of the strategies of classical film theory appear foreclosed. This calls for another alternative to be explored.

An Alternative to the Classical Evaluation of the Moving Image: The Pluralistic-Category Approach

What we had hoped to inherit from classical film theory was a solution to the problem of the correct category. This problem is a pressing one for motion picture evaluation because if we are able to find a way to establish the correct category for evaluating a given film, then we are at least on our way to resolving rationally many – though not all – of the disagreements that arise when we attempt to assess motion pictures. Unfortunately, however, we have seen that so far classical film theory has failed in this regard. So, until classical film theory delivers on its promise, we must explore alternatives.

Undeniably, the failure of classical film theory is instructive. It shows us something, but we need to be careful about what we think it reveals. It does not entail that there cannot be correct categories for evaluating films. Rather, it only suggests that it is unlikely that we can evolve a unitary theory of evaluation based upon a *single* category, such as film as film. That is, at its strongest, the failure of classical film theory may only indicate that there is not a universal litmus test – such as the cinematic – for goodness in movies. But the failure of classical film theory does not imply that categories as such are irrelevant to motion picture evaluation.

The defects of classical film theory may incline us to be skeptical about whether there is a single evaluative category that subsumes all movies. But this should not make us skeptical about whether moving pictures fall into various different categories, many of which come with perfectly respectable standards of evaluation. That motion picture practices are too diverse to be all assimilated productively under the sort of essentialist category of the generality that classical theorists hoped to isolate hardly indicates that movies cannot be categorized.

In fact, isn't it overwhelmingly obvious that movies can be categorized? We have lots of motion picture categories, indeed, many that are perfectly unobjectionable, such as suspense, horror, structural films, melodramas, mysteries, thrillers, trance films, action films, war films, platoon films, German expressionist films, science fiction films, neo-realist films, bio-pics, comedies, mythopoetic films, art films, westerns, socialist realist films, ninja films, fantasy films, musicals, surrealistic films, Bollywood films, costume films, new talkies, fluxus films, *animé*, and various New Waves (add the country of your choice here – France, Germany, Taiwan, Hong Kong, South Korea, etc.). Of course, I've barely started; I could go on for pages.

Some of these categories are less widely known than others, though many of them can be found in the movie and TV listings in your daily newspapers as well as on the racks in video stores. Some of these categories may be genres, such as the soap opera, while others can be movements, like the New American Cinema, or styles, as in the case of film noir or montage films.

Of course, these categories are not necessarily exclusive and can, in many cases, be combined, as in *Outland* (which restaged *High Noon* on

Jupiter's volcanic moon of Io). Nevertheless, there is no reason to think that regarding certain motion pictures under some of these categories rather than others is not often correct. *The Gunfighter* is a western, not a musical; *Au hasard Balthazar* is an art film, not a romance picture; *L'Age d'or* is surrealism, not socialist realism. And so on.

Furthermore, many of the aforesaid categories (and scores and scores of others unmentioned) come with subtending purposes and standards of excellence attached to them. For example, some movies are correctly categorized as melodramas. Part of the point of a melodrama is to incite the audience to feel – at least for some portion of the duration of the movie – sadness or pity for one or more of the protagonists. A correctly categorized melodrama that failed in this respect would be prima facie defective. A correctly classified melodrama, as opposed to a parody thereof, that set us laughing at the mishaps of the protagonists, as arguably John Cromwell's *Made for Each Other*, with its excessive agenda of relentless misfortunes, does, would be a disaster. But a melodrama, like *Back Street*, that reduces us to tears at the plight of its central characters is prima facie a good melodrama.

Likewise, a correctly identified classical detective movie that fails to prompt speculation about whodunit – perhaps because the butler answer is too blatantly obvious from the get-go – or a comedy whose gags are so badly timed that every laugh line falls flat are both presumptively failures. For they do not measure up to the standards of the categories to which they are *known* to belong. If nothing can be said to justify the ways in which these movies deviate from the criteria of worthiness for the categories by which they are justly described, then we can rationally ground our negative assessments of them.

To return to the question of *Inside Man*: you said that it is good; I said that is bad. However, in the course of our discussion, it became apparent that the likely basis for my disparaging assessment of *Inside Man* was that I placed it in the wrong category. I situated it in a comparison class along with *Fast, Cheap & Out of Control*, an essayistic documentary in the lineage of Werner Herzog with aspirations to be meditative – that is, aspirations to invite an active exploration of certain philosophical issues on the part of the viewer. But clearly the aims and standards relevant to this type of documentary differ wildly from those appropriate to thriller-suspense films (of the heist and hostage variety). Among other things, meditative documentary essays are designed to invite abstract rumination, and, though some suspense fictions may also do this (think *Vertigo* here), explicitly provoking philosophical rumination is not a standard expectation that we require every (or even any) suspense thriller qua thriller to fulfill.

A meditative documentary ought to be philosophically provocative. If a suspense movie is not philosophically intriguing – as *Inside Man* is not – that should not count against it (given its category); if a suspense thriller is philosophically interesting, then that's icing on the cake, as they say (though "icing" that needs to be philosophically interrogated, as frightening as that sounds). On the other hand, were an intended thriller-suspense movie philosophically ambitious, yet not suspenseful in the least, we would find it wanting and probably discount it as deadly dull, would we not?

However, in any event, the failure to engender philosophy is not a basis for charging that a motion picture correctly classified as a suspense thriller is bad, since philosophizing is not wherein excellence in the suspense genre primarily resides. Thus, if you can adduce objectively creditable reasons for categorizing *Inside Man* as an exercise in thriller-suspense, while also challenging my attempt to compare it with meditative documentaries, then you have a reasonable basis for dismissing my dissing of *Inside Man*. And if I cannot undermine your categorization with reasons, nor defend my categorization, I should (rationally speaking) concede your point.

In this example, a great deal of weight has been placed on the role of reasons in supporting or rejecting categorizations. But this may strike the reader as somewhat obscure. What are these reasons and in what sense are they objective? Where do they come from? In this regard, three kinds of reasons come into play most frequently in classifying motion pictures.

The first kind of reason pertains to the structure of the work: if the work possesses a large number of features that are typical of the motion pictures inhabiting a certain category, then that is a strong reason to subsume it as, for example, under the category of a suspense thriller. Conversely, the fewer features a movie contains of the sort that are typical for a certain category, the less likely it is that the movie belongs to that category. *Inside Man*, for example, possesses a great many of the features common to suspense thrillers – like a daring escape against the odds – but it has few of the salient features of meditative documentaries (since, for example, it is neither a documentary nor meditative). So it is far more reasonable to regard *Inside Man* as a suspense thriller and to award it high marks for being good of its kind.

The number of relevant structural features a motion picture possesses or lacks, as well as the degree of salience those properties project, may not always provide conclusive reasons in favor of one categorization over another, but statistics such as these generally provide evidence in the direction of one classification versus another. Moreover, these reasons are objective inasmuch as it can be a matter of inter-subjectively verifiable fact that a movie possesses or lacks a certain number of clearly defined features and that said features are typical of a certain category of moving picture. That *Inside Man* contains a daring escape is not a figment of personal opinion; it is incontrovertible. That daring escapes are a mark of suspense thrillers is likewise a matter of historical record.

Another kind of reason that is pertinent to the question of the correct categorization of a movie involves authorial intention. How a moviemaker or a group of moviemakers intend a work to be classified is quite often an inter-subjectively determinable matter of fact, and, in a great many of the remaining cases, a highly plausible hypothesis about the intended categorization of a given movie is available. We know as well as we know anything, for example, that Martin Scorsese intended *The Aviator* as, at least, a bio-pic.

Many scholars in the humanities today are chary of attributing intentions to artists, including movie directors. But their anxieties are generally misplaced. There is nothing more chancy about recognizing the intentions – especially the categorical intentions – of moviemakers than there is about divining the intentions of others in everyday life. Just as one cannot typically doubt that the conductor on the train is reaching out for your ticket, can anyone really doubt that Howard Hawks intended *Bringing Up Baby* to be a comedy or that Henri-Georges Clouzot meant *Diabolique* to be a thriller? In a great many cases, there is nothing arcane about determining a moviemaker's categorical intentions. It is only academic fashion that seems to make it seem so.

Of course, authorial intentions may not always provide conclusive reasons for a specific categorization. Sometimes we may suspect the authors of dissembling (this is often said of so-called "snuff" films) or possibly of being confused. Or the evidence may be indeterminate. Nevertheless, very often our information is adequate enough to support a presumption in favor of one categorization over another. And when evidence of authorial intention can be wedded to structural evidence, of the sort alluded to previously, the grounds for rationally preferring one categorization over another mount appreciably.

Further reasons on behalf of the categorization of a motion picture can be gathered from the historical and/or cultural context in which the moving picture emerged. That is, if a certain category of moviemaking is alive and abroad in the historical and/or cultural context in which the film was produced (especially when competing categorizations are not), then that supplies rational grounds for classifying a movie one way rather than another.

Notice that this too is generally a question of fact. Whether a certain kind of motion picture is common or can be found in a given moviemaking community at a certain time period is not up for grabs. Were spaghetti westerns being produced in Hollywood in the 1920s? No. Is this just my opinion? No. It is a verifiable, historical datum.

That thriller-suspense films are a staple in the cultural enclave of the Hollywood-type, mass-market moviemaking whence *Inside Man* originated gives us some warrant to think that thriller-suspense is the category or comparison class to which it belongs, especially in contrast to the suggestion that it be assessed as a meditative documentary of the ilk of *Fast, Cheap & Out of Control*. For meditative documentaries are not native to the kinds of popular venues for which *Inside Man* was crafted and distributed; their venues are far more specialized than even Michael Moore's screeds. Of course, historical and/or cultural reasons of this sort are not absolutely conclusive, but like structural and intentional reasons, they supply us with some rational motivation to move in the direction of one classification rather than another, particularly where the rival classifications are less convincing historically and/or contextually.

Structural, intentional, and contextual considerations, then, provide us with reasons, often strong reasons, for categorizing motion pictures a certain way. Where we have reasons of all three kinds, their combined force may sometimes be conclusive, or at least as conclusive as things get in this vale of tears. Often, these kinds of reasons dovetail. For example, contextual considerations frequently count as evidence for – and, thereby, reinforce attributions of – authorial intention, since moviemakers usually have an interest in addressing audiences in terms of categories with which they are familiar. Most moviemakers (save certain avant-gardists) are not invested in confusing their target audiences. Moreover, moviemakers typically signal the category they have in mind by exhibiting in their motion pictures well-entrenched and readily recognizable structural features of the kind associated with the type of moving picture they are presenting. That is why so many horror pictures begin on dark and stormy nights and westerns open with panoramas and expansive musical scores.

Of course, in some cases, our categorizations may not depend on all three kinds of reasons in concert. Sometimes structural (*or* authorial *or* contextual) reasons alone will be sufficient. This is especially likely to be the case where there are no persuasive, countervailing reasons available for competing categorizations.

Where does the current discussion of motion picture categorization leave us? First, it lends support to our earlier conviction that there are objective grounds for categorizing films one way rather than another. Thus, if the objective evaluation of motion pictures rests upon our ability to categorize movies correctly, then we have shown that this requirement can be met sometimes, if not often. Furthermore, if we possess the means to categorize moving pictures correctly – and to defend certain categorizations over others – then we can rationally settle some – indeed, I suspect many – disagreements with respect to evaluating movies.

In order to defend our own evaluations of motion pictures against competing ones, we will often proceed by demonstrating that our evaluation is grounded on a correct categorization, while also arguing that rival evaluations depend on incorrect, unlikely, or, at least, less plausible ones. Moreover, insofar as this procedure of invoking objective categorizations enables us to adjudicate a significant number of evaluative disputes, it establishes that motion picture evaluation is, at least to this extent, a rationally governed activity. Let us call this procedure for evaluating motion pictures the *pluralistic-category approach*, since it depends upon countenancing many diverse categories of moving pictures.

Admittedly, the pluralistic-category approach will not dissolve every disagreement about motion picture evaluation. Even if the correct category is identified, there may be debates about how to apply it – disputes, for example, about how a given movie fits the category or categories in question; disagreements about how to weigh the different standards that may be pertinent to the category or categories at issue, and debates about their underlying purposes. Perhaps most often, these controversies need to be worked out on a case-by-case basis (which is not to say that they cannot frequently be resolved objectively). As well, some further matters, involving cross-categorical rankings – which we will address in the next section of this chapter – require an approach different from the pluralistic-category approach. Nevertheless, it remains the case that a great many of our disputes over the merits of moving pictures can be settled by establishing the correct category, as when the husband disparages a movie because it lacks gunfights, but the wife points out that it is a light and frothy, adolescent romantic comedy (rather than, say, a dark one like the recent *Mr. and Mrs. Smith*).

One objection to the pluralistic-category approach is that it is inherently formalist, since it primarily involves assessing a movie in virtue of the kind of motion picture it is, referring its evaluation to the formulaic canons of certain categories, whether they be genres, movements, styles (period and otherwise), and so forth. One idea behind this criticism is that if movies are evaluated in terms of categories, they will be insulated from cognitive, moral, or political evaluation in favor of whatever comprises the internal standards of the category.

But this anxiety is ill founded for at least two reasons. First, many motion picture categories quite clearly presuppose criteria of cognitive, moral, and political excellence. For example, many nonfiction films, as a matter of the kind of documentaries they are, are committed to educating their audiences cognitively as well as often enlightening them morally and politically. Furthermore, a social problem picture that failed to portray injustice effectively would be a defective specimen of its category

Moreover, even in cases where the categories in question are not as straightforwardly connected to other-than-formalist criteria of excellence, cognitive, moral, social, political, spiritual, and other "extra-aesthetic" considerations are usually not irrelevant to the evaluation of the movies that fall under their rubric. Suspense pictures, for example, given the argumentation of the previous chapter, will have to abide by a recognizably pro-social ethic, if they aspire to enlist the care and concern of typical audiences on behalf of those protagonists hanging from the cliffs. Melodramas will have to reassure us that those whom we are intended to pity are morally deserving; most normal viewers will not cry for the remorseless Nazi commandant who dies in a car accident while trying to run over an ailing grandmother and her infant grandson; many may even applaud. In cases like these, the morally flawed perspectives of the movie will patently count against them.

Likewise, cognitive gaffes can also be demerit-making features in a movie that is not overtly committed to enlightenment, as in the case of the adventure flick in which the hero announces that he is running out of bullets but continues blasting away for the next thirty-five minutes or so. Being an action movie does not automatically get you a pass for outright dumbness. In short, things like cognitive and moral defects can enter our deliberations not only with respect to motion picture categories that are designed to address such issues directly, as part of the nature of the kind of category they are, but also with respect to the evaluation of movies in many other categories as well.

Another objection to the category approach is that it makes a fundamental ontological mistake. It seems to suppose that there is one and only one category into which each motion picture neatly fits with no remainder. And this is just false. But, of course, we may readily concede that movies may inhabit more than one category. However, that does not show that the approach is flawed. It only entails that evaluation may be more complicated than examples so far have indicated. Motion pictures may combine categories and, therefore, may need to be evaluated in light of several moving picture kinds. *Bride of Frankenstein*, for instance, blends horror and dark comedy. This is a case where the mesh is nearly perfect. However, this kind of category splicing can also lead to mixed results. A movie may turn out to be good with respect to one category to which it belongs, but bad with respect to another. The humor component of a comic mystery of the *Cat and Canary* variety may be superlative, while the mystery element is utterly and disappointingly transparent.

This sort of situation, however, should come as no surprise. Mixed results often figure in our assessments of movies. Even with respect to a single category, more than one criterion of excellence may be relevant in evaluating a film. Several *Batman* spectacles have been especially commendable for their production designs, while being leaden narratively. Of course, if one comes to think about it, probably most of our assessments of movies – indeed, of most artworks, save the most magnificent masterpieces – are mixed. Mixed results are just something – like gravity – which those of us who evaluate movies have to learn to live with. Thus, the fact that the pluralistic-category approach to motion picture evaluation leads to mixed results should not be taken as a shortcoming. In fact, that it can usually clarify the sources of the mixed results should probably be scored in its behalf.

Some may fear that relying so heavily on motion picture categories is too conservative. It appears to presume that the pertinent categories are fixed. But moving picture categories are also mutating. Some are disappearing, others are changing (often by combining with other categories), and sometimes, in addition, new categories are coming into existence. Can the category approach handle motion pictures that are in the process of evolution, not to mention movies that herald the very onset of new genres? For, certainly any approach is of dubious value, if it ignores evolutionary phenomena like these.

But the pluralistic-category approach need not deny or otherwise repress these phenomena. In defense of the approach, however, it is important to remember that the pertinent categories, like the movies that fall under their umbrella concepts, do not hail from nowhere. New categories arise from earlier ones by well-precedented processes of development – such as hybridization, amplification, repudiation, and so forth. Consequently, it is possible to track emerging categories along with their purposes and their subtending standards *in medias res*.

Perhaps this seems doubtful when it comes to the avant-garde. But with respect to avant-garde cinema, the identification of new categories, purposes, and their correlative criteria of accomplishment is typically facilitated by the existence of manifestos (signaling authorial intent) and the lively motion picture culture that surrounds such film and video production (which supplies pertinent historical/contextual information) as well as, frequently, information that comes through the existence of related aspirations (and similar structural features) articulated in adjacent artforms, like painting and music, which limn the rationale behind new developments in cinema (that is, which afford even more informative historical/contextual background).

For example, the avant-garde category of the New Talkie – which appeared in the late 1970s and early 1980s – was comprehended virtually with the arrival of the first examples of this tendency due to the manifestos and discourse that enveloped it. Thus, there is no reason to fear that talk of categories precludes receptivity to novel forms of motion picture making, even in the face of the persistent challenges of avant-garde visionaries. There is always a social context that prepares for "the unexpected." When something is called "unprecedented" or "unexpected" in the world of cinema, that is, more often than not, promotional rather than descriptive.

The defense of the pluralistic-category approach in the preceding paragraph is likely to ignite the ire of those who think that there are motion pictures that stand outside of any category – works of such exceeding uniqueness as to be reckoned one of a kind. But there are grounds to be extremely skeptical of this view. A motion picture that was truly, ontologically incomparable with any other would be, honestly, an equally incomprehensible artifact. Faith in the consummately singular motion picture derives from a romantic-modernist fantasy of the genius. But the creature dreamt up in these philosophies is a psychological impossibility. No artist comes from nowhere. And, in any case, the artist as a young wolf-child or an apprentice to Kasper Hauser would be indisputably incapable of making a movie.

A recent motion picture that has been proffered as one that defies the category approach is the *Cremaster* series by Matthew Barney. This is a brilliant, sprawling work with often elusive imagery of gay import and radical juxtapositions. But it does fit into a tradition and it does belong to a category – namely, that of the mythopoetic cinema, as christened by P. Adams Sitney, which includes *Inauguration of the Pleasure Dome* by Kenneth Anger, *Heaven and Earth Magic* by Harry Smith, *Dog Star Man* by Stan Brakhage, and others. There is no doubt that this category is not on the tip of every viewer's lips – as is the label *musical* mostly is; however, the obscurity of the category does not militate against either its reality or its relevance.

In this regard, it pays to note that one function that motion picture critics can perform for the general public is to inform them of the existence of categories that are not widely known and to explain their points, purposes, and virtues. It is unfortunate that journalistic film criticism is often assigned to writers who possess nothing other than the ambition to write – thus presuming that anyone can write about movies – whereas a really accomplished motion picture critic should have a capacious enough knowledge and understanding of motion picture history that she ranges widely over its stunning diversity of categories, subgenres, visionary movements, stylistic tendencies, and so forth. One of the most significant services that a motion picture critic can perform is to enable plain viewers to place puzzling work in unfamiliar categories where the goodness to be had from the movie in question becomes available to viewers upon the elucidation of the subtending purposes of the relevant categories.

Clearly, the pluralistic-category approach to motion picture evaluation, as its very label advertises, is not as unified as the one proposed by classical film theory. Since classical film theory acknowledged only one category, it supplied a unitary metric according to which every motion picture, genre or style notwithstanding, could be ranked on a single scale. That is, every movie could be compared for its degree of cinematicity. The pluralistic-category approach is far more fragmentary, since it maintains, quite credibably I would argue, that there are many different categories that we can and indeed should call upon to evaluate different types of moving pictures.

Some may find this disheartening. They might complain that the pluralistic-category approach makes the qualitative comparison of motion pictures from different categories impossible. This may be a big disappointment, especially when contrasted to the capacity of the classical tradition to rate all movies along a single grid. But, these lamentations may be exaggerated, on the one hand, and utopian on the other.

The objection that the pluralistic-category approach makes all comparisons between motion pictures of different categories impossible is hyperbolic for at least two reasons. First, as noted earlier, many movies inhabit more than one category. Consequently, a high-spirited, comic spy film can be compared qualitatively to a comedy *simpliciter* in terms of humor. Moreover, there is no reason to suppose that there are never shared, cross-categorical dimensions of evaluation, such as narrative coherence or the deft and not-so-deft manipulation of point-of-view structures.

At the same time, the wish to be able to compare every motion picture with all other motion pictures is frankly unrealistic. Why imagine that a near-perfect ciné-dance like Hilary Harris's *Nine Variations* can be weighed against an estimable social drama like *Once Were Warriors*? And even supposing one could find some points of tangency between these two moving pictures, note that in virtually every respect that we care about with reference to these two achievements, the two candidates are effectively incommensurable.

Indeed, sometimes the attempt to compare certain films with others cross-categorically seems almost silly. When I was young, my friends and I would get into shouting matches over whether Sherlock Holmes was smarter than Captain Nemo, or whether Mighty Mouse was tougher than Superman, or, my favorite: could Frankenstein's Monster take Godzilla? This was a pleasant enough way to blow a summer afternoon, but, in point of fact, these arguments were ridiculous, since the comparisons were being made between non-overlapping fictions whose make-believe worlds were utterly unconnected. Similarly, but for different reasons, it often is simply nonsense to attempt to appraise every movie on a single axis.

This is especially obvious with regard to masterpieces. Which is greater – *A Midsummer Night's Dream* (the play) or the *Goldberg Variations*? Who knows? How would you go about deciding the issue? And, basically, who really cares? At a certain level of achievement, trying to parse the precise difference in quality between masterpieces, even if possible, seems feckless. Both the aforesaid works belong to the highest strata of artistic excellence; calibrating a differential between them seems akin to determining whether Captain America is stronger than Batman. Both artworks are just "top of the line."

Just as Captain America and Batman are the *non plus ultra* human warriors of their respective, ontologically disjoint fictional worlds and, consequently, not suitable for direct comparison, so *A Midsummer Night's Dream* (the play) and the *Goldberg Variations* dwell at the summits of at best weakly commensurable artistic categories. Turning to motion pictures, judging whether *Some Like It Hot* is better than John Huston's *Maltese Falcon* seems likewise beside the point. It is questionable whether it can be done, how it could be done, and, most of all, why it needs to be or should be attempted at all.

Because it may not make sense to attempt to weigh every motion picture against every other motion picture, it cannot be a failing of the pluralistic-category approach that it is unable to do so. Perhaps this alleged shortcoming of the pluralistic-category approach is actually a reflection of its underlying good sense.

But ...

Maybe sometimes, even often, it is silly, or imponderable, or both to try to evaluate comparatively certain works of radically disjoint and virtually incommensurable categories. Nevertheless, it is not always silly to do so. Aren't there cases where we are willing to indulge in this sort of comparison with great confidence? Does anyone feel squeamish in asserting that *Tokyo Story* is a better film than *The Big Broadcast of 1938* or that *Pather Panchali* is superior to *Glen or Glenda*? However, these are not the sort of evaluations that the pluralistic-categorical approach is well suited to advance, since it seems fruitless to attempt to situate either of the preceding pairs of motion pictures informatively in the same category or categories. Consequently, the pluralistic-category approach to motion picture evaluation has to be *supplemented* to manage cases like these (and probably other sorts of cases as well).

One task for the philosophy of a practice, including the practice of moving picture evaluation, is to strive to establish the premises upon which reasoning in that practice proceeds. So far we have tried to show that a great deal of movie evaluation rests on trying to place the moving picture on the docket in the correct category (or categories). But that cannot be the whole story about movie evaluation, since there appear to be perfectly acceptable motion picture evaluations where the category approach appears inapplicable. *Tokyo Story* and *The Big Broadcast of 1938*, on the one hand, and *Pather Panchali* and *Glen or Glenda*, on the other, are so categorically remote from each other that it seems pointless to suppose that they share any aims concrete enough to motivate the differential assessments we are willing to make here.

Nevertheless, with these particular examples, it is not difficult to hypothesize the principle that makes the evaluations at issue compelling. *Tokyo Story* and *Pather Panchali* number among the most excellent achievements in their class, while *The Big Broadcast of 1938* is at the bottom of its particular heap and *Glen or Glenda* is the worst of its lot. The pairs in question, though not profitably situated in shared categories, can be compared evaluatively vis-à-vis their relative status in the categories to which they do belong. And where one motion picture is an excellent example of its type and another makes a very poor showing in its class, we are likely, all things being equal, to rate the former above the latter.

Yet the preceding possibilities do not exhaust the field. Isn't it fair to suppose that most informed motion picture goers would be prepared to agree that *The Bicycle Thief* is a better moving picture than *Beetlejuice*? In this case, we have two motion pictures, each of which is at the top of its category – humanist realism (*The Bicycle Thief*), on the one hand, and horror-comedy (*Beetlejuice*), on the other. The narration in both films is flawless and the performances perfect. It is tempting to think that this might be one of those cases where we think it is fatuous to ask whether one of these really splendid motion pictures is better than the other. And yet it does not sound silly or strained to maintain that *The Bicycle Thief* is better than *Beetlejuice*, even to someone like me who really adores *Beetlejuice*. Why not?

The value or disvalue of a motion picture is connected to its purposes. As we have seen, moving pictures belong to various categories, which categories, in turn, are devoted to the realization of certain points and purposes. A movie that accomplishes its aims succeeds as the kind of motion picture it is; a mystery, for example, that sustains our curiosity throughout achieves its objective and is objectively valuable for doing so.

However, assessing a motion picture from the perspective of its category (or categories) does not address the question of the value of the purpose that the category is intended to attain. Nevertheless, it would appear to stand to reason that an overall evaluation – a.k.a. an "all-things-considered judgment" – of a motion picture should take into account not only the movie's success or failure by its own (category-relative) lights, but the value or disvalue of the purpose or purposes to which the category is committed.

Moreover, the achievement of some purposes is clearly more valuable than the achievement of others. For example, the discovery of the polio vaccine was more valuable than my managing to get out of bed this morning (or any other morning, for that matter). Likewise, the dramatist who succeeds in disclosing the deep secrets of *ressentiment* produces something of greater value than the *New Yorker* cartoonist who captures perfectly the quaint foibles of a Greenwich Villager complaining about out-of-town bagels. In both cases, the works in question are good of their kind, but we rank the purposes of the one kind more highly than the purposes connected to the other kind.

Returning to the case of *The Bicycle Thief* versus *Beetlejuice*, it seems likely that we are inclined to rank *The Bicycle Thief* more highly because, all things being equal, we think that cinematic works of humanist realism are more valuable than works of horror-comedy in cases where each of the candidates in question are superb with reference to their own respective kind. On the other hand, we may be less willing to rank *The Bicycle Thief* and *La Grande Illusion*, since both realize their purposes magnificently *and* neither purpose seems obviously more valuable than the other. Indeed, their aims seem of a piece.

Movies are evaluated in terms of whether they succeed or fail in realizing their purposes. Generally, these purposes are rooted in the categories the motion pictures under evaluation inhabit – which categories include genres, subgenres, cycles, styles, movements, and so forth. Some of these categories may belong exclusively to the history of motion pictures, such as the ciné-dance, but many belong to more than one artform, such as the melodrama.

Yet, in either case, it is primarily from its presiding category (or categories) that the movie, so to speak, gets its marching orders. If the motion picture reaches its destination, then it is good as the kind of moving picture it is; if not, not. This kind of evaluation might be thought of as *movie* evaluation, narrowly construed, since it is tethered to the specific kinds of movies there actually are and have been. Evaluation of this sort is the type of evaluation to which movie critics and connoisseurs may lay special claim, because it relies upon a sophisticated knowledge of motion picture history, its modes, and its varieties.

Yet sometimes we also incorporate into our overall evaluation of movies an assessment of the value of the purpose which the motion picture at hand successfully realizes. Where does this evaluation come from? The short answer is that it comes from the culture at large. In this respect, this species of judgment might be thought of in terms of the evaluation of motion pictures, broadly construed. Moreover, this is the kind of evaluation in which we are involved when we pronounced *The Bicycle Thief* to be better than *Beetlejuice*. We are expressing the conviction, *ceteris paribus*, that *The Bicycle Thief* and the kind of purpose this category of motion picture making implements serves more important cultural interests than *Beetlejuice* and the genre of horror-comedy.

Indeed, even within a single category, we appear willing to rate one very excellent example of a kind over another very excellent instance, where one of the pair, in addition to being splendid of its type, also serves some higher purpose. Thus, we may feel that *Vertigo* is better – all things considered – than *The Lady Vanishes*, since, although both films do an especially fine job engendering suspense, *Vertigo* offers insights into the philosophy of romantic love as well, thereby contributing more than simply a thrilling adrenaline surge.

Of course, once we start to issue estimates of this variety, we are no longer simply speaking as movie critics and/or connoisseurs with narrowly specialized knowledge about the history of movies. *Movie* evaluators can say what makes for a good splatter film, but they have no special authority when it comes to attesting to the value of a good splatter film, like *Halloween n +1*, versus a satiric exposure of hypocritical posturing, like *Team America*. To enter the discussion about the value of the cultural interests served by different cinematic categories, or even by different individual movies, is undoubtedly to broach questions of general axiology. To assert, for example, that even a very remarkable splatter film is, *ceteris paribus*, not as valuable as an equally well executed satire of contemporary affairs obviously requires taking a stance upon the status, aims, and needs of the civilization in which this particular discussion makes sense. That is, this discussion involves a shift from movie evaluation, narrowly construed, to cultural criticism – a transition that requires that the best prepared evaluators of movies not only know film history, but be generally informed intellectually as well.

Although the very best movie evaluation requires an informed and refined understanding of the actual history of the moving image, it does not entail that, in our evaluations of motion pictures, we should stick to the narrow gauge – in fact, far from it. Instead, there would be something peculiar about trying to sequester movie evaluation solely inside the history of the moving image. For motion pictures penetrate the life of the culture in every way, and therefore the discourse about them, including the evaluative discourse, should also be multi-layered. Unquestionably, movie evaluation requires specialist knowledge, but it also calls for an engagement with the life of a breathing civilization.

In some cases, evaluating some motion pictures may require summing up the value of the movie in terms of the kind of moving picture it is plus some estimate of the social value of the purposes that category of moving image usually serves. With reference to our previous discussion of *The Bicycle Thief* and *Beetlejuice*, talking crudely and only heuristically, we might try to represent this by saying that on a scale of -10 to $+10$, both films get a $+9.9$ for category excellence. But on a similarly calibrated scale for cultural importance, let us say that *The Bicycle Thief* gets a $+9.9$ again, but *Beetlejuice* only garners a $+6$. Overall, then *Bicycle Thief* would merit a score of $+19.8$, while *Beetlejuice* racks up a $+15.9$, where the hypothetical point spread is explicable in virtue of the variable cultural weight that we assign to the purposes we attribute to these different kinds of movies.

Although we may often feel uncomfortable in admitting it, when we are confident in claiming that, of two excellent motion pictures of barely commensurable categories, the latter is superior to the former, it is reasonable to conjecture that that is probably because we are convinced that the latter (or the category to which it belongs) is more important because the civilizational interests it serves are more important than those served by the former. That is what really grounds our evaluations. Indeed, it is difficult to imagine what other grounds there might be. The only reason that we feel nervous about confessing this is that many of us are still in the grip of the ideology of the autonomy of art, including motion picture art, which dictates that considerations of social importance are somehow beyond the pale. And yet as members of society we cannot but help to harken to its claims when it comes to assessing almost everything, including art and even movies.

Does this entail that it does make sense to compare every film in this way? Probably not. When we have excellent motion pictures, such as masterpieces, from disparate categories where the there is no assignable difference in cultural value between the purposes of the categories in question or where the difference is imponderable or indeterminate, it is likely that an attempt at comparison will either be beside the point or silly. Of course, as the preceding sentence concedes, there may be cases where the cultural weighting to be assigned to the different categories will be disputed by reasonable people. In those cases, our evaluative debates may sometimes go unresolved. Nevertheless, there are no grounds for thinking that none of our disagreements will ever be resolved. The cartoon "Godzilla Meets Bambi" is perfectly delightful enough on its own terms, but no one can seriously maintain that it is of the same order of cultural heft as Lanzmann's *Shoah* and its like.

Some, even many, evaluative disputes will be settled. Some will be beside the point. And some may remain intractable. However, the fact that some evaluative disagreements concerning motion pictures remain unsettled is not a reflection of some special weakness of moving picture evaluation in contrast to other cognitive enterprises. For we should not expect to resolve every dispute concerning the evaluation of moving pictures. After all, we have not done that in any other field of inquiry.

The Value of Cinema?

So far, we have been stalking the question of value in relation to cinema in terms of the evaluation of particular motion pictures. However, a number of previous theorists and philosophers have also been invested in claiming a value for cinema as such – albeit cinema generally understood as film. For example, Bazin thought that we value film as such as a kind of celluloid mortuary, a means to immortality (since on photographic film, Greta Garbo will be eternal); Kracauer maintained that film redeemed physical reality for a civilization that had become overly abstract; and Stanley Cavell suggests that film might serve as a symbol or talisman against the anxieties of solipsism, inasmuch as film shows us a world past, a world that, despite our absence from it, persists.

It would be wonderful to conclude this book with a comparable flourish. However, as the argument of this chapter and others suggests, there is no single, unique value that film, or, more broadly, the moving image as such achieves. Unlike Bazin, Kracauer, and Cavell, we have defined our object of inquiry functionally rather than in terms of a specific medium. The function of the artifacts in question is their capacity to impart the impression of movement, a function that can be multiply realized in a number of media, including film, obviously, but also video, broadcast TV, CGI, and technologies yet to come.

Moving imagery, in turn, can obviously serve a multitude of agendas, from the documentation of scientific experiments, the analysis of movement, security surveillance, animal studies, the diagnosis of football strategies, ballistics testing, and weather forecasting to producing video and computer games, advertising, political propaganda, the delivery of the evening news, and, of course, fictional movies.

Moving imagery can implement many purposes and gets its value (and its disvalue) from the uses to which it is put, and its successes and failures with respect to discharging them. It has no end in itself; the moving image is a means to an end, and each use of moving imagery ultimately derives its value through factoring into account the worth of its goals and its actual facility in accomplishing them.

The moving image as such has no particular value, unique or otherwise. No one watches a moving image for the intrinsic value of seeing movement in the image. There has to be a point to be made by the movement. And from thence – the point and its making – comes the value.

Historically, the capacity of the moving image to project motion pictures that can be combined into visual narratives, generally of a fictional sort, has been its most prominent function in Western culture, and in others. Throughout the twentieth century, visual narration – as art and/or entertainment, as cinema and/or movies – has been the purpose that has driven the evolution of the moving image and the refinement of its technical capabilities. That is why so much of this book has been devoted to questions pertaining to art and narrative. For as a philosopher of a practice, one must go where the practice does.

However, things are changing. Motion pictures are no longer creatures that inhabit just movie houses. They have taken over our homes (TV), our offices (computers), and even our pockets (cellphones). They dominate not only our lives, but our children's lives (video and computer games).

In some big cities, moving picture billboards are cropping up on subway entrances; huge ones vault certain major intersections. On large airplanes, the stewardess no longer recites the safety instructions; the monitor on the back of the seat in front of us illustrates them. A videocassette or a DVD tells us how to assemble our computer. And so on.

Moving images are not only for Friday nights or rainy Saturday afternoons. They are everywhere, all of the time. We are becoming a moving image culture, not merely in the sense that motion pictures are our leading form of art and/or entertainment, but in the sense that they are beginning to play a role in a remarkably diverse and comprehensive range of our communicative activities. Perhaps someday they will be a part of almost every one of our channels of exchange.

Thus, one predicts that in the future the philosophy of the moving image will have a far larger waterfront to cover than the one that has been surveyed in this text.

Suggested Reading

As indicated in this chapter, the question of motion picture evaluation has not been the subject of much recent philosophical and/or theoretical discussion. Nevertheless, sometimes explicitly, but often implicitly, the question of film evaluation – as it relates to the notion of the cinematic – was a preoccupation of much of the film theory produced through the 1960s by what might be called the classical tradition. See the suggested reading at the end of chapter 2 for citation of several of the most relevant texts.

One participant in that conversation who is specifically interested in laying the foundations of rational film evaluation is Victor F. Perkins. His book *Film as Film: Understanding and Judging Movies* (Baltimore, MD: Penguin, 1972) is probably the most ambitious and thoughtful treatise on film evaluation to date.

The discussion of the pertinence of categories for motion picture evaluation was inspired by Kendall Walton's very important article, "Categories of Art," *The Philosophical Review* 79 (1970), 334–67. An earlier version of the pluralistic-category approach can be found in Noël Carroll, "Introducing Film Evaluation," in *Engaging the Moving Image* (New Haven, CT: Yale University Press, 2003). A useful response to that article is Cynthia Freeland's "Evaluating Film," *Film Studies* 8 (Summer 2006), 154–60.

Daniel Kaufman has recently published pioneering work on the philosophy of evaluation. See Daniel Kaufman, "Normative Criticism and the Objective Value of Artworks," *Journal of Aesthetics and Art Criticism* 60:2 (Spring 2002), 150–66, and Daniel Kaufman, "Critical Justification and Critical Laws," *British Journal of Aesthetics* 43:4 (Oct. 2004), 393–400. Both of these pieces are highly recommended to any readers interested in pursuing further the topics broached in this chapter.

A very influential approach to movie criticism that has not been discussed in this chapter is what is called auteur theory. Originated in France by members of the New Wave, it was imported to the United States by several critics, the most notable of whom is Andrew Sarris.

A founding document of the auteurist persuasion was the 1948 article by Alexandre Astruc entitled "The Birth of a New Avant-Garde: Le Caméra-Stylo," which is reprinted in *The New Wave*, edited by Peter Graham (New York: Doubleday, 1968). This anthology also contains other statements of the theory. A variant of the approach inflected by structuralism is available in Peter Wollen, *Signs and Meaning in the Cinema* (Bloomington, IN: Indiana University Press, 1972).

For the version of auteurism that probably had the most impact on critics in the United States, see Andrew Sarris, "Notes on the Auteur Theory in 1962," in *Film Theory and Criticism*, 3rd edn., edited by Marshall Cohen and Gerald Mast (New York: Oxford University Press, 1985). Pauline Kael criticizes this approach in her "Circles and Squares," which appears in the same edition of *Film Theory and Criticism*. The auteur theory is also criticized in Noël Carroll's introduction to *Interpreting the Moving Image* (New York: Cambridge University Press, 1998).

The topic of evaluative disagreement which motivates a great deal of this chapter finds its *locus classicus* in David Hume, "Of the Standard of Taste," in *David Hume: Selected Essays*, edited by Stephen Copley and Andrew Edgar (Oxford: Oxford University Press, 1993). For a useful overview of the twentieth-century debate among analytic philosophers about the evaluation of art and, in addition, for a provocative theory of art evaluation, see George Dickie, *Evaluating Art* (Philadelphia, PA: Temple University Press, 1988).

Select Bibliography

Richard Allen, *Projecting Illusion* (Cambridge University Press, 1996).

Richard Allen and Murray Smith (eds.), *Film Theory and Philosophy* (Oxford University Press, 1997).

Joseph Anderson, *The Reality of Illusion* (Southern Illinois University Press, 1996).

Rudolf Arnheim, *Film as Art* (University of California Press, 1956).

Alexandre Astruc, "The Birth of the Avant-Garde: Le Camera Stylo," in Peter Graham (ed.), *The New Wave* (Doubleday, 1968).

Bela Balász, *Theory of Film* (Dover Publishers, 1952).

André Bazin, *What is Cinema?*, 2 vols. (University of California Press, 1967).

Walter Benjamin, "The Work of Art in the Age of Mechanical Reproduction," in *Illuminations*, ed. Hannah Arendt, trans. Harry Zorn (Schocken Books, 1968).

David Bordwell, *Narration in the Fiction Film* (University of Wisconsin Press, 1985).

—— *Making Meaning* (Harvard University Press, 1989).

David Bordwell and Noël Carroll (eds.), *Post-Theory: Reconstructing Film Studies* (University of Wisconsin Press, 1996).

John M. Carroll, *Towards a Structural Psychology of Cinema* (Mouton Publishers, 1980).

Noël Carroll, "Address to the Heathen," *October* 23 (1982/3), 89–163.

—— "The Power of Movies," *Daedalus* 114:1 (1985), 79–103.

—— *Mystifying Movies* (Columbia University Press, 1988).

—— *Philosophical Problems of Classical Film Theory* (Princeton University Press, 1988).

—— *The Philosophy of Horror* (Routledge, 1990).

—— *Theorizing the Moving Image* (Cambridge University Press, 1996).

—— *Philosophy of Mass Art* (Oxford University Press, 1998).

—— *Interpreting the Moving Image* (Cambridge University Press, 1998).

—— *Philosophy of Art: A Contemporary Introduction* (Routledge, 1999).

—— *Beyond Aesthetics: Philosophical Essays* (Cambridge University Press, 2001).

—— "The Wheel of Virtue," *Journal of Aesthetics and Art Criticism* 60:1 (2002), 3–26.

—— *Engaging the Moving Image* (Yale University Press, 2003).

—— *Comedy Incarnate* (Blackwell Publishing, 2007).

—— "On the Ties That Bind: Characters, the Emotions and Popular Fictions," in William Irwin and Jorge Garcia (eds.), *Philosophy and the Interpretation of Popular Culture* (Rowman & Littlefield, 2006).

——— "The Problem with Movie Stars," in Scott Walden (ed.), *Photography and Philosophy* (Blackwell Publishing, forthcoming).

Noël Carroll and Jinhee Choi (eds.), *Philosophy of Film and Motion Pictures* (Blackwell Publishing, 2006).

Allan Casebier, *Film and Phenomenology* (Cambridge University Press, 1991).

Stanley Cavell, *The World Viewed*, enlarged edn. (Harvard University Press, 1979).

——— *Pursuits of Happiness* (Harvard University Press, 1981).

——— *Contesting Tears* (University of Chicago Press, 1996).

——— *Cities of Words* (Harvard University Press, 2004).

Jinhee Choi, "All the Right Responses," *British Journal of Aesthetics* 43:1 (2003), 308–21.

——— "Fits and Startles: Cognitivism Revisited," *Journal of Aesthetics and Art Criticism* 61:2 (2003), 149–57.

——— "Leaving it up to the Imagination," *Journal of Aesthetics and Art Criticism* 63:1 (2005), 17–25.

Amy Coplan, "Empathic Engagement with Narrative Fictions," *Journal of Aesthetics and Art Criticism* 62:2 (2004), 447–69.

Donald Crawford, "The Uniqueness of the Medium," *The Personalist* 51 (1970), 447–69.

Gregory Currie, *Image and Mind: Film, Philosophy, and Cognitive Science* (Cambridge University Press, 1995).

——— "The Moral Psychology of Fiction," *Australasian Journal of Philosophy* 73:2 (1995), 250–9.

——— "Visible Traces," *Journal of Aesthetics and Art Criticism* 57:3 (1999), 285–97.

Arthur Danto, "Moving Pictures," *Quarterly Review of Film Studies* 4:1 (1979), 1–21.

Gilles Deleuze, *Cinema*, 2 vols. (University of Minnesota Press, 1989).

Jan B. Deregowski, *Illusions, Patterns and Pictures: A Cross-Cultural Perspective* (Academic Press, 1980).

Mary Devereaux, "Beauty and Evil," in Jerrold Levinson (ed.), *Aesthetics and Ethics* (Cambridge University Press, 1998).

George Dickie, *Evaluating Art* (Temple University Press, 1988).

Umberto Eco, "On the Contribution of Film to Semiotics," in Gerald Mast and Marshall Cohen (eds.), *Film Theory and Film Criticism*, 2nd edn. (Oxford University Press, 1979).

Sergei Eisenstein, *Selected Works* (BFI Publishing/Indiana University Press, 1988).

Cynthia Freeland, *"The Naked and the Undead"* (Westview Press, 2002).

——— "Evaluating Film," *Film Studies* 8 (2006), 154–60.

Cynthia Freeland and Thomas Wartenberg (eds.), *Philosophy and Film* (Routledge, 1995).

Berys Gaut, "On Cinema and Perversion," *Film and Philosophy* 1 (1994), 3–17.

——— "The Enjoyment of Horror," *British Journal of Aesthetics* 35:3 (1995), 284–9.

——— "Cinematic Art," *Journal of Aesthetics and Art Criticism* 60:4 (2002), 299–312.

——— "Identification and Emotion in Narrative Film," in Carl Plantinga and Gregory Smith (eds.), *Passionate Views* (Johns Hopkins University Press, 1999).

—— "The Movies: Cinematic Narration," in Peter Kivy (ed.), *The Blackwell Guide to Aesthetics* (Blackwell Publishing, 2004).

Alan Goldman, "Specificity, Popularity, and Engagement in the Moving Image," *Film and Philosophy* 5:6 (2002), 93–9.

Karen Hanson, "Minerva in the Movies," *Persistence of Vision* 5 (1987), 5–11.

Gilbert Harman, "Semiotics and the Cinema," in Gerald Mast and Marshall Cohen (eds.), *Film Theory and Film Criticism*, 2nd edn. (Oxford University Press, 1979).

—— "Eco-location," in Gerald Mast and Marshall Cohen (eds.), *Film Theory and Film Criticism*, 2nd edn. (Oxford University Press, 1979).

Elaine Hatfield, John T. Cacioppo, and Richard L. Rapson, *Emotional Contagion* (Cambridge University Press, 1994).

Brian Henderson, *Critique of Film Theory* (Dutton, 1980).

Mette Hjort and Sue Laver (eds.), *Emotion and the Arts* (Oxford University Press, 1997).

Julian Hochberg and Virginia Brooks, "Pictorial Recognition as an Unlearned Ability," *American Journal of Psychology* 75:4 (1962), 624–8.

David Hume, *Selected Essays* (Oxford University Press, 1993).

Ian Jarvie, *Movies and Society* (Basic Books, 1970).

—— *Philosophy of Film* (Routledge, 1987).

Pauline Kael, "Circles and Squares," in Gerald Mast and Marshall Cohen (eds.), *Film Theory and Film Criticism*, 3rd edn. (Oxford University Press, 1985).

Andrew Kania, "The Illusion of Realism in Film," *British Journal of Aesthetics* 42:3 (2002), 243–58.

—— "Against the Ubiquity of Fictional Narrators," *Journal of Aesthetics and Art Criticism* 63:1 (2005), 47–54.

Daniel Kaufman, "Normative Criticism and the Objective Value of Artworks," *Journal of Aesthetics and Art Criticism* 60:2 (2002), 150–66.

—— "Critical Justification and Critical Laws," *British Journal of Aesthetics* 43:3 (2004), 393–400.

Haig Khatchadourian, "Film as Art," *Journal of Aesthetics and Art Criticism* 33:3 (1975), 271–84.

—— "Movement and Action in Film," *British Journal of Aesthetics* 20 (1980), 349–55.

Soren Kjorup, "George Inness and the Battle of Hastings, or Doing Things with Pictures," *The Monist* 58 (1974), 216–35.

—— Pictorial Speech Acts," *Erkenntis* 12:1 (1978), 55–71.

Peter Kivy, "Music in the Movies," in Richard Allen and Murray Smith (eds.), *Film Theory and Philosophy* (Oxford University Press, 1997).

Deborah Knight, "Aristotelians on Speed," in Richard Allen and Murray Smith (eds.), *Film Theory and Philosophy* (Oxford University Press, 1997).

Siegfried Kracauer, *Theory of Film* (Oxford University Press, 1960).

Joseph Kupfer, *Visions and Virtue in Popular Film* (Westview Press, 1999).

Flo Lebowitz, "Apt Feelings, or Why 'Women's Films' Aren't Trivial," in David Bordwell and Noël Carroll (eds.), *Post-Theory: Reconstructing Film Studies* (University of Wisconsin Press, 1996).

Jerrold Levinson, "Film Music and Narrative Agency," in David Bordwell and Noël Carroll (eds.), *Post-Theory: Reconstructing Film Studies* (University of Wisconsin Press, 1996).

Andrew Light, *Reel Arguments* (Westview Press, 2003).

Paisley Livingston, "Cinematic Authorship," in Richard Allen and Murray Smith (eds.), *Film Theory and Philosophy* (Oxford University Press, 1997).

Dominic McIver Lopes, "The Aesthetics of Photographic Transparency," *Mind* 112:447 (2003), 433–48.

Joseph Margolis, "Film as Art," *Millennium Film Journal* 14–15 (1984–5), 89–104.

—— "Le Significant Imaginaire, malgré lui," *Persistence of Vision* 5 (1987), 28–36.

—— "Mechanical Reproduction and Cinematic Humanism," *Film and Philosophy* 5–6 (2002), 114–30.

Patrick Maynard, "Drawing and Shooting: Causality in Depiction," *Journal of Aesthetics and Art Criticism* 44:2 (1985/6), 115–29.

Aaron Meskin and Jonathan Cohen, "On the Epistemic Value of Photographs," *Journal of Aesthetics and Art Criticism* 62:2 (2004), 197–210.

—— —— "Photographs as Evidence," in Scott Walden (ed.), *Philosophy and Photography* (Blackwell Publishing, forthcoming).

Aaron Meskin and Jonathan Weinberg, "Emotion, Fiction, and Cognitive Architecture," *British Journal of Aesthetics* 43:1 (2003), 18–34.

Paul Messaris, *Visual Literacy: Image, Mind and Reality* (Westview Press, 1994).

Richard Moran, "The Expression of Feeling in Imagination," *The Philosophical Review* 103:1 (1994), 75–106.

Hugo Munsterberg, *The Photoplay: A Psychological Study* (Dover Publishers, 1916).

Alex Neill, "Fear, Fiction and Make-Believe," *Journal of Aesthetics and Art Criticism* 49:1 (1991), 47–56.

—— "Empathy and (Fiction) Film," in David Bordwell and Noël Carroll (eds.), *Post-Theory: Reconstructing Film Studies* (University of Wisconsin Press, 1996).

Victor Perkins, *Film as Film: Understanding and Judging Movies* (Penguin Books, 1972).

Carl Plantinga, *Rhetoric and Representation in Nonfiction Film* (Cambridge University Press, 1997).

Carl Plantinga and Gregory Smith (eds.), *Passionate Views* (Johns Hopkins University Press, 1999).

Trevor Ponech, *What Is Non-Fiction Cinema?* (Westview Press, 1999).

Jesse Prinz, *Gut Reactions* (Oxford University Press, 2004).

V. I. Pudovkin, *Film Acting and Film Technique* (Vision Press, 1958).

Colin Radford, "How Can We Be Moved by the Fate of Anna Karenina?," *Proceedings of the Aristotelian Society*, supplement 49 (1975), 67–81.

Jenefer Robinson, *Deeper Than Reason* (Oxford University Press, 2005).

William Rothman and Marion Keane, *Reading Cavell's The World Viewed* (Wayne State University Press, 2000).

Bruce Russell, "The Philosophical Limits of Film," in Noël Carroll and Jinhee Choi (eds.), *Philosophy of Film and Motion Pictures* (Blackwell Publishing, 2006).

Edward Sankowski, "Uniqueness Arguments and Artist's Actions," *Journal of Aesthetics and Art Criticism* 38:1 (1979), 61–74.

Andrew Sarris, "Notes on the Auteur Theory in 1962," in Gerald Mast and Marshall Cohen (eds.), *Film Theory and Film Criticism*, 3rd edn. (Oxford University Press, 1985).

Roger Scruton, "Photography and Representation," in Noël Carroll and Jinhee Choi (eds.), *Philosophy of Film and Motion Pictures* (Blackwell Publishing, 2006).

Alex Sesonske, "Cinema Space," in David Carr and Ed Casey (eds.), *Explorations in Phenomenology* (Martinus Nijhoff, 1973).

—— "Aesthetics of Film," *Journal of Aesthetics and Art Criticism* 33:1 (1974), 51–7.

—— "Time and Tense in Cinema," *Journal of Aesthetics and Art Criticism* 38:4 (1980), 418–26.

Gregory Smith, *Film Structure and the Emotion System* (Cambridge University Press, 2003).

Murray Smith, *Engaging Characters* (Oxford University Press, 1995).

Susan Sontag, "Film and Theater," in her *Styles of Radical Will* (Farrar, Straus & Giroux, 1966).

Francis Sparshott, "Vision and Dream in the Cinema," *Philosophic Exchange* 1 (1971), 111–22.

—— "Medium and Convention in Film and Video," *Millennium Film Journal* 14–15 (1984–5), 72–88.

Kevin Sweeney, "Constructivism in Cognitive Film Theory," *Film and Philosophy* 2 (1995), 33–44.

Malcolm Turvey, "Seeing Theory," in Richard Allen and Murray Smith (eds.), *Film Theory and Philosophy* (Oxford University Press, 1997).

Kendall Walton, Categories of Art," *The Philosophical Review* 79 (1970), 334–67.

—— "Fearing Fictions," *Journal of Philosophy* 75:1 (1978), 5–27.

—— "Transparent Pictures: On the Nature of Photographic Realism," *Critical Inquiry* 11:2 (1984), 246–77.

—— *Mimesis as Make-Believe* (Harvard University Press, 1990).

—— "On Pictures and Photographs: Objections Answered," in Richard Allen and Murray Smith (eds.), *Film Theory and Philosophy* (Oxford University Press, 1997).

Nigel Warburton, "Seeing Through 'Seeing-Through' Photographs," *Ratio* (1988), 64–77.

Thomas Wartenberg, *Unlikely Couples* (Westview Press, 1999).

Thomas Wartenberg and Angela Curran (eds.), *The Philosophy of Film: Introductory Text and Readings* (Blackwell Publishing, 2005).

Thomas Wartenberg and Murray Smith (eds.), *Thinking Through Cinema: Film as Philosophy* (Blackwell Publishing, 2006).

Trevor Whittock, *Metaphor and Film* (Cambridge University Press, 1990).

George Wilson, *Narration in Light* (Johns Hopkins University Press, 1986).

—— "On Film Narrative and Narrative Meaning," in Richard Allen and Murray Smith (eds.), *Film Theory and Philosophy* (Oxford University Press, 1997).

—— "*Le Grand Imagier* Steps Out: The Primitive Basis of Film Narration," in Noël Carroll and Jinhee Choi (eds.), *Philosophy of Film and Motion Pictures* (Blackwell Publishing, 2006).

Peter Wollen, *Signs and Meaning in the Cinema* (Indiana University Press, 1972).

Richard Wollheim, *Art and its Objects* (Cambridge University Press, 1980).

Sol Worth, "Pictures Can't Say Ain't," *Vegas* 12 (1975), 85–108.

Index